DATE DUE

MAR 11 92			

IT
STARTED
IN
EDEN

IT
STARTED
IN
EDEN

How the Plant - Hunters
and the Plants They Found
Changed the Course of
History

Bertha S. Dodge

McGRAW-HILL BOOK COMPANY
New York   St. Louis   San Francisco
Düsseldorf   London   Mexico   Sydney   Toronto

Copyright © 1979 by Bertha S. Dodge.

All rights reserved.

Printed in the United States of America.

No part of this publication may be reproduced, stored in a retrieval system, or transmitted, in any form or by any means, electronic, mechanical, photocopying, recording, or otherwise, without the prior written permission of the publisher.

1 2 3 4 5 6 7 8 9 0 B P B P 7 8 3 2 1 0 9

LIBRARY OF CONGRESS CATALOGING IN PUBLICATION DATA
Dodge, Bertha Sanford, 1902–
    It Started in Eden.
    Bibliography: p.
    Includes index.
    1. Botany, Economic—History. 2. Plant collectors—History. 3. Botanists—History. I. Title.
SB 107.D62   581.6′09   79–15049
ISBN 0–07–017290–0

Book design by Marsha Picker.

CONTENTS

ACKNOWLEDGEMENTS

The preparation of a book such as this involves a great deal of reading, which, in turn, involves the securing of appropriate books. This is not always a simple task, since material which may be valuable and interesting can turn up in the most unexpected places—a limited-edition book published by an eccentric English traveler, a book of poems, an early Spanish chronicle of life in a high Andean city, travelers' accounts from almost everywhere. All these must be read if the nuggets hidden within are to be mined. Fortunately, in addition to my own rather extensive library, I have always been able to turn to the Bailey Library of the University of Vermont, where I have ever found ready help. I must therefore here express my appreciation of the librarians who have always been ready to provide such help, for permission to roam the stacks freely, for assistance in procuring information I have needed, and, especially, for securing for me by interlibrary loan such books as were not to be found on the library shelves.

FOREWORD

When they had tested all other food resources in the Garden of Eden, Adam and Eve—so the Bible tells us—turned their attention to the one tree whose fruit they had so far refrained from tasting. Thereby they started something that has not yet come to an end. It was not just that now overtouted sense of sin and prudery that has most influenced man's world but the consequences of the awareness which led them to stitch together fig leaves to cover their nakedness—in other words, to exploit such plant resources as were available to fill man's suddenly recognized needs. As the potential of plants to fill such needs and possibly to better man's life became recognized, there followed the urge—men being what they are—to find out whether better and yet more useful plants might not exist somewhere. Adam's descendants were presently vying with one another to gain monopoly of the more valuable and rarer plant species. As nations grew, such rivalries would grow to national proportions until the history of men and nations has become inextricably involved with the history of plants.

More than the fruit and leaves plucked in the Garden of Eden, it became every kind of thing belonging to the plant kingdom. Plants and their products were eventually to pervade all aspects of increasingly complex human life. In fact, most of those aspects could not have come into existence without plants. Nearly three and a half centuries ago, a herbalist put it succinctly: "Give me leave onely to tell you That God in his infinit goodnesse and bountie hath by the *medium* of Plants bestowed almost all food, clothing, and medicine upon man. And to this off-spring we also owe (for the most part) our houses, shipping, and infinite other things, though some of them *Proteus* like, have run through divers shapes, as this paper wereon I write. . . ."

IT STARTED IN EDEN

The
Staff
of
Life

What men are, their plants—for better or worse—have made them. Cave dweller of prehistory, city builder of today, tomorrow's citizen of outer space—such progressive levels of human achievement imply human survival, and while it is conceivable that men might survive without animals, it is totally inconceivable that men or animals could survive without plants or even have come into existence had not plants been here first. Our bodies, as well as those of our animal brethren, lack that one gift of the gods without which all other gifts must prove worthless—the power to take from earth and air inanimate atoms and simple molecules and from these to create complicated molecules endowed with that power we call life, of creating more molecules after the same patterns. Plants have that power, the most crucial endowment of all.

Molecular nitrogen is by far the largest component of the air we breathe, yet we have no power to use it though our bodies may be crying for the nitrogen compounds they need. That need is filled through a long and complicated process that begins with single-celled bacteria which can break apart molecules of nitrogen and incorporate the atoms in compounds which, in turn, support the larger plants that men and their animals must have if they are to continue on earth.

This dependence, as unavoidable as it is unchosen, has been faced by every living animal from dinosaurs to doodle bugs. It is a heritage fraught with conflict—initially over access to food supplies, later over access to the other plants no-longer-hungry men came to covet. If men starve, nations cannot survive. This is a fact which rulers of nations have ever been uncomfortably aware of, for a starving populace can be a menace to even the most absolute of rulers, whose policies must be shaped to avoid such a confrontation. For the men who could devise ways and means of abating the threat of starvation, there would be a royal reward.

Seventeen centuries before Christ, an imprisoned Israelite slave named Joseph was to win such a reward from the Pharaoh of Egypt. Interpreting the strange dreams that the Pharaoh had had as a warning that the current fat years were to end in widespread famine, Joseph counseled the Pharaoh to avoid the inevitability of disaster by laying up stores of food against those lean years which, incidentally, were almost certain to return periodically to that land. With such a dream-warning from God, Pharaoh, impressed by the wisdom of the dream interpreter, "said unto Joseph... 'Thou shalt be over my house, and according to thy word shall all my people be ruled: only in the throne will I be greater than thou' "—a meteoric rise which almost nothing but forecasting famine could have achieved for the then penniless slave.

Joseph's activities, however, would have come to naught had there not been growing in Egypt crops which could survive lengthy storage. Such were and are the grains, the most important of which was wheat, which had, for thousands of years, been cultivated in the lands over which the Pharaoh ruled. Sarcophagi of 6,000-year-dead Egyptian mummies, dated with some accuracy, include recognizable seeds of wheat. The bricks of their tombs show wheat straw used as binding. In that same era China was also cultivating wheat. Such widespread cultivation suggests that the plant was already then an ancient crop, the key to survival and to power. To assure a continuance of that power, sowings and harvests were celebrated, often with bizarre fertility rites that should persuade the appropriate deities to protect the crops from ever threatening disasters.

WHEAT

Today no one can tell where wheat first grew wild, where its food value was first recognized, who were the first men to sow it, harvest the crop, recognize its durability in storage and perceive that this, combined with its high food value, set it apart from most of the other plants they knew. We know that it is now one of the world's most important food plants for whose yields great nations continue to vie. Those endless wheat fields, with the towering grain elevators that loom over our Midwestern landscapes, testify not only to the fertility of the fields, the ingenuity of men who sow and harvest such crops, but also to the political power that would fade were the fields to remain unsowed, the crops unharvested, the elevators unfilled.

Expanded planting of wheat was bound to come up against the limitations of climate, since the earlier types of wheat, unlike oats and buckwheat, cannot tolerate the colder climate which prevails in areas otherwise best suited to the raising of wheat. Wheat is a choosy grain. Where lands are too warm or too cold, fertilization of the flowers is inhibited and no seed sets. Even if seed is set, it cannot mature unless there is sufficient time before frost blasts it. A ten-day difference in the length of the growing season between the last frost of spring and the first of autumn can spell the critical difference between a harvestable crop and one frost-killed on the stalk. With climate still uncontrollable, it becomes of crucial importance to have a variety of wheat that can mature in a relatively short growing season.

This is where plant breeders come in. They are men absorbed in science, not politics, yet whose activities are bound to have tremendous political clout. Plant breeding is a long, repetitive undertaking demanding infinite patience and promising no certain success. Success, if attained, is rarely dramatic and often illusory. Nevertheless, as populations explode and come to demand more and better food, men's inescapable reliance on food plants has made the production of new, hardier, and better kinds of crop plants almost the only way left to fight man's ancient and universal enemy—hunger.

It was during the 1880s that Dr. William Saunders, a Canadian, visualized a wheat that could flourish and mature in previously marginal climates such as that of the Canadian wheat-growing area. From cool lands all over the globe, including the chillier high elevations of warmer lands, he imported seeds of native wheats. It was to be one of his sons, Dr. C. E. Saunders, who would bring the scheme to completion. Year after year, selecting and crossbreeding numberless strains of wheat, Dr. Saunders finally, in 1903, came upon an ear which, his instincts suggested, might be the kind of wheat he was looking for. In the following year, seed from that single spike was to yield twelve plants which produced less than a pound of seed—too little for the crucial baking tests needed. However, Dr. Saunders devised a chewing test and, from the elasticity of the chewed mass, guessed that he might really be on the track of the wheat he was seeking.

By 1907 there were twenty-three pounds of grain—enough for the milling and baking tests. These, fortunately, gave encouraging results. Two years later this "Marquis" wheat was being judiciously released to farmers. Soon there was enough growing for 100,000 bushels to be exported as seed to the United States. By 1918 in Minnesota alone the yield of Marquis wheat was computed to be about thirty-five million bushels—testimony both to the value of wheat, of wheat breeders in particular, and of plant breeders in general.

Other grains have been bred for special qualities. However, the most spectacular grain breeding has resulted in the production of a totally new grain, now, as triticale, available in markets. This grain, whose name as well as inheritance is a cross between wheat (*Triticum*) and rye (*Secale*) is the product of a century of dreams and forty years of active pursuit of the all-but-impossible. The first wheat-rye cross, attempted in Scotland in 1876, proved sterile, as so often happens with man-made crosses. Some thirteen years later, a similarly sterile accidental cross appeared in Germany. Another half century was to pass before men developed a chemical means of making plant crosses fertile.

By 1974 triticale was being grown on about a million acres in fifty-two different countries, including Ethiopia, Mexico, and India, where it has been outyielding the best wheat. Combining the important high-protein content of wheat with the ruggedness of rye, triticale could afford improved nutrition for dwellers in underdeveloped lands. Whether it will do so, whether such dwellers will accept this new grain any more readily than some have the new variety of rice that was to have sparked a green revolution, is a decision that individual peoples will make and world politicians cope with.

RYE

Probably as ancient a crop plant as wheat, rye has been, in general, less popular as a food, though with a far more dramatic impact on people's lives. Like wheat, ancient enough for its origins to be beyond men's memories, it certainly was growing in Egypt in Joseph's day. Certainly it was there three centuries later when Moses undertook to chasten the Pharaoh of his day with a storm of hail: "And the flax and barley were smitten: for the barley was in the ear and the flax was bolled. But the wheat and rie were not smitten; for they were not grown up."

For long, fastidious upper classes cared as little for rye as did the Roman Pliny, writing a few decades A.D.: "it is very poor food and only serves to avert starvation . . . it is of a dark sombre color. . . . Wheat is mixed with this to mitigate its bitter taste, and all the same it is very unacceptable to the stomach." Acceptable then or not, rye was destined to win eventual popularity for the very qualities that Pliny decried.

The more sinister potential of rye was not to be recognized until the mid-nineteenth century, though even ancient men had been vaguely aware of it. Amos, prophet of Israel about eight centuries before Christ, furiously rebuked his people for their too worldly ways, threatening them that if they did not reform, they should lose their grain crops through blights, both red and black. Red blight would have been a leaf rust of the kind that still infests wheatfields and seriously reduces crop yields. Black blight, a fungous disease of rye which was not to be recognized as such until nearly two thousand years after Amos' day, has consequences far more traumatic than those following upon wheat rust.

Both kinds of blight have something in common. They are the consequences of infestation of crop plants by microscopic plants—fungi—though the ones responsible for the two blights are more different from each other than the grains they infect. The fungus that turns rye black in the ear bears the scientific name *Claviceps purpurea* and the common name "ergot." *Claviceps*-invaded grain turns into hard black kernels, but the plant itself does not die back so that these dark kernels may, at harvest time, be mingled with uninfected grains and, along with them, be milled into flour. The flour would be darker than usual, but could poor people afford to be choosy about the color of the bread they ate, since to have bread at all was something to be grateful for?

To people living during the ninth and tenth centuries of our era, life itself was a doubtful matter. Wars, looting, pestilence—all these were commonplaces, so why make a fuss over so small a matter as a darker-than-usual bread? Some people may have wondered what evil genius might have cast a spell over their grain, but nearly a thousand years would pass before their descendants came to realize that infections of plants, animals, and men are not a form of punishment by an outraged God but the result of microscopic plants growing enthusiastically as well as impartially where they can find the right conditions of nourishment, moisture, and temperature.

To citizens of Limoges in the year 943 A.D. it seemed not illogical that the death of some children in a grain field—probably as described by a child witness who had escaped the fate of the others—had been the work of a "grain witch," with tangled hair, bony arms, and pitch-black breasts who actively enticed the children into the fields, then forced upon them bread she had smeared with something as black as tar. When the children tried to reject this food—so the account ran—she seized them in her bony arms and smothered them to death.

Had there really been some demented evil woman wandering in the grain fields in the hope of entrapping and destroying innocent children? Might she not have been altogether the figment of some child's overstimulated imagination—a child, perhaps, who had gone trespassing with other hungry children and watched them chew the grains, finally being persuaded to taste one? Such blackened grains are said to be of sweetish taste. The ugly witch and the repulsively black bread—these might explain the otherwise inexplicable—that the children who had had the most massive doses of ergot (one of its several active principles being LSD) had gone almost at once into convulsions, then died after the pattern of that periodically recurring but now rarely encountered disease known as "ergotism." The child who merely tasted a grain could have hallucinated sufficiently to have "seen" the witch at work.

Within the city limits of Limoges, evil spirits were soon taking possession of adults, too. Men collapsed in the streets, shrieking and wailing. Indoors, a man might suddenly become aware of pain, stand up from his table only to fall to the floor and roll about in agony.

Epileptiform convulsions seized upon some who foamed at the mouth, vomited, and screamed, "Fire! I'm on fire!" A chronicler of the horror told of people perishing by hundreds in "intolerably excruciating pain." They complained of a fire in their bodies which "permeates the wretched people with such cold that no means suffices to warm them." In addition, the limbs of some became gangrenous (this now known to be due to a second active principle of ergot), turned black and seemed to rot off.

Where did it all come from, that dreadful plague which no kind of medicine seemed able to abate? Those were times when men accepted the fact that medicine could cure very little, especially when pitted against the devils and witches who must have joined forces against the city of Limoges. Devils were best combatted with prayers and, should prayers fail, with holy relics. The bones of martyred St. Martial were brought to Limoges and seemed to frighten off the evil spirits, though not before thousands had died in misery. At another time and place, such a plague was dealt with through relics of St. Anthony, patron saint of the poor. And because the poor always formed the largest portion of those afflicted, the "pestilence" acquired the picturesque name "St. Anthony's Fire."

Periodically throughout the Middle Ages, St. Anthony's Fire flamed up, wreaked havoc, flickered out. It appeared during years of especially heavy rainfall when fields remained damp enough to encourage fungous growths. With bread made of already damaged flour susceptible to yet further infestation by ergot, there were times that rye loaves, when cut, oozed a tarry substance like that the witch of Limoges was supposed to have forced on her young victims. Even those wise men, the philosophers, would have been hard put to it to recognize the sequence of plant infection, darkening flour, human disease. In fact, some six centuries later, witches were very much alive in the minds of men as sober and learned as those who belonged to the British Royal Society. Only a few of the most scientifically enlightened then rejected the thought of witches interfering in the lives of men. For many it seemed the only way to explain the inexplicable.

The poor, shabby old women upon whom accusations of traffic with evil spirits were most likely to fall were possibly themselves already victims of St. Anthony's Fire. A perceptive scientist of our own day has pointed out the close analogy between symptoms of ergotism and manifestations of witchcraft as described by writers of seventeenth- and eighteenth-century New England. The scientifically unsophisticated, however, would find in the symptoms proof positive of possession—the convulsions, the hallucinations which led the unfortunates to describe supernatural visions they had seen and weird creatures they had conversed with and in whose company they had traveled to strange places and taken part in fantastic ceremonies which the unpossessed saw as witches' sabbaths. The free admissions of traffic with evil spirits were most likely to fall rary examiners that the old women might not be evil witches but poor, sick, suffering fellow human beings. The cruel destruction of such persons must be added to the score against ergot and that microscopic plant *Claviceps purpurea*.

Throughout the centuries people were vaguely aware of some connection between those years when rye turned black in the ear and when St. Anthony's Fire flared up. Both happenings were ascribed to witchcraft.

Not until the 1850s was *Claviceps purpurea* identified as the villain and the word *ergotism* invented to indicate the symptoms of ergot poisoning. Even today, unless growers and millers are alerted to the risks, epidemics of ergotism may break out during years when growing conditions favor the development of the fungus. The best control is to plant clean rye seed in areas where the ergot fungus has not previously appeared and hence could have left behind no spores to start a new infection.

Interestingly, and as a postscript, biochemists have found among the ergot alkaloids several that have demonstrated medical value so that in some areas deliberately infected rye is grown. Otherwise, in eliminating that plant poison entirely, civilized men seem to have been less successful than primitive casava growers of the American tropics who long ago recognized the poisonous potential of the root which serves as their staff of life and who developed an ingenious process of turning it into an acceptable food.

CORN

If the early Americans had no problem with ergotism, it was not because they had developed particularly effective rituals for propitiating the deities of their grain. All the human sacrifices an Aztec priest could achieve in his lifetime would not alter the inherited, inbred characteristics of a plant. No orange could thereby be made to grow on an apple tree nor *Claviceps purpurea* on any grain not endowed, in part at least (as in triticale), with genes belonging to rye.

It was in 1492 that newly arrived adventurers from the Old World were to encounter that grain, so alien to European eyes, that had supported the great ancient civilizations of the Americas—the Aztecs of Mexico and the Incas in Peru. Unsophisticated natives of less highly developed Cuba, without the slightest premonition of the troubles Europeans were presently to bring them, received the new arrivals hospitably and served them "a sort of grain they call *maiz* which was well tast'd, bak'd, dry'd, and made into flour." It must have tasted especially good to mariners so recently cooped up on small ships where too long they had subsisted on monotonous, vitamin-poor ships' rations. Of the recognized essential vitamins, maize lacks only two, belonging to the Vitamin B complex—niacin and riboflavin—which for native Indians had been supplied by beans and squashes.

With Columbus' return to Spain, ears and kernels of maize were making their very first bow on the European scene. Having so far failed to locate the anticipated fabulous treasures of the Orient, Columbus was trying to compensate with samples of minerals he believed to be valuable (but which were not) and samples of plants that might, at least, rouse the interest of his royal sponsors, Ferdinand and Isabella. Inevitably, those Spanish monarchs were disappointed, for they could have no way of knowing that a few strange ears from an alien grain were eventually to represent, though for other lands, more total wealth than the oriental treasure that Columbus had failed to lay at their feet.

With or without that golden treasure, there was, from the start, much about the New World to fascinate both the sixteenth-century Spaniards who went thither and those who did their traveling by hearsay. Strange scenes, strange peoples, strange plants—all these were being discussed in Spain, with men on every returning ship met by eager questioners and listened to with openmouthed wonder, the small material mementoes of their travels examined and commented upon.

This interest continued long after, in Mexico and in Peru, there began to be realized that hope of finding precious metals which had first stimulated Spaniards to take the risks of crossing wide seas to explore and conquer new lands, then kept them there to guard what they had seized. The soldiers were mainly a rough lot, illegitimate sons of nobles as well as nobodies of humbler origins, all vying not too scrupulously for the prizes of wealth and of status that might assure a soldier that his own son should be a *hidalgo*—*hijo d'algo*—son of a somebody.

Yet among them there was an occasional thoughtful, observant man who looked on the strange new environment and peoples with appreciative eyes. Such a one must have been the Pedro de Osma, who, in 1568, sat down to write a fan letter to a learned physician-author, Nicolas de Monardes, of Seville. De Osma had just read de Monardes' recent book, an account of plant novelties of the New World. "I doe write your worshippe these thynges"—thus, in part, runs the letter which so moved de Monardes that he published it in its entirety in a later edition of his work (rendered into contemporary English in 1577 by one John Frampton, Merchant)— "whereby ye maie consider how many more Hearbes and Plantes of great vertue . . . this our Indias hath."

In his book, entitled *Joyfull Newes from the Newe Founde Worlde,* de Monardes makes approving comment on Pedro de Osma and his letter: "The gentleman of the Peru, which wrote me this letter although I know hym not . . . I have hym in great estimation. For because that the office of a Souldiour is to handle weapons, and to sheed bloud, and to do other exercises apertainyng to Souldiours, he is much to be esteemed, that he will enquire and search out Hearbes and Plantes, to know their properties and vertues . . . I doe much esteeme this Gentlemanne, for the labour which he taketh, in knowyng and enquiryng, of these naturall thyngs."

Implicit in de Monardes' words was an acceptance that plants belonged inextricably in the lands where God had placed them. Several centuries were to pass before *men* would undertake on a large scale to do such placing. Meanwhile, if plants' special virtues were to be exploited by men of distant lands, it must be through samples of plants sent by men, like de Osma, alert to "naturall thyngs." What the learned "phisition" wanted to find out was, first, what served as the staff of life to natives of the new lands, then what plants provided them with medicines of special value.

What for instance, was the "bread" of natives of Santo Domingo, that Caribbean island where Columbus planted his first colony? Being informed, as he wrote, "I have caused that they shoulde bryng me from Sancto Domingo, a Leafe of that Plante which they doe make the Casavi, and they brought it me." He goes on to describe the leaf with its spreading points, giving a still recognizable description of the growing manioc plant as told him by retuning travelers—that "Hearbe that the Indians dooe call Yuca." The "fruit"—actually a fleshy root—has an appearance "after the maner of grosse Turnepes." Peeled and grated, its juice is squeezed in an ingeniously devised press. From the solid residue are made flat cakes which are then heated, probably to make certain the last traces of the juice are removed.

The final processing of the cakes follows. The cake they "putte in the Sunne, that it may drie, and of this

cake thei eate for breade, which is of much substance:
and these cakes be a long tyme without corruptyng, and
thei bryng them in Shippes which cometh from those
partes and thei come into Spaine without beyng corrupted and it serveth for bisket to all the people."

Presumably remaining mold-free—"without being
corrupted"—even in the damp tropics, the product
must have served well as ship's biscuit in vessels making
that long return journey to Spain. Today in our land we
know the product as tapioca. Brazilians call the coarsely
ground "bisket" *farinha,* which is universally used in that
land as thickening for soups and stews, sometimes
cooked in the pot, sometimes sprinkled on top at time of
serving. Occasionally farinha is made into a sort of
porridge. In any case, it is as much a staple of Brazilian
diets as wheaten bread is of other lands.

Nicolas de Monardes expressed mental reservations
about eating that "casavi," for there had come to his
notice definitely disturbing accounts: "It is a marvellous
thyng of the juice which cometh out of this fruite, which
is spoken of, that if any manne or beaste doe drinke it,
or any parte of it, incontinent he dieth, with the most
strong venome in the worlde." This is now generally
recognized, so that we have to wonder how savages
worked out a way to process a root which they all knew
to have a lethal juice. De Monardes, in an age before
chemical composition had been worked out, correctly
compared that juice to the poison, now known to be a
cyanide, which is found in peach pits. Though prolonged boiling—"seethyng"—can make certain the last
traces of volatile cyanide are driven off, the cautious
physician wanted none of the product.

"How so ever it bee," he wrote, "havyng in the Indias
so much Maies, and so common in all partes of it, I

would not eate Casavi, seyng that the Maies is of so much substaunce as our Wheate, and in no parte hath neither venome nor poyson, but rather it is healthful and doe make a good stomache: and there is breade made of it, and with water thei knede it, and in a frying panne of yearth thei bake certaine cakes thei make of it, and it must be eaten freshe, as sone as it is made: for being drie, it is sharpe and troublesome to swallow doun and doeth offend the teeth"—which will be heartily seconded by anyone who has tried to chew and swallow stale tortillas.

Wherever conditions were right for maize to grow to maturity, ancient Americans were using it for food, but whether as tortillas, boiled, or simply roasted by tossing unshucked ears into the embers, we cannot know. Nor can we know exactly what the original maize plants looked like in those far-distant times when Americans began bringing wild maize under cultivation. No one today has located a maize plant that corn experts agree must be the ancestral type. Certainly, like the people who cultivated it, maize has undergone changes and has continued sparking changes in its cultivators. Upon their decisions as to which ears to eat, which to lay aside for the next year's plantings has, undoubtedly, rested the gradual change in size and general character of the yield.

Though the type of maize first cultivated remains unknown, we can get some idea of the hoary antiquity of the crop plant through that very modern technique of radiocarbon dating. This rests on the fact that when an incoming cosmic ray strikes a carbon atom of atomic weight 12, two units are added to that atomic weight, thereby producing a radioactive carbon atom of atomic weight 14. As far as plants are concerned, a heavier carbon dioxide is as usable as the lighter form, so that they take C-14 in and incorporate it into growing tissues just as long as they remain alive to build tissues. Meanwhile, the radioactive atoms begin to decay so that, in 5,700 years, half will be gone. Another 5,700 years again reduces the remaining radioactivity by another half to one-fourth the original, and so on. By comparing the percentage of radiocarbon remaining in those long-dead tissues of corncobs and kernels with that in tissues which have grown in our own day, we get a fair approximation of the age of the ancient specimen.

Such dating technique has revealed that pumpkin seeds in the prehistoric kitchen middens of Oaxaca, Mexico, date back to 7800 B.C., long before the most ancient events of Bible record. Corn, from various levels of Bat Cave, New Mexico, is more recent, though still antedating Biblical events. The lowest level of Bat Cave suggests that men were living there and eating corn some 5,000 years ago, the upper levels that the place was thus inhabited for a span of perhaps 3,000 years. All levels tell us that corn was a diet staple for thousands of years and, during that period, was accidentally or by design undergoing changes.

The maize that made its bow in Europe after Columbus returned from his first voyage could not have been the maize of those earliest New Mexicans. Maize was soon a matter of written record in sixteenth-century Europe, for there were many men like Nicolas de Monardes who shared his fascination with strange plants. They planted corn kernels, watched the plants tenderly to maturity, describing what they observed and often picturing it in one of those delightfully drawn and hand-colored woodcuts such as are to be found in herbals like John Gerard's.

"This Corne is a marvellous strange plant," wrote a Dutch herbalist in 1578 (his work was translated into English some fifty years later), "nothing resembling any other kind of grayne; for it bringeth forth its seed cleane contrarie from the place where the Floures grow, which is against the nature and kinds of all other plants, which bring forth their fruit there, whereon they have borne their Floure . . . at the highest of the stalks grow idle and barren eares, which bring forth nothing but Floures or Blossoms." All this is a way of saying that the corn plant has at the top tassels (male flowers) whose pollen fertilizes the female flowers growing below on the corn stalk, thereby producing the ears.

For men of the sixteenth century, corn's strange habit of growth must have supported the view that America was an altogether wild place where even crop plants disdained to grow by accepted European standards. Except for the eager herbalists, Europeans long remained stonily indifferent to the new grain save as a curiosity.

As a food plant, American maize has never found much popularity in Europe, though today it may be a shade more acceptable than it was during the 1840s when a blight was destroying Ireland's staff of life, the white potato. Corn meal then shipped from across the sea seemed to most Irish only a shade better than starvation. Recipes supplied along with the meal added little persuasion to people long accustomed to living on huge quantities of boiled potatoes—over ten pounds per day per person. Even today, when there have been bred varieties of corn able to mature in the shorter growing season, between last and first frost, near London, the grain remains a questionable food to most people on that side of the Atlantic.

As with other grains, plant breeders have gone to work at improving corn. Today's hybrid seed has produced fields of maize that would not only astonish agricultural Indians of ages past but also earlier generations of non-Indian farmers in our own land. It represents an annually renewing fortune that has long since outdistanced in money value the total metallic treasure garnered in America to enrich the monarchs of sixteenth- and seventeenth-century imperial Spain and to finance their futile wars.

A NEW ROOT FOR THE OLD WORLD

Plants chosen by primitive folk to supply their staff of life must grow native in the environment of the choosers. The jungles of Santo Domingo, at the time of Columbus, offered no good alternative to casava, for the hot tropics do not favor the maturing of grains. Not all the tropics, however, are jungle-ridden lowlands. Equally inhospitable to grain crops are the Andean highlands, still in tropical latitudes, where frost can strike almost any month of the year and with a climate colder and harsher than any the conquistadors could have experienced at home. Spaniards would gladly have avoided such places, but since precious metals were there to be mined, sixteenth-century Spaniards found ways to endure the misery which had for eons been familiar to Andean Indians living thereabouts.

A chronicler of the famous silver-mining city of Potosí in today's Bolivia (about 20° south latitude and situated at an elevation of over 13,000 feet) recounts the only slightly exceptional snowstorm that kept the city's inhabitants isolated for many days during August 1557:

"After the snowfall continued for two days, yet another threat made its appearance—hunger. . . . After six days, it was learned that some five of the seven Indians who were bringing various foodstuffs had been buried in the snow at Carachipampa, a league [about three miles] from this city . . . where they had frozen to death. . . . After the snowfall had continued eight days, a sharp and penetrating wind arose, during which fourteen Spaniards perished in their own homes for want of wood, charcoal, or straw."

In all, that snowfall amounted to over five feet in protected spots. Where the penetrating wind could reach, drifts piled up to unbelievable heights. In a place where nothing woody grew and no familiar plants matured, Spaniards had to learn to be thankful for strange plants that could produce edible seeds or roots. Pedro Cieza de León, one of the early chroniclers living in the Viceroyalty of Peru (which then included Potosí), wrote feelingly of the Altiplano: "The climate is so cold that there is no maize, nor any kind of tree: the land is too sterile to yield any of the fruits which grow in other parts. . . . [The Indians'] principal food is potatoes which are little earth nuts." (In Europe, "earth nuts" meant truffles, the underground fungi dug for food, and no kind of relative to the potato.)

With potatoes literally their staff of life and even the regular harvesting of those an uncertain matter, Peruvian Indians developed ways to process them so that they might remain unspoiled for months and tide over the failure of a harvest. Cieza de León explains: "They dry these potatoes in the sun and keep them from one harvest to another. After they are dried, they call these potatoes *chuñus* and they are highly esteemed and valued among them. . . . They have no water in channels for irrigating the fields, so that if the natural supply of water required for the crop fails, they would suffer from famine and want if they had not the store of dried potatoes. Many Spaniards enriched themselves and returned prosperous to Spain by merely taking these *chunus* to sell at the mines of Potosí." The grim corollary, of course, was that by taking the *chunus* the Spaniards, in enriching themselves, might well be condemning the Indians from whom they took them to die of hunger.

Garcilaso de la Vega, the half-Spanish, half-Incan chronicler of the conquest of Peru, gives a more detailed description of the preparation of *chuño* (as it is now written) in the region near Lake Titicaca, altitude about 12,500 feet. The process has hardly changed in the intervening centuries: "In all that province called Colla, more than a hundred and fifty leagues in length, maize is not produced because the land is too cold: much *quinoa*"—a large-seeded pigweed, *Chenopodium quinoa*—"is harvested, which is like rice, and other grains, and vegetables which fructify beneath the soil"—one being the tuber-forming sorrel, *Oxalis tuberosa*, known as *Oca*—"and among them is one called *papa* [potato]. To preserve it, they spread it on the ground on straw, which is very good in those parts. They allow it to freeze many nights, for in that province it freezes hard all year, and after the freezing has softened it as though it had been cooked, they cover it with straw and tread it carefully and gently to remove the moisture which the potato has within itself and which the freezing has caused to be loosened: after they have extracted all the moisture, they place it in the sun and keep it in the open until completely dried. Prepared in this way, the potato lasts a long time and its name changes to *chuñus*."

Indians may place great value on these *chuños*, which

even some of today's upper-class Bolivians are said to like. However, to a foreign visitor, this favorite Indian food looked much like old cork and was of about the same taste—"a horrible article of diet." As alternatives to starvation, *chuños* are certainly not to be scorned. Moreover, at elevations where the temperature at which water boils is so low that potatoes might take a very long time to cook soft, and where fuel is always at a premium, already processed potatoes might offer further advantages.

About 2500 miles to the south of Potosí and some 13,000 feet lower are the damp, foggy, chilly islands of the Chonos Archipelago off the coast of southern Chile. And it was there the physician-naturalist of H.M.S. *Beagle*, Charles Darwin, was to encounter in 1832 a very close relative, if not the identical species, of the potato—*Solanum tuberosum*—that was already known to grow at Andean heights.

"Among the Chonos Islands," Darwin wrote, "a wild potato grows in abundance, which in general habit is . . . similar to the cultivated kind. These potatoes grow near the sea-beach in thick beds . . . the tubers were small and few in number. . . . Nevertheless, I found one which was of oval form, with one diameter of two inches. . . . So close is the general resemblance with the cultivated species, that it is necessary to show that they have not been imported. The simple fact of their growth on the islands, and even small rocks, throughout the Chonos Archipelago, which has never been inhabited and seldom visited, is an argument of some weight. But the circumstance of the wildest Indian tribes being well acquainted with the plant is stronger. . . . The simple fact of their being known and named by distinct races, over a space of four or five hundred miles on a most unfrequented coast, almost proves their native existence. . . . It is remarkable that the same plant should be found on the sterile mountains of central Chile, where a drop of rain does not fall for more than six months, and within the damp forests of the southern islands." Clearly, potatoes have those qualities required for survival in a competitive world—endurance and adaptability.

Two and a half centuries before Darwin, Sir Francis Drake had passed the same way with the object of profitably harassing Spanish settlements along the American west coast. The chronicler of that voyage, preacher Francis Fletcher, described the Chilean landfall in *The World Encompassed*: "We continuing our course fell the 29th of November (1578) with the island of La Moucha, where we cast anker . . . and went with ten of the company to the shore where we found people . . . whom the cruel and extreme dealings of the Spaniards have forced for their own safetie and libertie to flee from the maine, and to fortifie themselves in this Island. We being on land, the people came downe to us at the water side with shew of great curtesie, bringing us potatoes, rootes and very fat sheepe." Clearly, potatoes were already known to Drake by reputation, at least.

The "cruell and extreme dealings" of the Spaniards were, for the English of those days, a matter of conviction. Since gentle Sir Francis was about to annoy such Spaniards, it could hardly have done for him to stop by for watering and victualing at one of the truly Spanish ports. Thus he was privileged to experience what must have been the first direct encounter between an Englishman and a potato, though, with many long, uncertain months of sailing ahead, he would not then have brought home to England a living tuber from which to propagate yet more tubers.

Whoever may have been responsible for the first act of transportation, potatoes as botanical curiosities had spread far and wide in Europe by the 1590s. Gerard describes "Virginia" potatoes, though why so named remains a mystery: "It groweth naturally in America, where it was first discovered. . . . I have received roots thereof from Virginia, otherwise called Norumbega, which grow and prosper in my garden as if in their own native country." He went on to assert that they were a good food, "being rosted in the embers, or boyled and eaten with oyle, vineger, and pepper, or dressed any other way by the hand of some cunning in cookerie."

With such commendation from a herbalist of standing—herbalists being presumed to know an edible plant from a poisonous one—the easily cultivatable potato should have been well on its way to general acceptance. The impressively huge herbal written by a man closely associated with the great Lord Burghley should have sufficed to convince the hesitant. However, even this failed to persuade the general public, always notoriously conservative as to diet, to take kindly to a new and foreign root.

Added to the always questionable fact of foreign extraction was the sinister fact that the potato was a *Solanum*, and the family of Solanaceae were known to include many poison-producing nightshades. Strangely, one member of that family, the eggplant, had long provided accepted food to lands of eastern Europe. The eggplant, however, had a pleasing appearance, whereas a potato was a dark, dirty, scruffy-looking item, and that, to people of that era, was a highly sinister matter.

In 1619 the Swiss botanist Gaspar Bauhin recorded, "I am told the Burgundians are forbidden to make use of tubers because . . . the eating of them causes leprosy."

Why leprosy? By the then current "doctrine of signatures," the general appearance of a food was designed by Higher Powers to warn of the effect such an article might have on folk eating it. And leprosy, which in those days was taken to include all repulsive skin diseases, was clearly indicated by the external appearance of potatoes. By 1630 the Parliament of Besançon had issued its verdict: "In view of the fact that the potato is a pernicious substance whose use can cause leprosy, it is hereby forbidden, under pain of fine, to propagate it."

Presently it must have dawned on folk that there were many lepers who could never have been privileged to eat or even look upon so rare a foreign vegetable as the potato. Other diseases took turns in being traced to potato eating: scrofula—the skin irritation believed to be curable through the touch of a king—fever, rickets, consumption, what would you. Two centuries were to pass before any of the disease-causing plants we now call bacteria would be recognized as such.

New England had its own doubts about the edibility of potatoes. A contract between master and apprentice, drawn up during the 1770s, specified that the apprentice, whom it was the master's responsibility to house and feed, should not be fed potatoes. What saved the vegetable, perhaps, from complete rejection was the fact that it was a good, filling food in times when diets had to be quite limited. Strangely, potatoes had long been expensive enough to have acquired snob value, one would think. During the early 1600s, one pound of potatoes might cost, in England, the equivalent of $1.40 in today's U.S. currency.

Potatoes began to come into their own in England during the middle 1600s when philosophers began to concern themselves with the plight of poor folk for whom the periodic failure of grain crops meant starvation. Potatoes—being filling, nourishing, yielding manyfold when planted, and willing to grow where the climate might turn too cold for grain to mature—might not they be made an answer to the famines which too often darkened the land? As for cost, increased production and consumption would take care of that quickly enough.

In 1662 the philosophers of the prestigious Royal Society of London, having individually discussed the matter at length, met formally "to consider Mr. Buckland's proposition to plant potatoes through all parts of England. . . . Mr. Buckland's letter containing said proposition, together with the whole way of planting and ordering potatoes, and the benefit thereof in time of scarcity of food was read: and the substance thereof considered and approved with the result, 1. that all those members of the Society, as have land, should be desired to begin planting this root, and to persuade their friends to do the same, 2. that in order thereunto, Mr. Buckland should be desired to send up what quantity he could of the smaller potatoes to furnish those that have conveniency to plant them in order to which, Mr. Boyle offered to provide as many of them as he could: as also to communicate such notes of his concerning this root . . . as he could recover."

One of the publicity gimmicks devised by Royal Society members was to have John Evelyn, whose book *Sylva* on forestry was soon to appear, add a section pointing out the value of potatoes and giving information as to their planting and culture. The daily papers—"Diurnals"—were to publish the same kind of directions, adding notes on where seed potatoes might be had by those who "had a mind to plant them."

Those first English seed potatoes were to come from Ireland, where, on Sir Walter Raleigh's estate, they had long been growing happily, possibly introduced by Sir Walter. Robert Boyle's Irish estate lay next to Raleigh's in Youghal, whence, in 1663, Boyle's gardener sent tubers and an explanatory letter: "I have according to your desire sent a box of potato rootes; my care hath been to make choice of such, that are fit to be set without cutting. . . ." A few sentences of directions follow. He ends with "I could speak in praise of the roote, what a good and profitable thing it is, and might be to a commonwealth, could it generally be experienced; as the inhabitants of your towne can manifest the truth of it . . . but I will be silent in speaking praise of them, knowing you are not ignorant of it."

With the prestigious Royal Society sponsoring potato planting, lesser and perhaps more ambitious men began to climb on the bandwagon. In 1664, already, John Forster, Gentleman, was producing a book on the subject which he cannily dedicated to King Charles II. Potatoes, he averred in the dedication, were not only to help fill the stomachs of the poor but also to fill the equally empty royal treasury by the simple device of licensing planters for a fee which should make the planting of potatoes a coveted privilege and—the clincher— "There is no reason why his most gracious Majesty should not benefit by this annual license money of 50,000 pounds, inasmuch as his loyal people would thus benefit by the cultivation of the potato."

Two centuries later, John Lindley, editor of the *Gardener's Chronicle,* would, at a time when the almost exclusive cultivation of potatoes in Ireland had brought disaster, comment sardonically on what he presumed to be the royal reaction to Forster's suggestion. Charles "could sanction any license—provided the license money should come into his private treasure. And he might thus forward the cultivation of the potato while he could not care whether or not it were brought to enlarge the comforts of the peasant. . . ."

By 1780, potatoes had become almost the only article of diet in Ireland, where a traveler noted that for ten months of the year people ate potatoes and milk, the remaining two months potatoes and salt. He estimated that a barrel containing 280 pounds might last an Irish family of five persons—two adults and three children—just a week. Forty pounds a day—eight pounds per person if the children consumed at the same rate as their parents. Such an incredibly limited starchy diet sounds disastrous, yet somehow the Irish peasantry, like the Indians of the Altiplano, managed to survive.

Aside from possible dietary insufficiency, the risks implicit in such dependence on a single crop are now obvious, though they would not make themselves so before the middle 1800s. Should the favored crop fail, there would be nothing to feed the millions that had become almost totally dependent on it. Moreover, a single-crop economy, with field after field of the same species growing in conveniently moist climate, was, as men would eventually learn, an invitation to disaster through those invisible plants that prey on living ones. Leaves would then develop strange spots, and these spots would enlarge until consuming the whole plant.

The grim news broke in the *Gardener's Chronicle* for August 23, 1845. Editor John Lindley wrote, "A fatal malady has broken out among the potato crop. On all sides we hear of the destruction that has overtaken this valuable produce. . . . In Belgium the fields are said to have been entirely desolated." Then he added a sentence that revealed how very little anyone in those days really understood the ways of plants in general and of infecting ones in particular: "The murrain seems to have been transferred from cattle to potatoes." Cattle diseases do not infect plants.

Letters to the *Chronicle's* editors soon came pouring in, most excitedly reporting new areas of infection: "A garden quite free last Saturday was quite offensive from decay on Monday," one shocked correspondent wrote. Presently there began to appear letters over the signature "M.J.B." This was the Reverend Miles Joseph Berkeley, then on his way to become one of the foremost botanists of Europe, his specialty being "lower plants," which included disease-causing fungi.

M.J.B.'s letters acknowledged correspondence with his Continental opposite numbers, among them a Dr. Montagne of France, who had sent him some infected leaves. Having viewed the leaves through his microscope—such microscopic study of biological material then being an altogether new technique—M.J.B. then wrote his French correspondent that he "purposed to call the microscopic organism thus revealed *Botrytis infestans**" As Lindley put it, "He does not undertake to say that the spots on the tubers are owing to the ravages of the *Botrytis*, or whether two causes of the disease coexist." This was typical scientific caution, for scientific proof of infection is a tricky matter even today. Editor Lindley was then inclined to believe the mildew was the result rather than the cause of the disease, yet he showed a conviction that something invisible to the naked eye must be at work on the potato crop with the words "Will those potatoes which to the eye are sound

*Now *Phytophthora infestans*

... contain already the seeds of the disease, and will they, too, rot in the long run?" For "seeds" substitute "spores," and you have a sentiment that might be expressed by a scientist of our own day.

It was to be some time before M.J.B.'s hint that microscopic organisms can be the cause of disease would find general acceptance. For the majority of mankind, it just didn't make sense that anything as tiny and invisible as microorganisms could be lethal in their effects. When a cholera epidemic appeared in India in 1817 and began to move first across Asia, then Europe, until finally in 1831 it reached England, few people had the slightest idea as to the whys and wherefores. All they could think of as preventative and cure was the prayer "Ah, Almighty God, who hast visited the nations near us with sudden death of thousands, spare, we beseech Thee, this Thy favored people the wrath which to our sins is justly due!"

Some physicians dared to doubt that it was all a matter of divine wrath. One, a radical of his day, having studied the patterns previously followed by cholera epidemics, stopped that epidemic cold in one region by having the handle of the Broad Street pump, in London, removed so as to deny people access to water which the doctor had reason to believe might be contaminated by sewage. Many, feeling their right to drink whatever water they chose interfered with, protested the doctor's high-handedness. Even he could not say what there was in sewage responsible for the terrible epidemic.

As for the potato plague, people of all kinds—on the basis of no knowledge, little evidence, much personal prejudice—were trying to fix the blame. Poor drainage, poor gardening habits, strange weather patterns—each in turn was pinpointed as the villain. Environmentalists got into the fray. They knew for a certainty that it was all due to electricity in the atmosphere, for electricity was then practically as little understood as disease. Such a one wrote to the *Gardener's Chronicle* casting all blame on railroads, those newfangled monsters which were taking people around the land at speeds never intended by the Almighty, who had designed horses specifically for the services railroads were usurping.

One resourceful writer managed to join railroads and electricity in his accusations. The disease was caused by "a superabundance of Electricity set free in the atmosphere by the thousands of locomotives traveling all parts of England, [which] might be so many traveling factories of electricity diffusing it through the atmosphere to an enormous amount."

No one, of course, was smiling at the plague nor at the grim facts of crop failure and human suffering which were, for many months, to grow increasingly grimmer. On September 13, 1845, Editor Lindley announced: "We stop the press with very great regret, to announce the Potato Murrain has unequivocally broken out in Ireland. The crops about Dublin are suddenly perishing." This, he did not need to remind his readers, was a tragedy far outdistancing the loss of potatoes to the English.

Editor Lindley pointed out the full force of the tragedy for the Irish: "It is said that 4,500,000 persons in Ireland are fed upon Potatoes alone. The usual allowance of Potatoes to a laboring man is 14 pounds per diem, and therefore we may assume that, making deductions for women and children, 10 pounds per diem are consumed by each of these persons; therefore 45,000,000 pounds of Potatoes per diem must be eaten in Ireland by this part of the population alone." He estimated that 800,000 tons of potatoes would be needed for each year's plantings, with 9,000,000 acres occupied in raising, for both food and seed, potatoes that should each weigh a total of between six and seven million tons.

With such a crop suddenly unattainable, many Irish were leaving their native land to find refuge and hope across the sea. They could not, however, totally leave behind the potato blight, which presently turned out to be worldwide (being, in fact, no stranger to the Altiplano), but they did leave behind the tremendous single-crop cultivation which invited preying fungi and made all but impossible control of such fungi once they had had a good start.

Americans were also striving to find answers to the same kind of questions that were being asked in Europe. In 1851 the Massachusetts legislature gave added incentive to seekers for answers with an offer of "$10,000 to any person who shall satisfy the Governor and Council that, by a test of at least five years, he has discovered a sure and practical remedy for the Potato Rot."

Over a hundred hopefuls communicated their views to Governor and Council, and these views, of course, included "atmospherical influences," this time caused by a planet that should fade away within that critical five years. Another writer announced scornfully that "the paltry sum of $10,000 would be no inducement to him to make known the cause and remedy of the disease." The paltry sum, as far as records show, was never to induce anyone in Massachusetts to produce the sure and practical remedy demanded.

By 1847 the editor of the *Gardener's Chronicle* was already admitting, "The mischief is felt to be past present remedy; the discovery of its cause, with any certainty, seems equally hopeless, all inquiries as to that subject ending in a negative; and the world has wisely resigned itself to its fate. 'What can't be cured must be endured,' and the Potato disease belongs to that category." This was almost as fatalistic in tone as that of some people in northern Ireland who were trying to console themselves with "The Almighty will never let us starve; some other food will be sent us."

As it turned out, it was not the Almighty but America that sent the food, Indian corn meal, which to the Irish was only a shade better than starvation. At best, it was too little, for by the time the Great Hunger had passed, well over a million Irish had died. A million more had tried to emigrate, many of those dying on shipboard, some so weakened as to be easy victims of that shipboard fever now called typhus. Still more of the thus weakened were to die after reaching their destinations. In all, the tragedy was beyond computation.

As time passed, that blight slowly receded in destructiveness. Then, in the 1880s and too late to undo the damage, accident revealed a method of controlling that plant disease as well as many others. In the vineyards near Médoc, France, small boys had been helping themselves to so many grapes that the owner sprayed on a mixture whose poisonous bright bluish-white color should act as a deterrent for the thieves. There, in 1882, the noted mycologist and plant pathologist Pierre Millardet made a visit in order to study the inroads of a mildew that had been damaging other vineyards. His educated eye soon perceived that the only healthy vines were those on whose leaves he could detect the poisonous deposit.

Thus began the career of the now famous Bordeaux

mixture (copper sulfate and lime) as a deterrent for many plant-infecting organisms. In 1885, Millardet made public the formula for that mixture—a milestone in the relationship between crop plants and the increasingly numerous populations that would come increasingly to depend on them.

A plant that, scattered in small garden plots, had for thousands of years supplied Andean Indians with the staff of life had been making it big in the Old World, where it came to feed millions to the exclusion of most other crops. When, in a year of especial dampness, the blight found conditions favorable to its spread, there was nothing to interfere with its progress across millions of closely packed acres of potato plants. No one then had either imagination or information to perceive that with such plants, as with people in crowded slums, disease could spread like wildfire. Thus the Great Hunger was bound to make its appearance there eventually, with no one having any idea as to how best it might be dealt with. The emigration and never assuaged bitterness that followed were an inextricable consequence of men's blindness and lack of understanding of the role a plant can play in the destiny of men.

Upon whom are we to blame the misery? Surely on more than the blight organism that might have been more successfully dealt with had it waited another forty years, until men had learned something of the ways of disease-causing plants. Surely not on the potato itself that in its native home had managed to coexist with the organism and that, undoubtedly, had brought the disease with it in specimens later discarded as rotted in transit. Should we try to fix the blame on those well-meaning philosophers who saw in potatoes only a cheap and satisfying food for the poor? Should we not also blame the planters of potatoes with their ever-expanding garden plots? Some of the blame must be fixed on incompetent government officials, bewildered by a situation they could not comprehend. Had any of the conditions been different, the potato plague might have been more successfully dealt with. It was the grim combination—plants with a plant's potential for disaster unrecognized, people who were well meaning, opinionated, lacking in understanding—that built up to a tragedy history will not soon forget, which history should not forget unless the pattern is again to be repeated.

BREAD FROM TREES

With its own kind of cereal—corn—growing in regions where it could mature and, where it could not mature, with other kinds of native plants supplying the staff of life, the New World had long been doing quite well without the Old. What, though, was the staff of life for the newer world—newer, at least, to most Europeans— of the South Pacific? Though European navigators had cruised the South Pacific during the sixteenth century, they had not been able to bring back, whole and viable, the kinds of plant samples Columbus had procured in his nearer New Found World. The alternate extreme heat and cold of ships' holds and the limited understanding of plants' requirements long militated against the transfer of living plants from the far reaches of the South Pacific.

Nevertheless, plants of that region had been wondered at and described long before eighteenth-century explorers would undertake to move them to more accessible areas. Already in the seventeenth century,

Fray Martín de Munilla, who kept a journal of one of the early Spanish voyages—that of Pedro Fernández de Quirós—had recorded one of the early encounters of Europeans with the local staff of life, clearly the tree that was to win fame as breadfruit. This memorable encounter took place on April 25, 1606, the feast of St. Mark, when the explorers reached an island they promptly named "San Marcos" and which today is identified as Star Island of the Banks group.

"All these natives," Fray Martín wrote, "were naked, the women also. Among the fruits they brought to the boats was one which was as large as a big pawpaw and it was green. The natives eat this fruit roasted. It was roasted on board ship and it seemed very good. It tasted like baked chestnuts."

Breadfruit had so long been cultivated by men of those areas—the Moluccas, Celebes, New Guinea, and, in fact, practically all the Pacific islands—that no one can say where its original home must have been. No one knows where first it grew wild. "In cultivated breadfruit," a botanical writer points out, "the seeds are almost always abortive which shows its cultivation goes back to remote antiquity." In the absence of such seeds, of course, propagation has to be "vegetative"—that is, by cuttings.

Captain James Cook was introduced to this fruit in Tahiti in 1769. He described it as about the size of a child's head, its surface finely pebbled, "covered with a thin skin and having a core about as big as the handle of a small knife. The eatable part of the breadfruit lies between the skin and core and is somewhat of the consistence of new bread. It must be roasted before it is eaten."

Again in 1772 Captain Cook was heading for the

South Pacific. With him as ship's master mate was William Bligh, who recorded with some enthusiasm the breadfruit (*Artocarpus communis*) he encountered: "Inside it is as soft and tender as a penny loaf. There is neither seed nor stone inside but all is pure substance like bread"—when roasted, of course, as today we do with potatoes. Eventually breadfruit was to play a critical role in William Bligh's life as well as in the lives of many other men.

It was to be Sir Joseph Banks, naturalist of Cook's 1769 voyage, whom the breadfruit haunted. If only it could be grown as well in the West Indies as in the East, it could help solve that constant problem of tropical plantation owners—how to procure bread in latitudes where the usual bread cereals could not mature or, where they might, must absorb too much of the slaves' time and efforts. Bread growing freely on trees would be an annually self-renewing crop to feed both planters and their many slaves. Definitely, the tree could confer a boon upon the West Indies!

Before all this could come to pass, breadfruit must be growing in the West Indies, and how was that to be achieved since breadfruit rarely produced any seeds and those doubtfully viable? The answer must be to transport thither young "seedlings." It was a fine idea but one more than a bit difficult to put into action. There had to be a ship exclusively devoted to such a mission. There had to be a captain who knew his way around in both East and West Indies, who appreciated the value of breadfruit and who could be relied on to see the undertaking through no matter what obstacles he might encounter. By late 1787 all these conditions seemed to have been met.

In August of that year Banks received a letter from

Captain Bligh: "I arrived yesterday from Jamaica. I have heard the flattering news of your great goodness to me with the command of the vessel you purpose to go to the South Seas."

From the Admiralty also came a letter to Sir Joseph, this one explaining that a ship had been commissioned, that she was to be called the *Bounty* and that Bligh had been selected to command her. Would Sir Joseph be so kind as to prepare instructions for the handling of the plants, especially directed toward the gardeners whom the Admiralty intended to send along to take charge of the so delicate nurslings.

Of course Sir Joseph would—and from a man of his high social and intellectual standing, the suggestions would be looked upon as commands: "The master and crew of the *Bounty*," Sir Joseph wrote, "must not think it a grievance to give up the best accommodations. . . . The difficulty of carrying plants by sea is very great: a small sprinkling of salt water or of the salt dew which fills the air even in a moderate gale will inevitably destroy them if not immediately washed off with fresh water. It is necessary therefore that the cabin be appropriated to the sole purpose of making a kind of greenhouse, and the key of it given into the custody of the gardener and that in case of cold weather in going round the Cape a stove is provided by which it may be kept at a temperature of the intertropical countries. . . .

"As the plants will frequently want to be washed from the salt dampness, which the sea air will deposit upon them, besides allowance of water, a considerable provision must be made for that purpose; but as the vessel will have no cargo whatever but the plants on board, there will be abundant room for water casks, of which she must be supplied with as large a quantity as possible, that the gardener may never be refused the quantity of water he may have occasion to demand."

It was, of course, necessary to emphasize to seamen who knew very little about any kind of plants how tender they might be to environmental changes. It should have been equally important to select seamen who could be made to understand the importance of the voyage's object and therefore might be willing to forego some of their very limited traditional comforts for the comfort of the plants. Someone should have anticipated the effect of the extreme coddling of plants on seamen who were never in the least coddled. Add to that the beguiling stay in Tahiti with its friendly natives welcoming the seamen to share their idyllic lives and thereby to regard themselves as more than human automata, and the makings of a mutiny might have been foreseen by any ship's master less unimaginatively disciplinarian than William Bligh.

Once the *Bounty* was well started on her homeward voyage, there flared up that mutiny which was destined to become famous throughout the civilized world. All those plants in whose future so much thought and money had been invested were tossed jeeringly into the sea. Captain Bligh in a boat overloaded with his partisans was set adrift to meet, everyone then expected, death by drowning or exposure. No one—so all believed—could take a boat like that across the 3,600 miles of ocean, to arrive at Timor, in the Dutch East Indies, forty-seven days later and with the loss of but a single life.

Emptied of seedlings and of the men who had gone with Bligh, the *Bounty* turned back to Matavai Bay. A few of the returned men decided to risk remaining there. Most, taking unto themselves Tahitian women and joined by several Tahitian couples, sailed off again in the *Bounty*—all but one never to be seen again by European eyes. Years later, on remote Pitcairn Island, there were encountered the surviving women and children together with the mutiny's then sole survivor, one of the gardeners whose mission had been to nurse the breadfruit seedlings on the voyage from Tahiti to Jamaica.

Captain Bligh's amazing odyssey in an open boat is today part of maritime legend. With the doggedness that had made his success in that doubtful undertaking possible, Bligh was determined to make a second and successful attempt at transplanting breadfruit. In 1793, assigned the command of the ship *Providence,* he was finally able to deliver young trees to the West Indies— 333 to St. Vincent, 346 to Port Royal, Jamaica.

"I give you joy of the success of your Plants," he wrote in a happy letter to Sir Joseph from St. Helena. "I am happily arrived with a beautiful collection in sight of this island. . . . I most sincerely pray you may live to hear they flourish and thousands are fed with their fruit."

Sir Joseph, as well as many other people, was to hear just that. One such person, George Washington, promptly made inquiry as to how he might secure a breadfruit cutting to start at Mount Vernon. Breadfruit being a strictly tropical tree, it was not to grow at Mount Vernon. However, descendants of the trees which formed the *Providence's* cargo are now to be encountered not only all over the Caribbean islands but throughout lowland Central and northern South America where few of the thousands who are fed by them have the vaguest idea as to how they got there and at what cost.

2

The
Spice
of
Life

For men never far from starvation should their crops fail, cereals and vegetables made the difference between life and death. Meats were a real luxury, though an impermanent one, since meats spoiled rapidly and had either to be eaten soon after slaughter or preserved by salting or drying or both. Where spices could be had, these offered a considerably better means of preservation since they could also hide the odors and taste of incipient putrefaction. It can be no mere accident of taste that the spiciest foods belong to hotter lands where there is never cold or frost to destroy putrefying bacteria and discourage molds. In part, at least, nature has compensated for such hot climates through the spices native to such lands. Men have completed the compensation by providing markets and means of transportation for the valued plant products. A taste for spicy foods developed in chillier lands and persisted long after the cost in money and human lives had risen to incalculable heights.

No historian writing of any part of Europe of the late sixteenth and early seventeenth centuries could overlook the impact of spices on the people and politics of that era. One such historian—John Lothrop Motley—put the spice trade in grim perspective.

"In that multitude of islands which make up the Eastern Archipelago," he wrote, "there were but five at that period which grew the clove—Ternate, Tydor, Motiel, Makien, Bacia. Pepper and ginger, even nutmegs, cassia, and mace, were but vulgar drugs, precious as they already were to the world and the world's commerce, compared with this most magnificent spice.

"It is wonderful to reflect upon the strange composition of man. The world had lived in former ages very comfortably without cloves. But by the beginning of the seventeenth century that odoriferous pistil had been the cause of so many pitched battles and obstinate wars, of so much vituperation, negotiating, and intriguing, that the world's destiny seemed to have almost become dependent upon the growth of a particular gillyflower. Out of its sweetness had grown such bitterness among great nations as not torrents of blood could wash away. A commonplace condiment enough it seems to us now, easily to be dispensed with, and not worth purchasing at a thousand human lives or so the cargo, but it was once the great prize to be struggled for by civilized nations. From that fervid earth, warmed from within by volcanic heat, and basking ever beneath the equatorial sun, arose vapours as deadly to human life as the fruits were exciting and delicious to human senses. Yet the atmosphere of pestiferous fragrance had attracted rather than repelled. The poisonous delights of the climate, added to the perpetual and various warfare for its productions, spread a strange fascination around those fatal isles."

Though the greatest violence of competition for spices belonged especially to the decades about which Motley was writing, spices had been a commercially valuable commodity since most ancient times. By King Solomon's reign (estimated about 1000 B.C.) when Sheba's queen undertook a lengthy journey to meet him, spices were representing a wealth to be classed with precious metals and flashing jewels: "And she came to Jerusalem with a very great train, with camels that bare spices, and very much gold, and precious stones. . . . And all the earth sought to Solomon, to hear his wisdom, which God had put in his heart. And they brought every man his present, vessels of silver, and vessels of gold, and garments and armor, and spices, horses, and mules, a [tax] year by year." (I Kings 10:2, 24)

About 1,100 years later when St. John was composing the Book of Revelation, spices remained an important item of exchange in that very commercial, sinful, doomed city, "Babylon the Great." "And the merchants of the earth shall weep and mourn over her, for no man bringeth their merchandise any more. . . . The merchandise of gold, and silver, and precious stones . . . and cinnamon and odours, and ointments."

Spices were still making it big on the international monetary scene some three centuries later when the Visigoth king, Alaric, managed to achieve through starvation what military strength alone had not been able to bring about. In 410 A.D. blockaded Rome surrendered to the barbarians who sacked it pitilessly, then demanded a high ransom, part of which—so it is told—was to be paid in pepper. In what remote land such pepper grew and by what long and devious route it had passed through middlemen's hands until it reached Italy can only be guessed at now.

Pepper, like most other spices, then grew as it grows

today in a very limited area of the earth's surface with just the right kind of soil, the right amount of atmospheric moisture, the right temperatures, and the right relationship between hours of daylight and of darkness. There are few lands where all such conditions are met at once, and though today spice trees grow in some areas far from the Spice Islands—the Moluccas—in the early days, even had plant transportation been undertaken, the journeys were too long and uncertain, plant requirements too little understood for that undertaking to prove successful.

Almost equally uncertain were the travels and fate of the harvested spices. Exactly by what route and agency spices would have arrived in Babylon the Great can now only be guessed. Since they grew on islands, their journeys had to start on native seagoing craft. By the time pepper was being paid as a partial ransom for Rome, it would have been unloaded at some Red Sea port, then reloaded onto camels for a trip to a spice emporium such as Alexandria, on the Mediterranean shore of Egypt.

In 1487 two Portuguese merchant-spies were reporting on the intricacies of the Alexandrian spice markets and on the very circumscribed lives endured there by non-Moslem European traders, who were permitted to remain only as long as the trading season lasted. According to their lands of origin, each group of traders—Genoese, Florentines, Venetians, Catalans, Narbonnese, what would you—was allowed a "fonduc" where European customs and religious observances might be followed and where no Egyptian could interfere. A fonduc was a walled settlement and included dwelling houses, warehouses, a chapel—all being surrounded by a wall whose gates, by the Sultan's orders, were to be locked each night. The men dwelling inside such foreign enclaves were not to emerge during hours of darkness and had to leave the city altogether once the annual trade in spices had ended. Each spice-trading nation had its own consul who could bring claims before Egyptian authorities in Cairo, but only for a limited number of times each year.

Foreign merchants had to buy spices in Alexandria as unsorted as they had been packed in the Spice Islands, whereas mercantile houses in Europe demanded spices that had already been sorted as to size and quality. Thus the European trader in Alexandria had to have a nice instinct as to when and how far he was being cheated, to weigh it all against the probable 100 percent profit in Europe, and to decide whether it all could be worth the insults and personal humiliations he had been made to endure. If some merchants dreamed of bypassing the Alexandria market in favor of direct dealings with the Far East, it is hardly to be wondered at.

Possibly it was mariners and merchants from Marseilles—the then Marsala—who may have secured in Alexandria the pepper which was to help buy off Alaric's hordes. By that time, Marsala was already a thriving Mediterranean port whence coveted Oriental specialties were further distributed in western Europe. In 1224, a Marseilles bride's dowry was being paid in ginger, mace, and cardamom.

Some fifty years later, the Polo brothers of Venice were taking the long overland route from the Near East to the Far East—a caravan route by which such Oriental luxuries as spices had been reaching the Occident. When, after an absence of twenty-five years, the two brothers, together with the son of one who had accompanied them, returned to their native city as world travelers, the riches, they had managed to bring with them on their persons and the further riches they could tell of helped to turn the eyes of many another European eagerly eastward.

What served further to make the Polos' journey of enduring influence was the book written in 1298 by the younger Polo—Marco—to while away the long dull hours he had to spend in prison after being captured by the Genoese during one of those too frequent campaigns then raging between Italian municipalities. *The Travels of Marco Polo* was destined to become a sort of bible for the adventure- and profit-minded of Europe.

Though the Chinese emperor had treated the Polos with great respect, the length of their stay at the Chinese Imperial court was not entirely of their own choosing. It had ended only when, the emperor being asked to send a young woman of his family as a bride for an Indian ruler and the land route thither being closed by wars, the emperor decided to send the lady by sea and to employ in that venture the nautical skills of the citizens of a nautical city-state. Thus released from Kublai Khan's immediate control, the Polos could start on the long, slow journey home. Along the way they were to see many things which, when recounted in Europe, were to stimulate European interest in the Far East.

Of a large island, possibly Java, Marco recorded: "It is under the dominion of one king only, nor do the inhabitants pay tribute to any other power. . . . The country abounds with rich commodities. Pepper, nutmegs, spikenard, galengal, cubebs, cloves and all other valuable spices and drugs, are the produce of the island: which occasion it to be visited by many ships laden with merchandise, that yields to the owners a considerable profit. The quantity of gold collected there exceeds all calculation and belief. From thence . . . also is obtained the greatest part of the spices that are distributed throughout the world."

Such riches to be wasted on naked, idol-worshipping natives!

Another island, presumably Ceylon, was equally likely to stir the cupidity of European men of business while challenging the missionary zeal of European men of God. "The people worship idols and . . . go nearly in a state of nudity. . . . The island produces more beautiful and valuable rubies than are found in any other part of the world, and likewise sapphires, topazes, amethysts, garnets and other precious and costly stones. The king is reported to possess the grandest ruby that ever was seen, being a span in length and the thickness of a man's arm, brilliant beyond description, and without a single flaw."

The Polos had not been privileged to view the fabulous stone, if indeed it existed, but they had managed to secure smaller stones, which they brought home concealed on their persons. The sight of these and the tales of gold, jewels, spices, drugs, perfumes sufficed to fire the determination of Europeans to increase traffic with the Far East and to find some way to dispense with the services of troublesome middlemen.

It was, of course, more than the Oriental middlemen that had been responsible for the high cost of Eastern products in western Europe. To the ever-present risks of total loss by storm at sea or accident along mountain caravan trails there had to be added the risk of hijacking by brigands on land and pirates at sea. Always to the original costs of the cargoes must be added the costs of months-long transport—the time for a spice cargo to reach England from the islands being two years or more. Small wonder that the prices paid for such a cargo could represent the ransom of an imperial city!

If only a ship could sail direct to those fabled islands and return thence, her hold full of spices, to her European home port! This was long the impossible dream, for not until the end of the fifteenth century did any European vessel succeed in reaching or rounding the Cape of Good Hope to penetrate into seas that were presently to give access to lands where spices grew. It would be well into the sixteenth century before any navigator should so much as believe it possible to reach the East by sailing west below South America.

Mariners had long accepted timidly and without challenge the dicta of early geographers who wrote, during the twelfth and thirteenth centuries, of the ocean that washed the westernmost shores of Europe—the "Sea of Darkness" called the Atlantic. "In that sea," wrote an early Arab geographer, "are places where flames of fire a hundred cubits high, perpetually rise into the air. Here too are enormous fishes of immense length, and other animals of strange form: there are cities floating in the air." In today's language that would mean volcanoes (possibly on Tenerife), whales, and the mirages encountered in hot, dry regions as along the African coast. In earlier centuries, wise mariners would regard such sightings as warnings not to let curiosity lead them on into unknown seas whence they could scarcely hope to return alive.

Other early geographers wrote more factually, though no more encouragingly: "No one knows what lies beyond in the Atlantic; no one has been able to discover anything for certain, on account of the difficulties of navigation, due to darkness, the height of the waves, the frequency of tempests, and the violence of the winds . . . no mariners dare venture to cross it, nor sail out into the open sea."

The open sea—therein lay the real problem. Up to the early fifteenth century, most navigations had been coast-hugging ventures either within the Mediterranean or, more daringly, south along Africa for a relatively short distance. Vessels had not then been built with thought for or knowledge of the possible stresses and strains of long ocean crossings nor for the excessive winds that might be encountered, especially in high latitudes. There were no reliable instruments. Men had long been conditioned both by legend and their own ignorance to believe that no man could safely undertake to sail south beyond Cape Bojador, lying far out on Africa's westernmost bulge and still about 25 degrees north of the equator.

One man, born during the last decade of the fourteenth century, was not prepared to accept the interdiction as final. Something lay beyond Cape Bojador as it lay beyond the many capes that seafaring men, through the centuries, had sighted and passed. Until Cape Bojador, too, was passed, nothing could really be known of what lay there, and all tales of the land being a cruel, uninhabitable waste could have no real basis save in the minds of timorous men. Thus reasoned a scion of the royal house of Portugal, a land whose shores were washed by the ocean he was bound to have explored.

Since he was born at a time and place where traditions of knightly derring-do still flourished, timorousness was not a quality to be tolerated by him either in knights or navigators. Though not himself a mariner and never guiding a vessel into those waters he wanted to have explored, the young prince became so enthusiastic a patron of geographers and pilots that he won for himself enduring fame as Prince Henry the Navigator (1394–1460).

Far out toward Cape Vincent, the westernmost point of all, Prince Henry had his castle built, and there, to the obbligato of pounding surf, he kept court for travelers and geographers and to them he made known his determination that Cape Bojador should be passed. Of this a chronicler wrote, "He sent out many times, not only ordinary men but such, as by their experience and great deeds of war, were foremost in the profession of arms. Yet there was not one who dared to pass that cape and learn about the land beyond it, as the Prince wished." Great deeds of war, unfortunately, could not equip a man to face, day and night, in a frail ship, the terrors of an as yet unexplored ocean.

"Not cowardice," we are assured, "nor want of good will were at the back of the failure." It was Portugal's neighbor and rival in exploration that had been spreading those dark rumors as to the dangers of such undertakings. Clearly, the seeds of international rivalry in exploration were already beginning to sprout.

At long last the prince found in his equerry and Master of Horse, Gil Eannes, a man willing to risk everything in the desired navigation. The first time he undertook this he was "touched by the self-same terror" as earlier adventurers, but the next year—1434— "despising all danger" he bravely tried again. This time he continued south beyond the cape to find there a land no more terrible than ones he already knew.

Not only had a forbidding cape been passed but a milestone in human thought and human vision as well. Cape after African cape were soon to be passed, with ships of newly courageous courtiers bringing back to

Portugal cargoes of ever-increasing value—gold dust, ivory, wax, skins, sugar, and the Malaguetta pepper which many insisted was no less desirable than that which came from the Spice Islands. They also brought back black slaves whom devout sons of the Church looked upon ambiguously both as pagan souls to be saved and strong bodies to be exploited. Rival nations, the prince realized, must soon learn of the profits thus to be made and would try to get possession of the lands whence the cargoes came.

Dreading lest his country should be excluded from the trade her navigators had established at so great a cost, Prince Henry sent an embassy to Pope Martin V, begging that the pontiff, in whose person was then embodied a sort of League of Nations, issue a decree stating that lands discovered by Portuguese navigators should belong to Portugal or, at least, be under Portuguese rule. The pagan natives, of course, were not consulted either by prince or pope, who granted the request, adding generously "a plenary indulgence for the souls of all such as should perish in the undertaking." Thus the seizure of newly discovered lands was elevated to the level of Crusades. Nevertheless—though it would take many, many decades for the fact to be realized—the profit motive thus stimulated by the passing of an unpassable cape was to threaten more lives more grimly than ever had the bloody hand-to-hand battles with Saracens.

When Prince Henry died in 1460, that ultimate African cape, presently to be known as the Cape of Good Hope, had yet to be passed. It would be over a quarter century later that the Portuguese navigator Bartholomeu Dias should be blown beyond that cape by one of the fabled storms of the South Atlantic. When the storm abated, Dias saw that as he sailed north, the land mass lay to his *left*—conclusive proof that there was a way around Africa as there had been around Cape Bojador. Dias, perceiving that his sailors, miserably sick with scurvy, were convinced their captain was taking his ships and them to certain destruction, knew that mutiny must follow should he continue his northward passage along Africa's east coast. Wisely, though reluctantly, he turned back and arrived in Lisbon during December 1488. Though he failed to reach the Spice Islands, he had opened a way thither and won for himself great honor and reward.

Meanwhile, a Genoese navigator named Christopher Columbus had been trying to persuade Portugal's king, John II, to sponsor his plan for a quick, easy voyage to the Spice Islands by sailing in a westerly direction, the earth having been conceded to be spherical but the diameter computed to be far less than it actually is. When King John showed no interest, Columbus moved himself and his pleas to the Spanish court and there presently found sponsors in Queen Ysabel "La Católica" of Castile and León and her royal spouse, King Ferdinand of Aragón. By March 1493 Columbus had returned from his first voyage to assure his sponsors he had found that new route to "India" and to receive tumultuous acclaim.

Disturbed by the realization of what he had rejected and thus had gone by default to rival Spain, King John determined to make as certain as possible that what his Portuguese navigators had won at so great a risk should not be seized by those greedy neighbors, the Spanish.

Spain was equally determined not only to hold what had been discovered in voyages sponsored by her monarchs but also to continue exploring until her mariners should arrive at the fabled islands, which should become her property, not Portugal's. The monarchs of both lands, being loyal and influential Catholics, turned for arbitration to the Holy See. The then reigning pontiff, Alexander VI, of the notorious Spanish Borja (Borgia) family, could hardly have been an altogether impartial judge. Yet through the famous treaty drawn up at Tordesillas in June 1494 Portugal emerged with a richer booty than Spain intended or Portugal may at first have realized.

The overseas world, known and yet to be known, was divided by an imaginary north-south line about 1,000 miles (by today's measurements) west of the Azores—Spain to hold all lands west of that line, Portugal the lands to the east. Where in the Orient the extension of such a line might run would long remain a matter of dispute between the contending lands. The intent was to give Spain undisputed claim to the Americas (not yet so named) and to Portugal, Africa and the Spice Islands already explored and exploited by Portuguese mariners. As it turned out, the imaginary line had allotted to Portugal the South American bulge which is now part of Brazil—a fact that suggests to some historians that King John knew exactly what he was getting and that some unusually closemouthed Portuguese mariners had already landed there. With or without treasure, it could serve as a most convenient landfall for any mariner on his way to the South Sea, as the Pacific was then referred to.

To anyone living nearly five centuries later, it seems almost incomprehensible that even a Vicar of Christ dared assume the right to sponsor a division of the oceans and lands of the earth between two clamorous Latin nations, no matter how good Catholics they might have been. Thereby he was ignoring the claims of the equally Latin Genoese and Venetians who had previously had a virtual monopoly of the European spice markets, of the French whose mariners were among the world's boldest and most skilled, and of the English and Dutch whose later apostasy had not yet provided excuse for such an exclusion.

The native rulers of far lands thus assigned to Spain and Portugal could have no rights worth considering beyond the one of saving their own souls by accepting conversion to the Holy Catholic Church. The pontiff, being a man of his times as well as of little conscience, would not have hesitated to issue the papal bull that followed upon the agreement at Tordesillas. After all, he carefully specified that voyages to heathen lands must include men of God and that all such voyagers, whether churchmen or not, were to strive continually to win new souls to the Holy Catholic Church. Whatever hesitation justice to alien peoples might have suggested to the mind of the pontiff, the near certainty of future bloody wars between professing Christians should have added the final persuasion.

With the treaty drawn up and signed, in 1494, by the disputing lands, the race to find and claim yet more spice-producing islands was on. While Columbus, cherishing the delusion that he had already arrived there, was consolidating Spain's claim to the Caribbean islands and nearby Central America, Portuguese Vasco da Gama set forth, in 1497, to extend Bartholomeu Dias' exploration of the seas on the far side of the Cape of Good Hope. After a year's voyage, da Gama arrived in Calicut, India, and was back in Lisbon a year later with spices purchased in Indian markets and with tantalizing tales of the magnificently wealthy Oriental monarchs he had encountered. No one then gave much thought to the sufferings or human losses such a voyage involved. A jubilant Portugal determined to expand her trade with and assert her claims over the fabulous lands of the East.

After Vasco da Gama had been received in Lisbon with noisy acclaim, arrangements were quickly made there to improve contacts with the Orient and to consolidate a monopoly of the spice trade. Navigator Pedro Alvarez Cabral set sail in March 1500, to return fifteen months later, his ship laden with a then priceless cargo of spices. On this voyage, as it was to be on most future voyages of Europeans to the Far East, the bulge of today's Brazil was a way station for securing water and fresh fruits—the latter then only vaguely recognized to be valuable antiscorbutics. Prevailing winds and ocean currents favored using Pernambuco or Bahía as stopping places. Meanwhile, Vasco dā Gama, in command of twenty vessels, set forth to close the usual route by which spices had previously been reaching Europe. Waylaying Arab traders, he denied their vessels access to Red Sea ports and their cargoes to Alexandria.

To govern the Indies he claimed, Portugal's king, Manuel I (1469–1521), sent out very able viceroys— Francisco d'Almeida in 1505, Alfonso d'Albuquerque (1507–1511). It must then have seemed that an increasingly brilliant future lay before the two Iberian lands that claimed dominion over vastly expanding empires. Yet the seeds of dissolution had already been sown, notably in Portugal, where the labor of black slaves purchased in Africa from black traders began undermining the once sturdy agrarian character of the Portuguese. Intrigue and corruption at home, exploitation abroad began to taint the aristocracy and forecast the downfall of that once great empire.

Already before Manuel I of Portugal died, Hernan

Cortés had conquered Mexico for Spain with the aid of a handful of Spanish adventurers and that fearful new secret weapon, the horse. Twelve years later, Francisco Pizarro and his brothers were adding to the golden wealth seized in Mexico the yet greater golden wealth of the Incas. None of the famed spices of the Orient were there found, and it would take decades for the "Joyfull Newes" of strange and valuable plants to stir interest in the martial Spanish. Yet it had been plant products that had provided the original impulse for exploration and exploitation of new lands and that would continue to set the men of Christian nations at one another's throats in a most un-Christian manner.

Only a firsthand account of a voyage of exploration can give an idea of the miseries men were prepared to endure in pursuit of spices and other valuable products of the East. We'd like to believe that those early voyagers were highly motivated through the same kind of challenge acknowledged by a notable mountain climber of our day when asked to explain why he had devoted so much effort toward climbing Mt. Everest—"Because it is there." Examination of the evidence, however, suggests that what motivated most of the early explorers of unknown seas could better be described as "Because it is there the profit is." For the seamen there was always great misery and small profit. For the commander there could be great honor as well as great profit—always assuming he survived to enjoy the rewards.

An account of one voyage of exploration can give an idea of most, for, despite exciting adventures along the way, there was a predictable sameness, though scarcely dullness, about all. They begin with a man obsessed by an idea and a determination to make that idea a reality. They continue with his search for a royal sponsor to lend legitimacy and authority to the proposed voyage and, it is hoped, thereby encourage private sponsors to add to the funds supplied from royal coffers. Detailed plans are then made, ships purchased, repaired, fitted out for a voyage of unknown duration into distant and dangerous seas. Always there must be men—common sailors of uncommon qualities, ships' officers to direct navigation, military men and officers prepared to fight any enemy, either European or Oriental—and, in Spain and Portugal, men of God undertaking, whatever the personal risks, to follow the directives of the Treaty of Tordesillas.

Ferdinand Magellan's voyage had all this plus something extra and altogether unique. His ship, *Victoria,* was to be the first of any land to set out in a westerly direction and arrive back home from an easterly, having demonstrated beyond the shadow of any doubt that the earth was a circumnavigable globe. The *Victoria* was the only vessel of that brave little fleet which had sailed forth from Seville in September 1519 to complete the historic voyage. One vessel, the *San Antonio,* turned tail and ran for home at the entrance of what would prove to be the straits Magellan had been seeking. Another vessel was wrecked off the coast of Patagonia. Of the three that limped to the Spice Islands, one, the *Concepción,* was scuttled and burned, possibly because it was too rotten to proceed farther. Another, Magellan's flagship *Trinidad,* foundered, perhaps overloaded with a cargo of spices. And of the men, reported to be 277 in all, only eighteen remained alive, though barely so, to arrive back in Seville on the *Victoria.* Magellan was there in spirit only, for his body had lain for over a year in the soil of one of those island groups, the Philippines, his venture had added to the Spanish Empire.

The *Victoria's* cargo of pepper and cloves was of sufficient value to excite the greed of stay-at-homes, not excepting the Spanish king who was also the Holy Roman Emperor, Charles V. Nevertheless, the most valuable yield of Magellan's voyage was the ocean-to-ocean passage that now bears his name and the journal of that voyage kept by an adventurous young Italian gentleman, Antonio Pigafetta of Vicenza, who enrolled himself under Magellan.

Portugal's expanding empire took Magellan first to service in India under Governor de Almeida where he had a chance to demonstrate his navigational skills, then to fighting the Moors in North Africa. Commended there for his courage, he imagined the king of Portugal would look with favor on his cherished plan of finding a shorter route to the Far East—shorter by the same computations that had misled Columbus. Like King John II a quarter century earlier, notoriously stingy King Manuel was not impressed with the plan save in that it must prove costly. Believing the undertaking impossible of realization in any case, he rejected Magellan's plans, thus insuring that his subject should look elsewhere to find a less parsimonious prince.

King Manuel might have hesitated thus to reject Magellan had some personal prejudice not blinded him to the fact that a disavowed Magellan would surely seek his fortune in a Spain as much committed as Portugal to the idea of claiming sovereignty over all the Spice Islands. By October 1517 Magellan had arrived in Spain, encouraged by the highly prosperous Diego Barbosa, whose daughter, Beatriz, Magellan presently took to wife. Barbosa was all for Magellan's plan and would have financed it himself had his funds been sufficient. He was able, however, to enlist the support of young King Charles so that by March 1518 articles of agreement between Magellan and his Spanish sponsors had been drawn up and signed.

Too late, the Portuguese monarch perceived his mistake and strove to remedy it by subterfuge, since, regretfully, he realized that it was no longer possible to detain Magellan in Portugal. Determined that a project so menacing to Portugal's spice monopoly should not succeed, King Manuel sent out a secret agent, Sebastian Alvarez, to spy on Magellan and to arrange that nothing should come of the grand design.

In July 1518 Alvarez was reporting at length to his royal employer, giving descriptions of Magellan's ships, personnel, armaments, victualing, and, in fact, any details he had been able to ferret out through the sly questioning for which he seemed to have a special talent. He told of visiting the captain-general—Magellan—with persuasions that included everything from appeals to the captain's loyalty to the land of his birth to subtle promises of advancement should he see the light and reject his agreement with the Spanish. "I will," wrote Alvarez, "watch the service of your Highness to the full extent of my power."

The "full extent" may have included arrangements for the total elimination of Magellan should such a course seem necessary. The secret agent, having considered this, explained, "It seems to me, that if Fernan Magellan were removed, that Ruy Faleiro would follow whatever Magellan did." Since the main object was to prevent the expedition sailing under any captain, Alvarez looked around for other means of stopping the expedition. To his employer, Alvarez expressed the pious hope: "Please God the Almighty, that they may make such a voyage as did the Cortereals!"—that is, never be heard of again—"and that your Highness may be at rest, and for ever be envied, as you are, by all princes." To this end, the so envied prince's agent was busily subverting suppliers and ships' captains.

Magellan would not have been a man of his land or age had he not had some suspicions as to the kind of schemes that were afoot. He must have realized that neither wind nor waves nor, even, some new terror of the sea would be his chief problem. Yet, devoutly putting his faith in God, he went purposefully ahead with preparations, enrolling men to a number variously given as 237 or 277. Of these, most were Spanish—men bound to resent having to sail under a Portuguese captain—while the thirty-seven Portuguese included could not assure Magellan loyalty, for some might already be in King Manuel's pay and others might be subvertible by the sly Alvarez.

Despite all obstacles, Magellan's little fleet had left Spain by late September and was heading south along the African coast. At Tenerife they stopped for fresh water and provisions. Somewhere in the equatorial regions they turned west to cross the ocean and reach, in late November, a cape near today's Recife in Pernambuco, Brazil. From there on, Magellan would keep close to the coast as he cruised southward in an attempt to locate the passage he so believed in. Every bay and inlet was examined for the opening which should lead to the South Sea. December saw the ships making a brief stay in the region of today's Rio de Janeiro. By the time the March fall equinox had passed, they were far to the south along the Patagonian coast and finding the winter days growing too short to permit effective navigation.

In Port San Julian, Magellan decided to outwait the long nights and fierce storms of the far-southern winter, and there a yet fiercer storm broke upon him in mutiny sponsored by the captains of three of his ships, who tried to seize their captain-general and destroy him. With the two ringleaders Magellan dealt swiftly and ruthlessly, as he had to if he were to survive the long months yet ahead. Another mutinous captain, who was thought to have the special protection of King Charles, was left behind on the Patagonian coast with a mutinous priest, both to be picked up by the *San Antonio* after she deserted at the entrance to the straits. The rest of the disaffected Magellan pardoned, hoping the example made of the others might have had a sobering effect and knowing that he could not afford to reduce the number of his companions by eliminating all mutineers.

During this Port San Julian interlude the *Santiago* was wrecked while attempting to explore the coast to the south. Crew, supplies, and most of the removable ship's gear, however, were saved. By late August 1520 the four remaining vessels were again heading south. Two months later and almost by accident they sailed into the inlet which is the entrance to the 350-mile-long, winding, stormy strait which now bears Magellan's name. This was where the *San Antonio* deserted, to head back for Spain with complaints and accusations against the captain-general. The remaining three ships kept on through the strait to emerge, thirty-eight days later, in the limitless ocean misnamed "peaceful"—the Pacific.

If the ships thought they were leaving their troubles behind them, they were soon to learn the bitter truth. Pigafetta recorded: "On Wednesday, 28th November, we left the strait and entered the ocean to which afterwards we gave the denomination Pacific, and in which we sailed for the space of three months and twenty days without taking any fresh provisions. The biscuits we were eating no longer deserved the name of bread; it was nothing but dust, and worms which had consumed the substance; and what is more, it smelled intolerably, being impregnated with the urine of mice. The water which we were obliged to drink was equally putrid and offensive. We were even so far reduced, that we might not die of hunger, to eat pieces of leather with which the main-yard was covered to prevent it from wearing the rope." Sawdust was also eaten and mice, which, when caught, sold for a ducat apiece.

All sickened with scurvy. Nineteen died of it, while many were so sick that they could do no work by the time, in late January, they reached St. Paul's Island in mid-Pacific. There they found a variety of sea foods, eggs of turtles and of birds as well as the birds themselves. They even succeeded in getting fresh water by collecting rain in sails and running the water thus collected into casks. Again they set sail and again experienced the miseries of bad food and water until, in early March, they reached the Marianas, whose inhabitants were, by Pigafetta's account, "poor, but very dexterous, above all in thieving." Thieves' Islands the group became—Los Ladrones.

By mid-March, Magellan's ships reached the islands that would eventually be known as the Philippines in honor of Charles V's bigoted son, Philip II, who was presently to stake Spanish sea power and overseas wealth on the subjugation of a wickedly Protestant England. For rest and refreshment Magellan chose to put in at an uninhabited island near Samar, whither came natives bringing offerings of strange foods—"figs more than a foot long," which were undoubtedly bananas or plantains, "and two cochos," obviously coconuts. Oranges were highly welcome to men recovering from scurvy. "We remained at this place eight days," Pigafetta wrote. "The captain went there every day to see his sick men, whom he had placed on this island to refresh them: and he gave them every day the water of this said fruit, the cocho, which comforted them much."

For the month following, the ships continued among the Philippines, and at Matan Magellan was lured into a battle by a chief who, claiming to have accepted Christianity, begged the captain's assistance in fighting another chief whose sinfulness was evidenced by his rejection of conversion. In this fight Magellan lost his life, probably to the gratification of his once mutinous fellow captains against whom he would not now be able to bear witness.

Inevitably, the surviving captains began bickering among themselves while the ships sailed on from island to island, looting and plundering as they could. A captain Carvalho had voted himself captain-general to succeed Magellan and began his rule by burning the least seaworthy of the three remaining ships, the *Concepción,* wherein were lost all Magellan's personal logs and records which otherwise might have borne witness against Carvalho and others.

On November 8, 1521, Carvalho reached one of the Spice Islands—Tidore, where the strangers were cordially welcomed by the island's king. Four days later the king had a shed built near the shore to accommodate the merchandise which, though the king could not know it, the newcomers had won by piracy of native junks. While observing closely and recording in some detail, Antonio Pigafetta did a bit of trading on his own.

"Thither we carried all we had to barter, and placed it in the custody of three of our men. For ten ells of red cloth of pretty good quality"—an ell being somewhat under a yard—"they gave a bahar"—about 400 pounds,—"of cloves. . . . For fifteen ells of middling quality, a bahar, for fifteen hatchets a bahar, for thirty-five glass cups a bahar; and the king in this manner had from us almost all our goblets. . . . Many of the above-mentioned goods had been obtained by us by the capture of the junks, which I have related; and the haste we were in to return to Spain caused us to sell our goods at a lower price than we should have done, had we not been in a hurry." Surely a tempting prize—these islands where spices were thus cheaply to be secured!

Pigafetta, at least, was eager to investigate the source of it all—the spice trees: "The same day I went ashore to see how the cloves grow and this is what I observed. The tree from which they are gathered is high, and its trunk is as thick as a man's body, more or less, according to the age of the plant. Its branches spread out somewhat in the middle of the tree, but near to the top they form a pyramid. The bark is of an olive colour, and the leaves very like those of the laurel. The cloves grow at the end of little branches in bunches of ten or twenty . . . are white when they first sprout, they get red as they ripen, and blacken when dry. . . . The leaf, the bark, and the wood, as long as they are green, have the strength and fragrance of the fruit itself. . . .

"There are in this island of Gialolo"—Gilolo—"some trees of nutmegs. These are like our walnuts, and the leaves are also similar. The nutmeg, when gathered, is like the quince in form and colour, and the down which covers it, but it is smaller. The outside rind is as thick as the green rind of our walnuts, beneath which is a thin web, or rather cartilage, under which is the mace, of a very bright red, which covers and surrounds the rind of the nuts, inside which is the nutmeg properly so called.

"They also grow in Tadore the ginger. . . . Ginger is not a tree, but a shrub, which sends out of the earth shoots of a span long like the shoots of canes, which they resemble in the shape of the leaves, only those of ginger are narrower . . . that which makes the ginger is the root."

Of the cinnamon-producing tree Pigafetta wrote, "It is a small tree not more than three or four cubits high"—a cubit being about eighteen inches—"and of the thickness of a man's finger, and it has not got more than three or four little branches. Its leaf is like that of the laurel. The cinnamon for use which comes to us, is its bark, which is gathered twice a year."

All Pigafetta's shipmates were now busily purchasing spices with whatever articles they could find to barter. The holds of both ships were overcrowded so that the *Trinidad,* which had started out as Magellan's flagship, burst her seams and was left behind for repairs while the other ship, the *Victoria,* took advantage of the monsoon season to head for home. In the end, nothing could make the old *Trinidad* seaworthy, and she had to be abandoned among those islands to which she had helped pioneer a route.

The men of the *Trinidad* were now at the mercy of people they had so recently been harassing and robbing. Somewhere along the way Captain Carvalho met an appropriate doom. Of the others on that ship it was later told: "From their departure from Ternate . . . there died eight individuals. What became of seven was unknown; two remained in the Moluccas, one in Malacca; and three reached Spain"—years later—"besides the licentiate and the priest."

Thus the *Victoria,* captained by the pardoned one-

time mutineer Juan Sebastian del Cano, was the one
ship to complete the navigation, bringing to Spain a
welcome cargo of spices and the even more welcome
tidings that a whole Far Eastern archipelago had been
discovered and claimed for the Spanish crown. Spain
now had a foothold within hailing distance of the Spice
Islands and a base for the rarely ceasing battles with
Portugal over dominion in the Far East.

It was, of course, the 100 percent Spanish Sebastian
del Cano, not Fernan Magellan, who received credit,
acclaim, and the rewards that should have been
Magellan's—a generous pension and a coat of arms on
whose center was a globe and the motto *Primus me
circumdedisti*—"You were the first to encompass me."
Supporting the globe were two crowned native kings,
each holding a spice tree branch. The armorial bearings
show two sticks of cinnamon, three nutmegs, and twelve
cloves.

Today, despite his sixteenth-century honors, Sebastian del Cano is a name known only to a few historians.
Every schoolchild has heard of the Straits of Magellan,
though few could bring themselves to believe it all
began because of plant products now to be found on the
shelves of every market.

Though del Cano may have received homage that
should have been paid Magellan's memory, his was yet a
real triumph in days when the return of any vessel in
any condition from so long a voyage was something of a
miracle. What Motley wrote of the Dutch navigators
applies with only slight modification to navigators of any
sixteenth-century European nation: "The instruments
of navigation, too, were but rude and defective. . . .
The small yet unwieldy, awkward, and, to the modern
mind, most grotesque vessels in which such audacious
deeds were performed in the sixteenth and seventeenth

centuries awaken perpetual astonishment. A ship of a hundred tons burden, built up like a tower at both stem and stern, and presenting in its broad bulbous prow, its width of beam in proportion to its length, its depression amidships, and other sins against symmetry, as much opposition to progress over the waves as could well be imagined, was the vehicle in which those indomitable Dutchmen circumnavigated the globe and confronted the arctic terrors of either pole. An astrolabe—such as Martin Behaim had invented for the Portuguese, a clumsy astronomical ring of three feet in circumference—was still the chief machine for ascertaining the latitude, and on shipboard a most defective one." Longitude was not to be determined with an approach to accuracy before the mid-eighteenth century and later, but in those earlier centuries "There were no logarithms, no means of determining at sea the variations of the magnetic needle, no system of dead reckoning by throwing the log and chronicling the courses traversed. The firearms with which the sailors were to do battle with unknown enemies that might beset their path were rude and clumsy to handle. The art of compressing and condensing provisions was unknown"—as also, until the mid-eighteenth century, was the fact that sauerkraut or citrus juices might control scurvy or prevent it entirely. Typically, that news was long in finding general acceptance.

Similarly, conservative navigators, though bent on exploring new lands, seem to have been hesitant to explore new designs in shipbuilding. Over two and a half centuries after the struggles for control of the Spice Islands began to obsess the nations of Europe, ships of the old unwieldy design were still carrying men to watery graves instead of Oriental ports.

Outspoken Dutch Captain Jan Splinter Stavorinus

was moved, in the 1770s, to give his opinion of the prevailing style of shipbuilding. A storm was battering his ship and "The force of the waves frequently made the ship heel so much that she was under water on one side as far as her masts, while the howling wind, bearing perpendicularly down upon them, pressed them, as it were, into the water and kept the ship for several minutes seemingly in the very act of oversetting.

"As nothing could now be done, by the art of man, we were forced to abandon the ship to the power of the winds and waves and the mercy of heaven . . . we owed our preservation, next to God, to the construction of our vessel; for although she was . . . often wholly overwhelmed by the waves, the water could not penetrate anywhere, but flowed off on all sides, when she rose again; whereas had she been a deep-waisted ship, she would infallibly have been water-logged and would, at least, have rolled away her masts, if not foundered.

"It is difficult to conceive why this manner of building has only been adopted for the East-India Company's ships by the chamber of Zeeland; for it is incontrovertible that a flush-decked ship is much more able to withstand the force of the waves, than a deep-waisted one"—such as adopted by the other Dutch "chambers."

Statistics available for the decades between 1720 and 1730 are grimly revealing. Of the 374 ships that were sent out from Holland to the Indies, only 303 returned. Somewhere in the seas between, 19 percent were lost. If the total number of crewmen was divided equally between those ships, 19 percent of 69,505 men were never to reach home. Over 13,000 men! Could dividends averaging over 23 percent outweigh that loss?

Clearly, such voyages demanded men of unusual

qualities—instinctive knowledge of navigation, personal dedication, courage, with a ruthlessness that could ignore the cost in lives, even including their own. If also greed and ambition were motivating forces, are we of the twentieth century to pass judgment on those brave eighteenth-century navigators?

Magellan's voyage had really settled nothing as to where, on the far side of the globe, Spanish influence might begin and Portuguese end. Portugal insisted that the Spice Islands were her exclusive domain. Spain continued to contest that claim, though some Spaniards even went so far as to doubt that the Philippines really lay within Spain's rightful zone. Actually, such questions were academic, for what did matter was that the Portuguese had established themselves firmly on the Indian subcontinent and the Spanish in the Philippine archipelago, and both were securing spices in the Moluccas whenever they could and eliminating rivals wherever such were to be encountered.

Clearly, though, if Spain were to consolidate her hold on the Philippines, a way must be found to get back with the treasure without being intercepted by Portuguese. That way east, without technically violating the papal interdiction, had been explored by Magellan and would be followed by others, notably a Captain Loaisa, who, in 1525, set out on Magellan's route with seven ships and 450 men under his command. Captaining one of Loaisa's ships was Sebastian del Cano, who would die on that voyage, which was to prove almost as disastrous as Magellan's. Only one ship out of the seven survived to arrive at its destination. Yet more fleets would follow, undeterred by scurvy, storms, and teredo worms. The way west to the East remained open.

For the Spanish, a satisfactory and legal way east

from the East had yet to be worked out, ships of five expeditions having arrived at the Spice Islands before a single vessel from any European land succeeded in making an easterly passage back across the Pacific to arrive safely at a Spanish port in Mexico. The prevailing winds made a direct course impracticable, yet that treasure could avail little unless some way was found to land the Oriental treasures on Mexico's west coast, whence they might be carried by pack train to Veracruz on the Gulf of Mexico to be reloaded on Spanish galleons for the final voyage to Spain.

It would be Friar Andrés de Urdaneta, who had served del Cano as a page on Loaisa's voyage, who would open the way west across the Pacific. Missionary to the Philippines and a navigator of great skill, Friar Andrés found the way to avoid those notoriously contrary winds which, in equatorial regions, could help sailing ships on their westward course but successfully denied easterly passage. From Cebú, he took his ship northeast until he had arrived at a zone of westerlies, and with the help of these he kept on eastward until he had arrived off the coast of California, somewhere near the Bay of San Francisco. There he picked up the Japan Current, with the help of which he headed south along the coast until he had arrived at the port of his choice, Acapulco. It was a triumph of navigation—this laying out of a course to be known, for long, as the Route of the Manila Galleons.

"Concerning the voyage from Cebú to New Spain," Urdaneta briefly and modestly reported, "we left from the place where our people remained on June 1st, 1565, and on September 18th, we sighted the coast of New Spain." After briefly describing his course to the Mexican port of his choice (New Spain then meaning

Mexico), he added matter-of-factly, "We suffered much hardship on the voyage through bad weather and illness. Sixteen men died before reaching port, and four others died after arriving." Such was the then expected toll of long ocean voyages, even of the most successful ones.

For long that route of the Manila galleons would be preempted by the Spanish, since no Portuguese would wish to take the risk of landing along the Spanish-dominated coasts of the Americas. It would take an extraordinarily brash and knowledgeable captain to challenge the Spaniards in their American ports. Such was the Englishman Francis Drake, who had personal reasons to detest the Spanish and who, during the 1570s, was to take special delight in bearding the Spanish on their home grounds.

It was, of course, beyond reason to expect that only mariners of Spain and of Portugal should be tracing routes across oceans, known and unknown. In an Age of Exploration, the urge to explore and, even more, the urge to win renown and wealth was not to be confined to any one land or people, especially since most of the lands were, explicitly or implicitly, rivals if not downright enemies.

The noisy public thanksgivings and boastful displays with which Portugal and Spain were vying with each other to publicize the successes of their respective mariners may have stirred regional pride but also served to add fuel to the fires of international rivalries. Both Portugal and Spain seem to have gone on the assumption that no men of other nations could have returned from dangerous explorations of unknown seas without making similar public demonstrations. Actually, already in 1365 and a full fifty years before Prince

Henry the Navigator had managed to persuade his reluctant mariners to explore the Guinea coast beyond Cape Bojador, Norman French captains from Dieppe had been there, to return with samples of the "Malaguetta" pepper, which most claimed to be quite as good as the Oriental pepper Italian merchants were offering at extortionate prices. Ivory and hides, too, came in Norman French ships, the cargoes proving valuable enough for the canny French merchant-navigators to prefer to keep their sources a secret rather than shout their exploits before a highly competitive world.

Eventually it was bound to leak out—the fact that the presumptuous French were daring to invade seas assigned by papal bull exclusively to the Portuguese. The news acted, if a pun may be forgiven, like a red flag to a bull. Any French vessel encountered by Portuguese vessels in seas claimed by Portugal (and by then she was claiming most of the Atlantic Ocean) was seized, the cargo appropriated, and all on board treated with a brutality that increased as it became increasingly evident that French mariners continued to trespass. Soon French vessels were arming in self-defense, and presently those arms might be used in anticipating attacks. With grim impartiality Portuguese were equally ready to attack English or Spanish vessels encountered in their seas.

For the French, who had as yet no footholds in the Far East, the situation was particularly menacing, especially since the French monarch was not well persuaded as to the value of overseas trade. In vain, Jean Ango, merchant prince of Dieppe, pleaded with his king, Francis I (1515–1547), "that God, when he made the sea, never intended it to be the private property of one nation." A half century later the queen of recently

Protestant England was to lend her own support to Ango's stand. In the early 1500s, however Francis I might sympathize with Jean Ango, he hesitated to act counter to a papal bull or to become embroiled with a brother king with whom he did not wish to war.

The issue came to a head in 1522 when some Portuguese in Pernambuco, Brazil, handed over a group of French captives to make a feast for the natives. Whether this act of vicarious cannibalism persuaded Francis I that the Portuguese were vicious and must somehow be restrained or whether it just gave him an excuse he had been hoping for, he finally consented to provide French sea captains with Letters of Marque and Reprisal—defined by Blackstone as "an incomplete state of hostilities." By such letters a sovereign might authorize private persons to fit out armed vessels to cruise as privateers and make prizes of vessels of an enemy, official or unofficial, thereby appropriating the enemy cargoes. This incomplete state of hostilities—complete in everything but name—while offering daring and abused private individuals a means to prevent or recoup losses, could easily become a thinly disguised piracy.

By 1525 two of Ango's mariners, the Parmentier brothers, were being dispatched to the Spice Islands, which they reached by a roundabout route that took them to Florida, the West Indies, Brazil, and Madagascar. The report one brother wrote on the Portuguese and their dealings with the natives suggests the same point of view that a half century later would lead Francis Drake to bemoan the cruel and inhuman dealings of the Spanish of Chile toward the Indians native there.

"Although this nation is the smallest on the globe," Parmentier wrote not too accurately of Portugal, "the whole world is not large enough to satisfy their cupidity." He further questioned the genuineness of the missionary zeal which the Portuguese claimed to have motivated them: "If the Portuguese, who claim to be masters of these lands"—the Spice Islands—"had had in mind the glory of religion, rather than the love of gain, one half at least of these people would have embraced Christianity, for many are anxious to understand our religion and willingly joined in our worship. The Portuguese, however, to whom the ignorance of the natives is profitable, do not allow them to be given a more complete knowledge of Christianity."

The Portuguese perhaps could not have cared less about this criticism of their religious fervor but would certainly have been speechless with fury at the final boast: "Having filled our ships with pepper and other spices, we left for Dieppe, where we arrived safely after a long and dangerous navigation, undertaken for the greater glory of God and of the Crown of France." No single nation, one gathers, had a monopoly on hypocrisy.

In those days of unquestioned royal prerogatives and numerous royal offspring, legitimate and illegitimate, there was almost always a simple and relatively effective way of cooling the heat of international disputes—international marriage. Thus, when John III of Portugal took unto himself as bride the sister of Charles V, the reigning Holy Roman Emperor who was also king of Spain, the violence of the disputes between Portuguese and Spanish expansionists was somewhat lessened. It was further reduced when, in 1529, Charles began planning for himself an ostentatious and inevitably costly coronation. Money he must have, and it must come more rapidly and directly than from the Spice Islands.

Royal prerogatives did not, even in those days,

extend to outright confiscation of subjects' possessions, especially since to attempt such meant impoverishing the more prosperous and thus could lead to a killing of the golden goose. The goose this time turned out to be Charles, who, for the sum of 350,000 ducats (possibly equivalent to one million dollars in today's currency), pledged to his Portuguese brother-in-law all Spanish claims to the Moluccas and their spices, the loan possibly to last indefinitely since no date for repayment was set.

Spanish merchants and mariners quickly perceived that they had been sold out. As one expressed it, "The emperor would have done better to pledge Estremadura, Serena or any other great cities and territories [of Spain] than Malacca, Sumatra, and the Moluccas." Some merchants even offered to raise the cash for paying off the debt at once, they to receive reimbursement by being allowed, for a period of three years only, all the profits accruing to the Spanish spice trade. The imperial answer was that "they should not . . . speak to him any more of this matter; whereat some marvelled, others were sorry, and all held their peace."

The great value of the spice monopoly was not to be concealed, and foreign merchants resident in Seville began to suspect that what Charles failed to value properly might, with skill and scheming, be made to fill the coffers of their own individual sovereigns. One such foreign resident in "Sivill" undertook to point this out in a letter to King Henry VIII of England. "Experience proveth that naturally all Princes be desirous to extend and enlarge their dominions and kingdoms," merchant Robert Thorne wrote in justification of his presumption in addressing a prince. After continuing in the same vein for about half of a folio page, he got to the essence of his proposal: "I know it is my bounden duety to manifest this secret unto your Grace, which hitherto, as I may suppose, hath been hid: which is, that with a small number of ships, there may be discovered divers New lands and Kingdomes, in the which without doubt your Grace shall win perpetuall glory, and your subjects infinite profite. To which places, there is left one way to discover, which is in the north."

This was a stroke of genius, for neither Portugal nor Spain had ever thought to reach the distant tropics by heading north. There was actually some logic in it, for the study of any terrestrial globe could quickly reveal that thousands of miles might be saved "could a passage to what was then called the kingdom of Cathay be effected by way of the north," as historian Motley justly pointed out. He also pointed out that in pursuit of the deluding northern passage—first to the northeast, then, for a much longer period, to the northwest—many lives of men of many lands would be sacrificed.

"It must be remembered," wrote Motley in extenuation, "that there were no maps of the unknown regions lying beyond the northern headlands of Sweden. Delineations of continents, islands, straits, rivers, and seas, over which every modern schoolboy pores, were not attempted even by the hand of fancy. . . . Many were the fantastic dreams in which even the wisest thinkers of the age indulged in as to the polar regions. . . . According to some . . . those seas enclosed a polar continent where perpetual summer and unbroken daylight reigned, and whose inhabitants, having obtained a high degree of culture, lived in the practice of every virtue and the enjoyment of every blessing. Others peopled these mysterious regions with horrible savages, having hoofs of horses and heads of dogs, and with no clothing save their own long ears coiled closely around their limbs and bodies; while it was deemed almost certain that a race of headless men, with eyes in their breasts, were the most enlightened among these distant tribes. Instead of constant sunshine, it was believed by such theorists that the wretched inhabitants of that accursed zone were immersed in almost incessant fogs or tempests, that the whole population died every winter and were only recalled to temporary existence by the advent of a tardy and evanescent spring . . . but it was universally admitted that an opening, either by strait or sea, into the desired Indian haven would have revealed itself at last."

What sixteenth-century seekers after the far northern passage did find were wastes of snow and ice, seas choked to impassability with floes, and the only inhabitants to dispute seriously with them their passage the towering polar bears to which several unfortunate navigators fell prey. Yet the apparently futile effort did have some positive yields—more accurate geographical, astronomical, and meteorological observations of regions previously unvisited—the ending of those naïve theories as to polar lands and their inhabitants—and some highly educational revelations as to the birds and beasts to be found there.

Notable among these latter revelations were the ones concerning the geese some Dutch explorers encountered near Spitzbergen and recognized to be the very same that visited Holland in flocks every summer. The Dutch had never before known where they laid and hatched their eggs, about which the diarist of the expedition, Gerrit De Veer, recorded solemnly: "Therefore some voyagers have not scrupled to state that the eggs grow on trees in Scotland, and that such of the fruits as fall into the water become goslings, while those which drop on the ground burst into pieces and become nothing. We see now that quite the contrary is the case, nor is it to be wondered at, for nobody has ever been until now where those birds lay their eggs. No man, so far as known, ever reached the latitude of eighty degrees before. This land was hitherto unknown."

De Veer might justly have added, "And biological processes not at all understood," for in biology as well as in geography men were groping for an understanding. Up to the middle of the nineteenth century men were still trying to locate a passable northern passage, still sacrificing not only human fortunes but human lives in the fantastic attempt, still unable to believe that polar regions were frozen wastes. Had he not been slain in the Hawaiian Islands in 1779, skilled, knowledgeable Captain James Cook, who had previously been keeping a sharp lookout for a supposedly tropical Antarctic continent, might well have become yet another sacrifice to the grim gods of the Arctic.

By the time Captain Cook was bracing to go in search of that presumed short northwestern passage, English mariners had already been long sailing the interdicted seas about the Spice Islands and meeting there, in the 1570s, with a cordial reception from native rulers. By 1574 Portuguese rapacity had become so unendurable to the initially hospitable inhabitants that Moslems there sparked an uprising during which the Portuguese were driven out of Ternate and their fortress there taken. Into the relative trading void thus left there sailed in 1579 the famous English ship *Golden Hind* and her even more famous captain, Francis Drake, on his own voyage of circumnavigation.

Drake's voyage had followed the pattern of Magellan's in more ways than one. Having crossed the Atlantic in a westerly direction, he, too, passed the shortest months of the year at Port San Julian. There, like Magellan, he found his fleet of five reduced by storms and reefs—his by two rather than one. Mutiny also raised its ugly head, and Drake, as had his predecessor, dealt quickly and ruthlessly with the ringleader as he had to if his voyage was not to be ruined. Drake's voyage through Magellan's straits was of shorter duration, but once out into the "peaceful" ocean, he encountered a storm so violent that two of the remaining ships disappeared, never to be heard of again.

Drake, left only with his *Golden Hind,* then undertook to harass the Spanish coast as far north as Callao, the port of Lima. There is no telling how much farther up along the coast he might have continued had he not picked up tidings of a Spanish ship, laden with Peruvian treasure, that had already left port bound for Panama. Drake quickly overtook and surprised the treasure ship, forcing her captain to yield, then removing her cargo before casting her adrift. After successfully twice repeating the same kind of venture, then coasting a considerable distance up North America, Drake decided "to go forward to the Islands of the Moluccas." A Pacific crossing of sixty-eight days took him, by early October, to the Ladrones. A month later he had sighted the Spice Islands.

"These are foure high piked Ilands," wrote Francis Fletcher, chaplain and diarist, in *The World Encompassed,* ". . . all of them very fruitful, and yeelding abundance of cloves, whereof wee furnished our selves of as much as we desired at a very cheap rate." The politics of spices was made evident when, the next day, they met a representative of the "King of Ternate," who urged the newcomers to avoid Tidore and visit Ternate with whose king "if he [Drake] once dealt, he should find that as he was a king so his word should stand; whereas if he dealt with the Portingals [who had command of Tidore] he should find in them nothing but deceit and treachery. And besides that if he went to Tidore before he came to Terenate, then would his king have nothing to do with us, for he held the Portingall as an enemy. On these persuasions our Generall resolved to runne with Terenate, where the next day very early in the morning we came to anchor: And presently our Generall sent a messenger to the king with a velvet cloake, for a present and as a token that his coming should be in peace: and that he required no other thing at his hands, but that (his victuals being spent in so long a voiage) He might have supply from him by way of traffique and exchange of merchandise (whereof he had a store of divers sorts) of such things as he wanted. . . ."

After a formal reception marked by considerable pomp and circumstance, the two parties got down to business which could include only a token cargo of spices, for Drake, unlike the captains of Magellan's fleet, was too canny to overload his ships even with so valuable a cargo. The *Golden Hind* was already, practically to the limit of safety, loaded with booty from those captured treasure ships. The important thing would not be the spices he brought home but that he had opened a way for English captains to share in the golden opportunities offered by richly laden Spanish galleons and richly bearing Portuguese spice trees. The first English navigator to have circumnavigated the globe, Drake was back home in Plymouth by September 1580, and there, on the deck of his *Golden Hind,* he was knighted by Queen Elizabeth I, who thereby was also announcing to the Spanish that what they claimed through a papal bull was of no import to a Protestant monarch.

The second Englishman and third of any nation to undertake a circumnavigation was "the worshipful and worthy gentleman, Master Thomas Candish"—now usually referred to as Thomas Cavendish. "Having therefore at his owne proper cost new built from the keele and furnished with all things necessarie for two yeares provision a brave shippe called the Desire of a hundred and fortie, and a lesser of threescore tunnes whose name was the Content, joyning thereunto a Barke of 40 tunnes named the Hugh Gallant, in which small fleete were six score and five men," Cavendish set out in June 1586. Once through Magellan's straits, he followed Drake's example with harassment of Spanish coast settlements until, by October 1587, he had arrived right across the route of the Manila Galleons off "the Cape of California, being the uttermost part of Nova Hispania."

In a published letter to the "Lord Chamberlaine," Cavendish describes one of the encounters with a treasure-laden galleon: "We lay off and on of this cape until the fourth of November, on which day in the morning wee espied the goodly shippe coming from the Phillipinas called the Saint Anna the great, being of seven hundred tunnes: we chased her until noone, so fetching her up, we gave them fight to the losse of twelve or fourteen of their men, and the spoyle and hurt of many more of them, whereupon at last they yeelded unto us: In this conflict we lost only two of our men. So on the sixt of the sayed November we went into the Port of Agua Segura, where we ankered and put nine score prisoners on land: and ransacking the great shippe, we laded our own two shippes with fortie tunnes of the chiefest merchandise, and burnt all the rest as well shippe as goods, to the quantitie of five hundred tunnes of rich merchandise, because we were not able to bring it away: This was one of the richest vessels that every sayled the Seas, and was able to have made hundreds wealthie, if we had had the meanes to bring it home." This account ends with the gleeful statement: "In this voyage we burnt twentie sayles of Spanish shippes, besides divers of their Townes and Villages."

Though, as with Drake's voyage, Cavendish's ships had little cargo space left for the spices of the East, he too headed west, stopping at the Ladrones and Philippines before dropping in on the Moluccas. He arrived back in England on September 9, 1588, two months after the destruction of the Spanish Armada had left England virtual mistress of the seas—that is, until Dutch navigators should challenge her and, what was more significant in the allotment of spices, break the power of the Portuguese in the East Indies.

For the Dutch there was a more urgent motive than for most European nations to covet the spice trade. Through royal marriages, royal purchases, and royal treaties, the Netherlands had gradually come under the dominion of Burgundy, then of Spain as Charles, Duke of Burgundy, became king of Spain and Holy Roman Emperor. When the northern Dutch states, now grouped together as Holland, embraced Calvinism, there was bound to follow trouble, first with the devout Charles V, then with his yet more devout son, Philip II. The Spanish army sent to garrison the Netherlands, the threat of a full-fledged Inquisition transplanted to Holland, the severe edicts against heretics often carried out with incredible brutality—all were bound to stimulate a subject Protestant people to find ways to increase and support an army of their own and to harass Spaniards wherever and whenever they could. For this, the first requirement was money, and to acquire money they had their native wits and skills—all stimulated by a long list of wrongs suffered at the hands of princes who had announced their righteous intent to extirpate heresy even should it require the extirpation of every heretic subject.

When, in 1579, the Portuguese king died without a male heir, the throne, after some dickering, went to the Spanish monarch (initially Philip II), where it remained until, in 1640, the Portuguese, being fed up with their Spanish cousins, revolted. While the dual monarchy lasted, however, it offered a fine double challenge to Dutch navigators and an opportunity to get control of the spice trade for their own country.

As historian Motley put it, when Spain, toward the end of the sixteenth century, swallowed Portugal, it "legally absorbed the East Indian possessions, and became proprietor of the whole new world under the Borgian grant.

"This was public law, religion, high politics, and common sense in those days, but the unsophisticated Hollanders could not be made to understand the theory.

"The same fishermen and fighting men, whom we have lately seen sailing forth from Zeeland and Friesland to confront the dangers of either pole, were now contending in the Indian seas with the Portuguese monopolists of the tropics. . . .

"But the spirit of change was abroad in the world. Potentates and merchants under the equator had been sedulously taught that there were no other white men on the planet but the Portuguese and their conquerors, the Spaniards, and that the Dutch . . . were a mere mob of pirates and savages inhabiting the obscurest of dens.

They were soon, however, to be enabled to judge for themselves as to the power and merits of the various competitors for their trade.

"Early in this year [1602], Andreas Hurtado de Mendoza with a stately fleet of galleons and smaller vessels, more than five-and-twenty in all, was on his way towards the island of Java to inflict summary vengeance upon those oriental rulers who had dared to trade with men forbidden by his Catholic Majesty and the Pope. . . .

"It so happened that a Dutch skipper, Wolfert Hermann by name, commanding five trading vessels, in which there were three hundred men, had just arrived in those seas to continue the illicit commerce which had aroused the ire of the Portuguese. His whole force both of men and guns was far inferior to that of the flag-ship of Mendoza. . . . To the profound astonishment of the Portuguese admiral the Dutchman with his five little trading ships made an attack on the pompous armada, intending to avert chastisement from the king of Bantam. It was not possible for Wolfert to cope at close quarters with his immensely superior adversary, but his skill and nautical experience enabled him to play at what was then considered long bowls with extraordinary effect. The greater lightness and mobility of his vessels made them more than a match, in this kind of encounter, for the clumsy, top-heavy, and sluggish marine castles in which Spain and Portugal went forth to do battle on the ocean . . . and thus Wolfert's swift-going galliots circled round and round the awkward, ponderous, much-puzzled Portuguese fleet, until by well-directed shots and skilful manoeuvring they had sunk several ships, taken two, run the others into the shallows, and, at last, put the whole to confusion. After several days of such fighting, Admiral Mendoza fairly turned his back upon his insignificant opponent, and abandoned his projects upon Java. Bearing away for the Island of Amboyna with the remainder of the fleet, he laid waste several of its villages and odoriferous spice-fields, while Wolfert and his companions entered Bantam in triumph and were hailed as deliverers. And thus on the extreme western edge of this magnificent island was founded the first trading settlement of the Batavian republic in the archipelago of the equator.

"Meantime Wolfert Hermann was not the only Hollander cruising in those seas able to convince the Oriental mind that all Europeans save the Portuguese were not pirates and savages, and that friendly intercourse with other foreigners might be as profitable as slavery to the Spanish crown."

Among such Hollanders were Captains Jacob Cornelius van Neck and Jacob Heemskerk and, of course, the crews of their ships. These men were motivated not only by a lively remembrance of Holland's sufferings under Spanish dominion but by the fact that the valuable cargoes they seized would, as was custom in those days, be divided among officers and crew of the ship that seized a prize. Holland's hold on the friendship of Eastern sovereigns was soon further bolstered by treaties as well as by transporting to Holland native ambassadors who might see and report home that the Dutch came from no crude and savage land.

For some time the profitable trade in spices and other Oriental commodities stirred many Hollanders to seek a piece of the trade. Relatively small trading companies with evocative names like "Company of Distant Countries" and "Company of Magellan" sprang up, soon to become involved in rivalries that could lead to national disaster. Through sheer necessity, as Motley wrote, "that great commercial corporation had been founded—an empire within an empire— . . . a counting house company which was to organize armies, conquer kingdoms, build forts and cities, make war and peace. . . . That it was a monopoly, offensive to the true commercial principles, illiberal, unjust, tyrannical, ignorant of the very rudiments of mercantile philosophy, is plain enough. . . . There can be no doubt that the true foundation of the [Dutch] East India Company was the simple recognition of iron necessity. Every merchant in Holland knew full well that the Portuguese and Spanish could never be driven out of their strongholds under the equator, except by the concentration of the private strength and wealth of the mercantile community. . . .

"So the States General [of Holland] granted a patent or charter to one great company with what, for the time, was an enormous paid-up capital, in order that the India trade might be made secure and the Spaniards steadily confronted in what they considered their most important possessions. All former trading companies were invited to merge themselves in the Universal East India Company, which, for twenty-one years should alone have the right to trade to the east of the Cape of Good Hope and sail through the Straits of Magellan."

This invitation was not the kind a recipient might freely decline—that is, not if he had any desire to continue sharing in Far Eastern trade. The Dutch commercial corporation thus organized intended, at all costs, to keep a firm hold on all that trade. Any and all other European traders, including would-be Dutch individualists, must bow to the company's power and to its laws. Governors of the Dutch East Indies, under that company, reigned with a power no less great and far more extensive than that of the Oriental potentates they were, for all practical purposes, replacing. The slight difference was that any supposedly offending and offended Dutchman might appeal his case in Holland should he live long enough and have the necessary funds.

The power monopoly was thought to be clinched by the fact that passage both by the Cape of Good Hope and Magellan's straits was sternly interdicted, the almost universal assumption then being that there could be no other way of passing from the South Atlantic to reach any part of the South Pacific. That any navigator might not share that assumption or, rejecting it, might have the courage and the funds to seek out another passage was not a thought that occurred to the monopolists.

The year 1619, however, saw the publication in England of the translation of a Dutch book, written within the two previous years and partially titled *A Voyage Around the World by a New Passage*. The translator, signed "W. P.," was one William Philip, who dedicated his translation to the director of the English East India Company, founded in 1600 under charter of Queen Elizabeth I just two years before the founding of the corresponding Dutch company. As Philip knew quite well, the book must be of considerable interest to the director of the English company, to whom he dedicated it.

As translator Philip pointed out: "The generall States of the United Netherland-Provinces, having granted their Letters Pattens to the East India Company resident in the sayd Provinces, to trafficke in the Indies, and none others but they onley, with a stricke prohibition unto all other Marchants, and inhabitants of the sayd Countries, not to sayle or trafficke Eastward beyond the Cape de bona esperance [Cape of Good Hope], nor through the Straights of Magellan Westward, either into India, or any other unknowne or not discovered countries, Isaack le Maire, a rich Marchant of Amsterdam, dwelling in Egmont, having a great desire to trafficke into strange and farre Countries, and William Cornelison Schouten of Horne [Hoorn] (a man well experienced in Seafaring, who before that time had sayled thrice into most partes of the East Indies, for Maister, Pilot, and Marchant) and yet very desirous to sayle into and discover new and unknown Countries, oftentimes speaking and conferring together, reasoned among themselves, whether they might not enter into the great South Sea by another way (then through the same wayes which in the East Indian Companies Letters Pattens are formerly forbidden and prohibited). . . ."

Decision being taken by LeMaire and Schouten, they secured two ships, the *Horne* and the *Unitie* (Philip's way of rendering into English the ship's Dutch name, *Eendracht*), had them outfitted, manned, and ready to sail by June 14, 1615. In December the *Eendracht* was lost by a fire that spread through her while she was being careened somewhere along the far southern coasts of South America. The *Horne* kept heading south and, on January 29 following, "about evening we saw land againe, lying northwest and north northwest from us, which was the land that lay South from the straights of Magellan, which reacheth Southward, all high hillie land covered over with snow, ending in a sharp pointe, which we called Cape Horne"—after both the ship and her city of origin.

When, some ten months later, the *Horne* reached the Dutch East Indies, no one there would believe she had not come by an interdicted passage. Ship and wares were seized, the owners to be shipped home to Holland as prisoners. LeMaire's son, Jacob, died in the East Indies. LeMaire senior survived to fight the company and, after two years of litigation, win his case and have his property restored. Cape Horn was thereby accepted as a reality, as was the passage through which the ships had sailed—the Straits of LeMaire—between Tierra del Fuego and the little far southern island named Staten after the Dutch States General. The discovery of that new route was an achievement of which all Dutchman should have been proud.

It was, however, not pride but profit that was the motivating force for Europeans. Control over Far Eastern realms and their commodities could send a formerly poor man home a millionaire, if he lived long enough to reach home. Robert Clive, having gone out to India in 1743 as an underpaid clerk of the English East India Company, was to return to London a millionaire and a peer, though a miserably ailing one. During the previous century the same company's agent and governor of a trading post in Madras, Boston-born Elihu Yale, accumulated a fortune sufficient to enable him to live in London in the style of an Oriental potentate. It was also to help convert the struggling young Collegiate School of Connecticut into Yale College.

The Dutch who risked life in the Batavia of 1616, were only too strongly aware of what they stood to lose, should they permit upstart countrymen like LeMaire and Van Schouten to challenge their monopoly of routes thither. Less than twenty years earlier, three ships directed by Cornelius Houtman had dropped anchor in the Texel, their holds full of spices garnered in the Far East. Two years later, four ships were arriving there with cargoes of mace, nutmegs, cloves, cinnamon, and pepper. By 1609, invoices were including "damasks" and by 1611 "indigo, silks, cotton-yarn, diamonds" had been added. In 1616, the year when the ship *Horne* dropped anchor off Batavia, the value of East Indian cargoes reaching the United Provinces of Holland amounted to over 566,000 florins, with the value of such cargoes soaring to over a million florins the following year and generally remaining about that level thereafter.

It was no new thought to Europeans outside the Netherlands that spices might be planted and harvested in tropical lands other than the ones where they grew native. At least one Spaniard had perceived that there were in the Americas places whose climates sufficiently matched that of the Philippines to encourage the growth of spice trees. By growing spices there, Spain might escape the risks and costs of shipping them from the Far East. Once Friar Urdaneta had scouted the route of the Manila galleons, the possibility of shipments of seeds and seedlings reaching Acapulco while still viable was greatly enhanced.

By 1571, a mere six years after Urdaneta's historic voyage, Nicolas de Monardes was recording one such venture as part of the "Joyfull Newes Out of the Newe Founde Worlde." He wrote, "Dom Frauncis de Mendosa, Sonne unto the Vise Roye, [of New Spain] Don Anthony de Mendosa, did sowe in the new Spaine Cloaves, Pepper, Ginger, and other spices, of those whiche are brought from the Orientall Indias, and that whiche by hym was begonne was loste, by reason of his death, onely the Ginger did remain, for it did growe verie well in those partes, and so thei bryng it greene from newe Spain, and other parts of our Indias."

Had the enterprising Don Francisco lived longer,

spices might have been domesticated in the New World two centuries before they were being harvested in other lands bordering the Caribbean. However, it seems that no one else in sixteenth-century Mexico shared Don Francisco de Mendoza's vision. Most Spaniards then living there were soldiers and fortune seekers whose eyes focused only on the wealth in the fabulous silver mines of Mexico and of Peru. For them there seemed little future in trees that demanded care and promised little in yields during the time they were to remain in the Americas. Men of other lands, however, were soon to follow in Don Francisco's footsteps, eventually bringing the transplantation of spice trees to reality, though in lands of other nations.

In 1672 John Evelyn, the noted English diarist who was a member of the Council of Foreign Plantations, was recording the council meeting that took place on February 12 of that year: "At the Council, we entered on inquiries about improving the plantations by silks, galls"—used in making ink—"flax, senna, etc., and considered how nutmegs and cinnamon might be obtained and brought to Jamaica, the soil and the climate promising success." Tantalizingly, nowhere else does Evelyn's diary mention the project, which must have been rejected since the obstacles to its success were greater than the council could have imagined. The thought had already been germinating in other British minds, as witnessed by a 1661 document in the British Museum entitled, "A proposall for Removing Spices and Other Plants from the East to the West Indies."

Despite such rumblings, the Dutch were holding firmly onto their monopoly and their profits by every means within their power. Since that power included control of planting, harvesting, and marketing spices, it would prove very hard, though not impossible, to break. Outspoken Captain Jan Splinter Stavorinus gives us a revealing account of the Dutch methods in comments written during the 1770's when he visited the Dutch Far Eastern holdings but not published until after his death: "The chief, if not the sole advantage derived to the Company from the possession of Amboyna and its dependencies, is the collection of cloves, and the mastery of this article to the exclusion of all other nations, by which they are enabled, at pleasure, to raise or lower the price.

"This gave rise, at an early period after the conquest of the island, to much jealousy and animosity between the Dutch and the English, and these disputes did not terminate with the expulsion of the latter from the island, but were made a pretense, many years afterwards, for declaring war against the republic: they were not formally settled till the conclusion of the Peace of Breda, in the year 1667.

"The Company would not, however, ever have succeeded in securing to themselves the exclusive trade in spice, which is spontaneously produced in all the adjacent Molucca islands, had they not endeavoured wholly to transfer and confine the cultivation of it to Amboyna; partly by subduing the princes of those islands by force of arms and prescribing to them such conditions of peace as they found convenient . . . compelling them not to sell any of the cloves produced in their dominions to any other nation; and partly by forcing them, about the middle of the last century"— that is, the middle 1600s—"to destroy all the clove trees which grew in their territories for which they were to receive an equivalent in money."

By December 1669 it was being decreed "that the

number of clove trees should not be allowed to exceed five hundred thousand, and it was further ordered, in the year 1773, that fifty thousand more should be destroyed, so that at present [1775] after three extirpations, the number of clove-trees, as near as could be ascertained, amounts to 513,268; whereof 320,491 fruit-bearing trees, 104,866 half-grown, 87,911 young plants, besides 22,310 *tatanamangs,* which are trees that are not comprehended in the clove plantations, but stand interspersed here and there, near the houses. Every Amboynese plants such a clove tree when a child is born to him, in order by a rough calculation to know their age. Although they do not oppose the extirpation of the clove-trees in the plantations, when the Company think it fit, yet to touch their *tatanamangs* would speedily be the cause of a general insurrection among them."

The captain then proceeded to discuss the costs of administrative services which, he pointed out, "must be defrayed out of the profits of the cloves, nutmeg, and mace . . . but can any favourable expectations of future advantage be entertained on this head, when we consider the great decrease which is experienced in the sale of the first named spice? Three million pounds remaining still in the warehouses at Batavia, of which no more than one fifteenth part can be annually disposed of in the Indies, together with the stock on hand in Holland, large enough to supply the consumption of Europe for the space of ten years, and the quantities of cloves that from time to time are committed to the flames by the Company, in order to lessen their superabundant stock, form proofs enough of the decrease of the clove trade."

Exactly what may have been responsible for this decreased consumption in Europe the captain does not attempt to say. Perhaps it was that, though still costly, those imported spices had ceased to be the kind of rarities whose use gave social distinction. Perhaps Europe's incessant wars had impoverished people who might otherwise have had money to spend on luxuries like spices. Whatever it was, the effect on the finances of the Dutch East India Company was far from favorable. Commenting on this costliness as compared with the low prices the Spice Islanders were receiving, Stavorinus points out: "If we go farther and consider that these three articles of trade"—clove, nutmegs, mace—"must bear the whole expense of the four eastern provinces, to which must be added the charges of seven freight ships, employed in fetching them, it will be found that they, in fact, cost very dear." Thus, the several hundred percent profit which spices appeared to bring in the Europe of the 1770s, when Stavorinus was writing, was largely illusory, though still sufficient to more than recompense the men and companies involved.

Administrators at the outposts of far-flung empires would not have been human had they not determined to keep all agricultural profits for themselves and the companies they represented, whatever the land to which they belonged. Citizens of those European lands that were being denied access to the profitable trade would not have been human had they not actively resented the monopolies and the prices such monopolies were forcing them to pay. The time had to come when the have-nots, in the matter of spices, would arrange to adjust the inequity.

Had the inequity been one of minerals or textiles, it would have been both harder and easier to adjust— harder because to break a spice monopoly no more than a few seeds or viable plants might suffice, easier because the relatively heavy cargoes of minerals or textiles were not perishable. In view of the small number of plants needed for eventually establishing large spice plantations, it seems strange that the seventeenth and much of the eighteenth centuries had passed before the men of any land should actively undertake to rob the Dutch of the envied monopoly.

Captain Stavorinus was only too well aware of this situation when he wrote: "Yet notwithstanding all this and how far so ever they may be able to extend their extirpations in the circumjacent countries, they will never be able to prevent other nations from procuring spices without their intermediation. There are too many islands, and too widely dispersed, that produce these commodities, of which neither they, nor their allies are in possession, or possibly can be, without entirely exhausting themselves by the erection of numerous fortresses, which are indispensably necessary, if all intercourse with foreign nations must be prevented." He might have gone further to point out that nations able to procure interdicted spices might equally well manage to procure both spice seeds and seedlings.

Here the editor-translator's note is more to the point: "A short time before the coming of the Portuguese to Amboyna, the Cerammers of Cambello secretly brought some mother-cloves in hollow bamboo from Machian, whence they were propagated all over Ceram, Amboyna, and the neighboring islands, and in the space of fifty or sixty years the whole of Hoewamoebil"—a peninsula jutting out from Ceram—"was covered with them. This was told to the Dutch when first they came to Cambello, and some of the trees first planted were shewn to them . . . the memory of it is likewise preserved in the traditionary songs of the Amboynese."

Such songs could put ideas into the heads of

foreigners able to understand them or, if the germs of such ideas were already there, could add the final bit of encouragement needed to get started the project of stealing spice trees. The idea certainly was already there, for as early as 1729 the French East India Company had drawn up plans for sending a vessel to one of the uninhabited islands of the Moluccas. The plan aborted. What was needed to carry it out was a person like the flamboyant young Frenchman, Pierre Poivre, endowed with an itching foot, a lively curiosity as to remote places of the world, and a gift for the mastery of languages. Born in 1719, Poivre enrolled himself at the age of twenty among the missionaries of St. Joseph and was on his way to mission stations in Cochin China (later Indochina, today Vietnam).

Once there, the young missionary spent less time on devotions than on the mastery of local languages and on making copious notes about the exotic peoples and crops of the strange world in which he found himself. Presently he was involved in some kind of scrape which so shocked his missionary superiors that, in 1744, they shipped him back home.

War between England and France being on, the French ship was attacked by an English one—a fight in which the young Poivre became sufficiently involved to suffer a serious wound in his arm. After holding him briefly as a prisoner, the English released him to the custody of the Dutch in Batavia, where he soon gathered all possible information about the clove and nutmeg plantations. By the time he was heading home again, his mind was full of schemes.

On that voyage he detoured via the French factories of Madras and Pondicherry on the Indian subcontinent, then stopped at Madagascar and the neighboring

French-owned Mascarenes—the islands of Bourbon, now Réunion, and France, now Mauritius. As he noted the soil and climate of these islands, his schemes had been further matured.

"There cannot be a doubt," he was to record, "but if our India Company who alone are in possession of the trade with the natives of this island [Madagascar] would give proper encouragement to agriculture, it would in a short time make rapid progress. . . . Our islands of Bourbon and France would here always find a certain resource against those dearths which too frequently distress the latter of these islands. Our squadrons bound for India, who put into the Isle of France for refreshments, would always find abundance of provisions brought from Madagascar, and of consequence would not be subjected to the necessity of losing their time at the Cape, or at Batavia, begging refreshments from the Dutch, whilst the enemies of France, as happened in the late war"—the Seven Years War—"are conquering their settlements and destroying their trade." From supplying ships with refreshments to growing cargoes of spices was not, for young Poivre's mind, a long delayed leap.

Reaching France after a second brief episode as a prisoner of the English, Poivre contacted the directors of the French Company of the Indies to urge upon them two projects he thought important. One was the building up of direct commercial relations with Cochin China, the other the securing and transplanting of spice-producing trees to the Mascarenes, notably the Isle of France. So convincing were his arguments that he was presently, as an appointed representative of the French monarch, returning to Cochin China, where he soon succeeded in arranging the first of his projects.

Next came the spice project in which he was to face a

quite different set of problems than would soon be challenging Captain Bligh in his attempts to carry breadfruit seedlings from Tahiti to the West Indies. For one thing, though spice trees might be grown from the seeds in spice fruits (which was impossible with the sterile breadfruit) the natives of lands where spices grew, having long been highly conscious of the trees' value to men of far lands, had a personal stake in helping maintain the monopoly (which was not the case with the original growers of breadfruit on Tahiti).

The Dutch, with their tremendous financial investment threatened, had even more urgent reasons for taking every possible means to keep the monopoly in their own hands. They excluded strangers from the islands where spice plantations grew. They extirpated trees that grew outside the confines of their plantations. Then, to make assurance doubly sure, they deprived spices that went to other lands of the power to sprout. Nutmegs were treated with lime which served that end while acting as a preservative. Other seeds, it was told, were subjected to treatment with steam or boiling water—as, halfway across the world, the Indians of Brazil were later similarly to deprive rubber seeds of the power to propagate. It was all in vain. Eventually Java was to have rubber plantations just as the Isle of France and other French colonies were to have spice trees.

Presumably it was from one of the uninhabited Moluccas, described by Captain Stavorinus, that Pierre Poivre secured, sometime during the 1750s, nineteen clove seedlings to carry back to the Isle of France. By the time he arrived there, only twelve little trees were still alive, and of these only five survived to take root and grow in the new soil. Meanwhile, at home in France, the company's directors were losing interest in giving support to Poivre's grand scheme. A discouraged Poivre left the few surviving seedlings to the tender mercies of a gardener and, in 1757, sailed back home to retire on his estate near Lyons.

What happened during the following ten years to reawaken the interest of the authorities in Poivre's scheme is not altogether certain. Certainly, the enthusiast would not have remained silent, nor would his equally enthusiastic scientifically minded friends have failed to use what influence they had with company and government. In any case, by 1766 Poivre was being offered the governorship of the Isle of France, where he would now have authority, as well as means for pursuing his dream.

He would send out two expeditions—one during 1769–1770, the second during 1771–1772—to gather spice seeds and seedlings from realms under Dutch control. By the time that second expedition returned, Poivre was able to welcome to his personal botanical garden, Mon Plaisir, 400 kidnapped nutmeg plants, 10,000 viable nuts, 70 clove seedlings, and a box full of mother-cloves, some already proving their viability by showing sprouts. The soil and climate proving acceptable to spice trees, Poivre was presently able to boast an orchard of 8,000 clove seedlings and some nutmegs, though the number of those is uncertain.

Until he left for home, Poivre was continually striving to import many kinds of plants from other lands—breadfruit, mangoes, mangosteens, tea-plants, camphor trees, date and sago palms, and, of course, cinnamon trees. He also tried plants better adapted to the climates and to the relative hours of night and day that prevailed in more northern parts of the world. Whether these apples, pears, and peaches bore fruit,

Poivre could have hardly been in a position to learn before he left the Isle of France in 1773.

After he had settled once more near Lyons, Poivre maintained his interest in those plantings, despite the conspicuous indifference of his successor as governor of the island, Jacques Maillart-Dumesle. Poivre's neighbor on the Isle of France, Jean Nicolas Céré, had caught Poivre's contagious enthusiasm for the promised new crops and was to spend many years caring for the spice trees already planted at Mon Plaisir. He was also to send seedlings to Isle Bourbon and to encourage planters there to raise spices through a lengthy correspondence.

In this Céré seemed to have no more official encouragement than Poivre had had, for Governor Dumesle was anything but helpful and Poivre's written pleas to the governor on behalf of his plants only managed to arouse antagonism. Finally, thoroughly exasperated, the governor gave vent to his feelings in an angry letter: "For you, M. le Poivre, the first and foremost care as Intendant of the Ile de France seems to have been to look after your precious spice trees. I have wider and more important things to consider. It is evidently not enough for you to have spoken to me about cloves and nutmegs for days, but now you continue to harp on the same subject. Let me tell you frankly I am sick of the very word, 'spice-tree.' "

Meanwhile, Poivre had been talking with and indoctrinating important people in France. Spices, he had already shown, could take root in the Mascarenes. His friend and late neighbor now was informing him that they had flowered and were bearing fruit. In a few years those trees would be producing profitable crops which could be sold in Asia, where, actually, more spices were used than in Europe. In addition to such profits, there was the important fact that once the Dutch learned their spice monopoly had been broken, the way would be open for an acceptable commercial treaty between France and the Netherlands. It was, then, important to the mother land that the planting and raising of spice trees on the Isle of France be continued under the guidance of a man willing to dedicate himself totally to the so important undertaking. Political issues, here as elsewhere, were never far below the surface.

All this spicy talk bore fruit when, in March 1775, Céré became the officially appointed director of the Jardin du Roi, as Mon Plaisir became after the king sanctioned the purchase of Poivre's estate on the Isle of France. This was to serve as a summer residence for that island's governors and, more important, was to become a botanical garden of note. From then on, all the thoughts and efforts of that garden's director were devoted to improving spice cultivation on the Mascarenes.

Under Céré's care, the clove trees were thriving and bearing fruit, though these were turning out smaller than had been hoped. By the time the second generation of cloves, grown from seed matured on the islands, came into bearing, the size was larger and the future looked more encouraging. The nutmegs, however, did less well. Few trees survived and few of the survivors produced fruit. For long this unfruitfulness seemed to frustrate all Céré's efforts until he discovered the important fact, long guarded as a secret by the Dutch, that nutmeg trees had sex, and until that fact of life was acknowledged no progress could be made toward the production of offspring. The sex life of nutmegs turned out to be a very important consideration.

Nutmeg trees share with a limited number of other

botanical species that interesting quality which botanists describe as *dioecious,*—that is, of being either male or female, not both at once as is the case with most of the trees we know. Of course other species—date palms in tropical lands and sumacs in more temperate climes— share this characteristic. What this results in is that no single plant of such species, if growing alone and whether it be male or female, can produce fruit. No female can bear fruit unless some male tree grows near enough for its pollen, by agency of wind or insect, to reach the sex organ of the female. Yet to the average eye the trees are indistinguishable.

Thus until a nutmeg tree has grown to a considerable size, no one unaware of the situation will begin to suspect why no nutmegs appear. M. Céré's letters to fellow planters on Bourbon are filled with the frustrations caused by such sex-conscious plants, even after he came to appreciate the basic problems. He has sent an indubitably female plant (secured by layering one that has borne fruit) to M. le Comte de Souillac, as requested. The slave, to whose care it has been entrusted, has directions to throw it overboard should an English vessel capture the French one carrying him to Bourbon. One lone tree, all now know, can produce no fruit, yet it's best to take no chances of letting the female tree fall into enemy hands.

The Count acknowledges receipt of the tree, then recounts a dispute between himself and a neighbor as to whose male plant should have the privilege of fertilizing it. A couple of months later, the Count asks for a male nutmeg. His little female is in flower, and there seems to be no male growing at the right distance and in the right stage of pollination to assure the female shall be properly served. In the end there is found a brilliant solution to the harrowing problems of sex-conscious plants. Male shoots are grafted onto female trees—and never the twain shall be parted.

As if sex problems had not been enough, internal French politics began to raise a threatening hand. The minister of Marine in his wisdom decided that the part of the French dominion to grow spices should be the French West Indies and Guiana. He ordered plants to be sent thither from the Jardin du Roi, while further culture of spices in the Mascarenes was to be discouraged. In this decision, one suspects the fine Italian hand of Governor Maillart-Dumesle, who had previously expressed himself so spitefully on the subject of spice culture on the Isle of France. Having previously held a government post in Cayenne, he undoubtedly wished to favor Cayenne with a crop every fool was insisting should be profitable. In doing this, he was also relieving himself of a great nuisance.

The planters of the Mascarenes were embittered as they considered the reward for all their efforts was now to accrue to the French West Indies. They argued and worked against the measure in vain and, though continuing to act as a way station for the transfer of spice trees, they would lose their monopoly as the Dutch had lost theirs and as, in the end, anyone attempting a total monopoly of any kind of plant was bound to lose.

Captain Stavorinus had insisted that "the propagation of spice-trees . . . will never succeed, except in the neighborhood of the Moluccas, unless in similar countries, situated in the same latitudes, heated by subterraneous fires." The latitude argument carries, of course, considerable weight, but, as the successful Isle of France experiment demonstrated, the services of an active volcano may be dispensed with. The special require-

ments of individual plant species were then not yet
understood and, in fact, were not to be understood for
decades to come.

When, in 1798, the Englishman Samuel Hull Wilcocke produced a translation of Stavorinus' book, he
could point out: "The clove-tree has, however, been
successfully introduced into the West India Islands, and
though the quantities hitherto brought from them, have
been very insignificant, yet their constant increase
suffices to show, that the culture is in an improving
state; in 1797, 350 lbs. were imported to London from
Martinico"—i.e., the French-owned Martinique—"and
in the present year 200 pounds from that island and
2,981 pounds from St. Kitts." No suggestion is given as
to how spice culture got started in the English-owned St.
Kitts. The timing, together with the known fact that a
clove tree begins to bear fruit when about nine years
old, suggests that those trees on St. Kitts were second-
generation trees for the West Indies, possibly bought or
stolen from a planter in Cayenne or one of the French
West Indian islands. By 1818, of the 78,000 pounds of
cloves sold in England for that year, 70,000 pounds
were said to have arrived from Cayenne, where a third
or fourth generation of clove trees might already be in
bearing. Such trees, surviving and bearing at the ripe
old age of eighty-five or more, could guarantee that any
Spice Island monopoly of spices was to remain a thing
of the past.

For peoples native to the New World, those hard
little black balls produced by Far Eastern pepper trees
would be more important as a source of income than as
a flavoring for their own food. The Indians of the New
World had always had "peppers" of their own which
Physician de Monardes described at length: "Also they

doe bring . . . a certaine kinde of Peper, which they call long Peper, which hath a sharper taste, than the Peper which is brought from the Orientall Indias, and it doeth bite more than it, and it is of more sweete taste and of better smell, than that of Asia, or the Peper of the East India, it is a gentle spice, for to dresse meates withall, and for this effect all the people in that countrie doe use it. . . . I have tasted it, and it biteth more than the black Peper doeth, and it hath a more sweet taste than it. I have caused it to bee put in to dreste meates, in place of the Orientall Peper, and it geveth a gentle taste unto that as is drest therewith."

Belonging to the large, strictly New World genus *Capsicum*, such peppers grow on small, shrubby plants or on vines and may appear in many sizes, shapes (from roundish bell peppers to elongated chili peppers), colors (yellow, green, red, purplish), and tastes (from sweet to very sharp). They all belong to that large plant family which includes numerous food plants, many of entirely New World origin—the Solanaceae. Tomatoes and white potatoes are notable New World members of this family.

One New World pepper, *Capsicum tetragonum*, is particularly notable in that long ago it was introduced into Hungary, to be cultivated there on a large scale and to emerge thence as Hungarian paprika. In addition to giving that "gentle" taste to meats, these Capsicums can supply what Oriental pepper cannot—valuable vitamins. However, they never did supply the spice to history that belongs to pepper grown in the Far East.

A spice expert of our day assures us that most of the spices, once thought to be the exclusive products of the Far East, now grow on Caribbean islands and in nearby Central America—allspice, ginger, nutmeg, mace, cardamon, cloves, black pepper. No one has a monopoly in growing them, nor has anyone a monopoly in marketing them, as witnessed by the variety of little cans and bottles on the spice shelves of our markets. What these also bear witness to is that the grim rivalries, for which so many lives and fortunes have been sacrificed, are now long since laid to rest.

3

Cups
That
Cheer

TEA

No American with the slightest awareness of history need be told of the importance of the tea plant—or, at least, of a certain Tea Party—to the politics and people of our land. Of course, if it hadn't been tea, it would have been some other imported luxury for which a habit had been sufficiently developed to create what was thought to be an insatiable demand. The issue was really not the tea itself but the tax on it. This was being publicly denied the government of King George III as the remains of shattered tea chests went bobbing along on the waters of Boston Harbor while phony Indians let out their not-at-all-phony whoops of triumph. What those whoops announced to the world of Tories was that even so coveted a luxury as tea was to be foregone rather than allow the minions of King George and Lord North to collect taxes the Colonials considered grossly unjust. They also made clear that the drinking of tea had by then become an important ritual to British subjects everywhere.

No more than a mere century and a half earlier,

neither tea drinking nor the North American colonies had seemed of much importance to most Britons. In fact, there is no record of a public tea auction in England before 1657—such an auction being the means by which imports were sold to wholesale merchants. Yet by the time of the famous Tea Party, as it is estimated, eighteen million pounds of tea were being used annually in Britain. By then tea had become more than a luxury to most Britons—and the American colonists were, of course, Britons only once removed. To the unimaginative home government, it seemed no more than logical that upon so necessary an item as tea there might be placed a tax which should force rebellious Colonials to share the costs of administering their government and protecting themselves from enemies, both native and foreign.

As a new habit in the England of the seventeenth century, tea drinking had been a matter of heated controversy. By 1699 there was published "An Essay Upon the Nature and Qualities of Tea," wherein the writer, John Ovington, gave explicit encouragement to tea drinking: "For it is generally acknowledged to be both Pleasant and Medicinal, at once to delight the Palate and correct the Disease, and to heal the Distemper without giving any Disturbance to the Stomach.

"And certainly were the custom of Drinking it as Universal here as it is in the Eastern Countries, we should quickly find that Men might be Cheerful with Sobriety, and witty without the Danger of losing their Senses; and they might even double the Days of their Natural Life, by converting it all into Enjoyment, exempt from the several painful and acute Diseases, occasion'd very often by a pernicious Excess of Inflaming Liquors, which render it rather a Burthen than a Blessing to us."

The quaint and dated wording of John Ovington's eulogy of tea drinking conceals truths that were certainly as much hidden to that writer as to all his contemporaries. In an era when sources of drinking water could so often and so undetectably be contaminated with sewage, a man who slaked his thirst at a well might be courting disease and death, as we now know, from typhoid or cholera. Such a drink was generally regarded with suspicion, though no one then could know anything about the mechanisms by which healthy people become mortally ill. Those "Inflaming Liquors," so generously imbibed and so explicitly decried by John Ovington, contained sufficient alcoholic content to be as lethal to microorganisms as to men. In that sense, they were actually safer drinks than much of the cold well water then available. The fact that boiling the water could make it safe for drinking would not be understood until the nineteenth century was well on its way. In any case, who wanted to drink boiled water—except, of course, in tea?

Tea, always prepared as by ritual with boiling hot water, was definitely safer to drink. If drunk in sufficient volume, as done by habitual tea drinkers, it could truly prove "medicinal" in effect by supplying enough safe water to keep in solution those substances now recognized to have been accumulating in places where they could cause pain and damage—uric acid in gouty joints, "stones" in kidney or bladder. During the seventeenth century, stones and gravel were so common and so painful an affliction that being "cut for the stone," in an era antedating anesthesia and any understanding of sepsis, was a risky undertaking resorted to only by the most harassed and hardy sufferers.

Samuel Pepys, in his famous diary that spanned the 1660s, describes the stone he hoarded as a memento of that operation in 1658 and proudly exhibited it every year at the party he held in celebration of the anniversary of its removal. Not every sufferer had the courage to face such an operation, as indicated in the diary of Pepys' equally famous contemporary, John Evelyn, under the date June 10, 1669: "I went this evening to London to carry Mr. Pepys to my brother Richard, now exceedingly afflicted with the stone. . . . [Mr. Pepys] had been successfully cut and carried the stone as big as a tennis ball to show him and encourage his resolution to go through the operation." Whatever the size of a 1658 tennis ball, the exhibit failed to convince Richard Evelyn, who was to die within a year in great agony.

For that also common affliction—gout—there seemed to be no such kind of possible escape. The continued consumption of high-protein diets and high-alcohol beverages only served to aggravate it. Those who forsook their frequent drinking of strong liquors for frequent cups of tea might well find reason to praise the new herb's medicinal qualities. They were presently to find it had social value also.

How such a habit first formed must be left to the imagination, as also must how the potential of any valuable plant comes to be recognized. The force of hunger could have served to drive our savage ancestors to try the grains and other foods which came to constitute their staff of life, especially if they had first seen wild animals eating them. Those alluring odors of spice-bearing plants could have served as temptation to men of more advanced food habits. These we can understand. But what in the world led men to tea? The answer is anyone's guess.

However much experts are supposed to disagree, experts in tea do agree that it all started in China long,

long ago. Of course the date—the century even—is shrouded in mystery, as are most dates that might help us pinpoint the time of discovery of any long-accepted useful plant growing within reach of resourceful men. One can imagine some Chinese of centuries gone plucking the leaves of a young shrub, chewing them absently while he gradually became aware of a mildly stimulant quality he found pleasant. Beyond that, the path that led to the tea drink is lost in the dimness of time and the quaintness of legend.

"In the reign of Yuen Ty"—so runs a Chinese legend of the third century A.D.—". . . an old woman was accustomed to proceed every morning at daybreak to the market-place, carrying a cup of tea in the palm of her hand. The people bought it eagerly; and yet from the break of day to the close of evening, the cup was never exhausted. The money she received she distributed to the orphans and the needy beggars frequenting the highways. The people seized and confined her in prison. At night she flew through the prison window with her little vase in her hand." The clear suggestion here is that witchcraft and tea must have much in common.

What of the plant itself—*Thea sinensis*—which does not figure directly in the legend? Of Asiatic growth and a close relative of the camellia, *Thea*, if left to itself, could develop into a tree as much as thirty feet high. However, if thus left to itself, it could not be producing marketable tea which represents an annual crop of young shoots gathered from what remains of a waist-high shrub. For centuries the raising and handling of tea in its native China remained practically unchanged from the ways described by an eighth-century Chinese tea expert: "Tea is generally plucked in March, April or May ... the tea shoots, four or five inches long, are plucked. ... From plucking to final packing, there are seven processes," which he proceeds to describe in loving detail as also he does the preparation of the drink from solid bricks of pressed leaves: "What is called cake tea is put into a jar or bottle after being pounded, and the boiling water is poured over it. Sometimes onion, ginger, ju-jube, orange peel, and peppermint are used and it is permitted to boil some time before skimming off the froth."

Some of these additives would not seem to us to contribute much to that drink which, incidentally, the prolonged boiling must have made bitter. Perhaps, though, to people previously accustomed to more inebriating beverages, something had to be done to give blander drinks like tea, coffee, and chocolate a special kind of bite.

European missionaries to China were the first to write of the tea-serving customs, then so strange to their own continent. A Portuguese Dominican friar, Gaspar da Cruz, visiting Canton in 1556, described the ritual of the social visits which, inevitably, included tea: "Whatsoever person or persons come to any man of quality's house, it is customary to offer him on a fair tray in a porcelain cup (or as many cups as there are persons) a kind of warm water which they call *cha,* which is somewhat red and very medicinal, which they use to drink, made from a concoction of somewhat bitter herbs; with this they commonly welcome all manner of persons that they do respect, be they acquaintances or be they not, and to me they offered it many times."

About twenty years later, another Portuguese friar, Martín da Rada, was being shown equal respect in the same city: "When one comes to visit another, after having made their bows and being seated, a household servant comes with a tray of as many cups of hot water as there are persons seated. This water is boiled with certain somewhat bitter herbs, and with a little morsel of conserve in water. They eat the morsel and sip the hot water. Although at first we did not care much for that hot boiled water, yet we soon became accustomed to it and got to like it, for this is always the first thing that is served on a visit."

Though experts are inclined to agree that the tea-drinking habit reached Japan from China, the when and how is now as much of a mystery as when it made its debut in China. In 1596 the Portuguese Archbishop of Goa (in India) arrived in Japan with his secretary, the Dutch Jan Hughen van Linschoten, who kept a record of impressions gathered during his far-flung travels. Of the Japanese tea habit he wrote: "And after their meat [they] use a certaine drinke, which is a pot with hot water, which they drink as hot as ever they may indure, whether it be Winter or Summer . . . the aforesaid warme water is made with the powder of a certaine hearbe called *Cha,* which is much esteemed, and is well accounted among them and all such as are of any countenance of habilitie have the said water kept for them in a secret place, and the gentlemen make it themselves and when they will entertain any of their friends, they give him some of that warme water to drinke; for the pots wherein they sieth it, and wherein the hearbe is kept, with the earthen cups which they drinke it in, they esteeme so much of them as we doe of Diamants, Rubies and other precious stones, and they are not esteemed for their newnes, but for their oldnes, and for that they were made by a good workman."

Such glowing accounts of a new drink, from the

fabled Orient Marco Polo's writings had first made known, could not fail to arouse curiosity, at least, in the people of Europe. Whether the writers of the just quoted accounts went further and managed to bring back home with them samples of that *cha*, either to exhibit to interested friends or to supply themselves with an occasional cup of a drink for which they had formed a habit, we cannot say. It is doubtful that they could have brought much home, for the journey was long and its outcome less than certain.

In any case, tea as plant or drink was so little known to sixteenth-century Europeans that neither John Gerard nor the editor of the 1597 edition of his herbal so much as mentions it, though the equally Oriental cinnamon tree is there described at length. If by then other contemporary European herbalists had described the tea shrub or tree, the great British herbal of the century would not have failed to include it, even to shamelessly lifting descriptions published by other authors.

Despite this neglect, the tea habit was soon reaching Europe. Even though at first their eyes seemed to be focused almost exclusively on the Spice Islands, Portuguese mariners and missionary friars were extending their interests to China and Japan and could have been the first to start the tea habit in Europe. Or it may have been the Dutch—both lands soon undertaking traffic with China. At home, the habit must have caught on quickly and well, for by 1635 the inevitable viewers-with-alarm began to make themselves known.

Had it been new to our own century, tea would have been denounced as an environmental hazard or, possibly, as a contributor to cancer. In 1635 the accusations were less specific and no more based on demonstrable facts. Dr. Simon Pauli, a self-consciously learned Danish physician, felt it incumbent upon himself to expose what he considered the great tea fallacy, not to mention those of equally new tobacco, coffee, and chocolate. After quoting miscellaneous authorities from Hippocrates to his own era, he came to the crux of the matter by reporting an account given him by a Danish friend just returning from the Indies: "In these Countries, vast sums of Money are laid out on this Herb, which is said to be possessed of very considerable Virtues; for it corroborates the Stomach, and produces a good Digestion; nourishes the Limbs, and dissipates and carries off by Urine, or otherwise all peccant and redundant humidity. It also cures the Gout, and prevents, or expels the Stone or Gravel. . . ." Not prepared to disprove such claims, whatever they might mean, Pauli concentrated his venom on the excessive extravagance of spending money on a Far Eastern herb when native European myrtle, he insisted, could serve equally well. In fact, he maintained that tea and myrtle were identical—a contention which, at least, demonstrated how limited and faulty was Pauli's botanical knowledge.

"As to the virtues they attribute to it," Pauli was generously ready to admit they just might exist under Far Eastern conditions, "but it loses them in our climates, where it becomes, on the contrary, very dangerous to use. It hastens the death of those who drink it, especially if they have passed the age of forty years." Of course Pauli gave no statistics in support of his claim—not even a single case cited, so one has to wonder just how he managed to equate deaths of people past forty and tea drinking.

The Dutch, who knew their Orient first hand, were not to be put off by a self-consciously learned stay-at-home. In early January 1637 the directors of the Dutch East India Company were writing to the governor-general at Batavia: "As tea begins to come into use by some of the people, we expect some jars of Chinese tea, as well as Japanese, with each ship." At about the same time, tea was reaching Russia by the long overland caravan routes. There, though it was slower to catch on, tea drinking was to develop an elaborate ritual centering around those handsome brass tea machines, the samovars.

Meanwhile, the Dutch East India Company had been putting on a public-relations effort intended to focus on tea the interest of all Western Europe. Soon the habit was reaching England, possibly through Holland, possibly directly as vessels of the English East India Company began to carry Far Eastern wares to home ports. Shortly after 1657 a London coffeehouse keeper, Thomas Garway, was offering, in a public advertisement, to sell tea, according to quality, at the then low, low prices of from about $4 to $35 per pound (the previous prices demanded having been from $30 to $50 per pound). He would, he promised, be serving the drink in his coffeehouse as well—and for both kinds of sales, his broadside must have served as an excellent stimulant.

"The Leaf is of such known vertues, that those very Nations famous for Antiquity, Knowledge, and Wisdom, do frequently sell it among themselves for twice its weight in silver. . . ." Continuing in such a vein for the remainder of a lengthy paragraph, Garway reaches a climax with a listing of tea's "vertues."

> It helpeth the headache, giddiness and heaviness thereof.
> It removeth the obstructions of the Spleen.
> It is very good against the Stone and Gravel, cleaning the Kidneys and Uriters, being drunk with Virgins Honey, instead of sugar.

It taketh away the difficulty of breathing, opening Obstructions . . .

It is good against Crudities, strengthening the weakness of the Ventricle or Stomach, causing good Appetite and Digestion, and particularly for Men of a corpulent Body, and such as are great eaters of Flesh . . .

It is good for Cold, Dropsies and Scurveys, if properly infused, purging the blood by sweat and Urine, and expelleth Infection.
It drives away all pains in the Collick, proceeding from Wind, and purgeth safely the Gall.

How could any man in his right mind resist the allure of so amazing, so potent a drink! Even should his health seem perfect, there was no security that it was not already on its way to change for the worse. Besides, tea drinking was now assuming a kind of snob appeal. It was becoming fashionable for men of culture, wit, and ambition to frequent those new coffeehouses—of which Garway's was one of the newest—so called in honor of that other alien drink whose arrival on the English social scene had preceded tea by a few years.

Of course that socially conscious, ever curious diarist, Samuel Pepys, had to find out for himself what it was like. He confided to his diary on September 25, 1660: "I did send for a cupp of tea (a China drink) of which I had never drank before." He does not record how he liked its taste or effect; he certainly had no need for an aphrodisiac, as tea then was reputed to be. His failure to mention tea for another seven years suggests either that it did not come up to his expectations or that it was so commonplace as not to merit special mention. In 1667 Pepys arrived "home and found my wife making of tea, a drink which Mr. Pelling, the poticary, tells her is good for her cold and fluxions." So it was still considered medicinal and, perhaps, Pepys found it too costly for other uses.

In those days, no king would scorn to receive a gift of tea. Twenty-three pounds of it (valued at 50 shillings a pound) were considered acceptable by King Charles II of England. It would have been yet more acceptable to his queen, the Portuguese Catherine of Braganza, who in 1662 brought to England a tea-drinking habit probably introduced into her own country by her own adventurous fellow countrymen. On the occasion of her birthday in that year, poet Edmund Waller sought to eulogize the new queen and the old beverage she favored:

> Venus her myrtle, Phoebus has his bays;
> Tea both excels, which she vouchsafes to praise.
> The best of queens and best of herbs we owe
> To that bold nation which the way did show
> To the far regions where the sun does rise,
> Whose rich productions we so richly prize,
> The Muse's friend, tea does our fancy aid,
> Repress those vapours which the head invade,
> And keeps the palace of the soul serene,
> Fit on her birthday to salute the Queen.

Had Waller actually turned to tea from the consumption of mind-fogging beverages? Certainly, as one of the acknowledged literary lights of his day, he would have been frequenting coffeehouses or, rather, some particular coffeehouse which was becoming known for the special talents of its patrons. There, over cups of the hot, stimulating but otherwise nonintoxicating drink, would be discussed the important issues of the day—literary, social, religious, political. And there, inevitably, might be sown seeds of dangerous ideas. By 1675 King

Charles II was beginning to feel the coffeehouses were places where seditious ideas were being spread—a tendency that must be nipped in the bud.

On December 29 of that year the king issued the following proclamation: "Whereas it is most apparent that the multitude of coffee houses of late years set up and kept within this kingdom . . . and the great resort of idle and disaffected persons to them, have produced very evil and dangerous effects; as well for that many tradesmen and others, do mispend much of their time . . . but also, for that in such houses . . . divers false, malitious and scandalous reports are devised and spread abroad to the Defamation of His Majesty's Government and to the Disturbance of the Peace and Quiet of the Realm; his Majesty hath thought fit and necessary, that the said coffee Houses be (for the future) put down and suppressed, and doth strictly charge and command all manner of persons, That they . . . do not presume from and after the tenth day of January next ensuing, to keep any Publick Coffee House, or to utter or sell by retail . . . any Coffee, Chocolate, Sherbett, or Tea, as they will answer to the contrary at their utmost perils. . . ."

As a Stuart, King Charles had to believe in the divine right of kings, which, of course, included the right to interdict anything and especially meetings for presumedly seditious purposes. However, as the second Charles, he had to remember the first Charles and that even a divinely appointed king could lose his head. So, when howls of indignation went up in coffeehouses all over London and increased in volume as days passed, it took no more than eleven such days to persuade the king that he would do well to indulge in a bit of "princely consideration and royal compassion" and withdraw the proclamation before the number of seditious protesters had increased beyond control.

As one commentator put it, "A battle for freedom of speech was fought and won over this question at a time when Parliaments were infrequent and when the liberty of the press did not exist." It was not, of course, a final victory. As another century was to demonstrate, the issue had not been permanently settled. If anything, the controversy probably helped to encourage sedition in the minds of some overseas Englishmen who were already in 1671, according to John Evelyn, one of the Commissioners for Trade and Plantations, "a people almost upon the very brink of renouncing any dependence on the Crown." Though the rambunctious New Englanders whom Evelyn was referring to would quiet down for a while, they remained altogether capable of future seditious thinking on the subject of taxing one of the drinks whose general use King Charles II had thought to interdict.

As tea continued to mount in popularity, the price began to drop and, therefore, its use increased still further. It was, therefore, inevitable that an anti-new-habit faction would form. By 1722 faddist James Lacy was declaiming vitriolically against tea, which, he asserted, caused "Hypochondriack Disorders," it being "A drug which of late Years very much insinuated itself, as well into our Diet, as Regales and Entertainments, tho' its Operation is not less destructive to the Animal Oeconomy, than Opium, or some other drugs, which we have at present learned to avoid with more Caution . . . tea may attenuate the Blood to any Degree necessary to the Production of any Disease."

In the strange medical language of his day, Lacy announced, "The Chearfulness of our Minds depends

upon the Quantity of Spirits secreted from the Blood
. . . by the frequent use of Tea the Spirits are so far
wasted as to be just able to perform the necessary
offices"—whatever that may mean. Perhaps it was not
intended to mean anything clearly defined, for the
Lacys of this world, then or now, thrive upon vague,
formless menaces.

The thought that tea might be deleterious was
shared by better men and for better reasons. In 1720
evangelist John Wesley was describing a hand tremor he
believed to have been induced by tea drinking. This
could have been the case had he prepared his drink, as
was not uncommon, by the prolonged boiling of a
considerable quantity of tea leaves. Today, having
learned that both tea and coffee contain the same
alkaloid—caffeine—and that, weight for weight, tea
contains more of it, we know that if the tea we drink is
prepared by the boiling that was once popular, it is
possible to take in enough caffeine to cause tremors. A
cup of tea, as it is now prepared by pouring boiling
water over tea leaves, usually contains much less of the
stimulant than a percolated cup of coffee. Had John
Wesley drunk a considerable quantity of well-boiled tea,
his tremor may not have been fancied. In any case, he
must have improved his method of preparation later in
life, for he happily resumed the tea habit.

Already in 1720 the annual import of tea into
Britain was amounting to over a million pounds, the
monopolist there in that trade, as in all other Oriental
commodities, then being the English East India Company. Duties on teas destined for British merchants were
much higher than those charged on teas being trans-
shipped to lands on the Continent, so that it did not take
long for enterprising smugglers to perceive how profit-

able they might find it could they secure English India Company teas in other lands, then sneak them into British markets without the interposition of domestic customs. Clearly, the escaping of taxes deemed to be unjust or burdensome was becoming a way of life for a certain kind of British subject. By December 16, 1773, when there was imposed a relatively trivial tax on tea—a tax whose payment might imply an acceptance of Parliament's right to impose taxes at will—tea-loving Colonials did not hesitate to cast their votes against the tea habit by dumping into the waters of Boston Harbor 340 chests of the East India Company's choice teas.

For some Bostonians it was, of course, a kind of matyrdom, as depicted by Oliver Wendell Holmes in his *Ballad of the Boston Tea Party* ("Bohea" here applying both to the district where tea grew and to the black teas derived from there):

> No! ne'er was mingled such a draught
>   In Palace, hall, or arbor,
> As freemen brewed and tyrants quaffed
>   That night in Boston Harbor! . . .
>
> O Woman, at the evening board
> So gracious, sweet, and purring,
> So happy while the tea is poured,
> So blest while spoons are stirring,
> What martyr can compare with thee,
> The mother, wife, or daughter,
> That night, instead of best Bohea,
> Condemned to milk and water.

It was a sentence not to be commuted for ten years and to be variously shared all over the colonies, most notably in the cities of Charleston, Philadelphia, and New York, which had celebrated their own kinds of tea parties.

It had been the English India Company's struggles to avoid bankruptcy that had contributed to the English government's insistence on making those fateful tea shipments. It was to be the company's need to find new, annually renewable sources of income that stimulated a search for ways to get the whole tea industry, from seed to marketable product, into British hands. Up to then the English had purchased teas in Canton, China, to be brought home in English bottoms. There now was an urge to try making tea a thoroughly English undertaking from start to finish.

As one writer put it in a confidential letter to the British governor-general of India, "It is therefore of considerable national importance that some better guarantee should be furnished for the continued supply of this article, than that at present . . . although the Chinese have at present a monopoly, it will be easy for us to destroy." A monopoly of so profitable an article in the hands of another people was definitely not to be tolerated any longer than necessary.

This just quoted letter was dated 1828. Could it have been mere coincidence that already in 1827 the Dutch East India Company was making discreet inquiries as to the possibility of introducing Chinese tea culture into Java, where their own colonial economy also seemed to need new sources of income? The man to whom much credit must be given for the success of this undertaking was the Dutch professional tea-taster, Jacobus Isidorus Lodewijk Levien Jacobson—a name so formidable that he was generally known as J.I.L.L. Jacobson. It was in 1827 that Jacobson undertook the first of six annual visits to China, ostensibly to taste China teas in the shipping port, Canton, but actually to learn all he possibly could about tea growing and manufacture. It was his intent to bring out of China not only information but also materials and workmen to help assure success to the proposed Java tea plantations.

It was, of course, a risky business, for the Chinese looked with doubtful favor on foreigners, whatever their motives for visiting that land, and must look with downright antagonism on any trying to undercut their own tea monopoly. Yet by his last visit—1832–33— though there was a price on his head by the time he left, Jacobson managed to take out with him fifteen skilled Chinese—planters, tea-makers, box-makers—plus about seven million tea seeds and a great quantity of other materials and instruments destined to start the tea industry in the Java hills.

Thus began there the first large-scale tea planting, though almost certainly Chinese laborers already working in Java would have kept growing near their homes enough tea plants to assure them a continued supply of that, to them, so necessary product. For fifteen years Jacobson presided over the developing Javanese tea plantations and industry—neither of which could long remain concealed from rival planters on the Indian subcontinent. It must, therefore, be more than a coincidence that by the end of 1848, when Jacobson returned to Holland, there soon to die, the English plant collector Robert Fortune was being engaged to try his hand and skills in securing for his own countrymen the same kind of materials and information Jacobson had brought out of China some fifteen years earlier.

During those years the English had not been idle. Though the news must have leaked out from Java that tea could be persuaded to grow in soils other than Chinese, the right soils must be found, also the right climate, in order to start plantations in other lands.

After much searching and argument, they decided that upper Assam and Darjeeling afforded suitable conditions. Now the big question remained—would tea actually consent to grow and thrive there? The English got their answer when, during the 1830s, botanical collectors found growing in Assam wild native plants that experts finally agreed to be a true tea. If one tea grew there, others surely would. Since the worth of that native tea was long questioned—China and high-quality tea being synonymous to potential British planters—it then became important to secure tea plants and seeds from China for the purpose of starting new tea plantations.

It was not unnatural to assume that only in China, whose teas must be the product of centuries of selection, could truly fine teas be found. So the English in India turned their backs on the native variety and determined to have workmen, materials, and plants of Chinese origin. To achieve this, they needed one of those men endowed with a quick eye, a keen mind, an itching foot, infinite discretion, and not a little personal courage—in short, a botanical collector—to penetrate into the remoter tea-growing areas of China, collect there the tea plants and seeds they needed, and use his persuasive powers to engage the services of enough Chinese to get the new tea industry of Assam started.

Incidentally and as a side line, he would bring out, for the gardens of the more prosperous British stay-at-homes, a miscellany of new ornamental plants to enhance their formal gardens. Among such plants is our common *Forsythia* (variety *Fortunei*), which every spring bears golden witness to the skill of that notable collector, Robert Fortune, who, in the course of six years—two expeditions—in China, acquired and brought out what was needed to help make those new tea plantations the success they were presently to become.

Fortune's published accounts—travelogues with a purpose—give a lively picture of the China he saw: "It was the harvest time for the principal crop of the season, and the natives were observed on every hill-side busily engaged in gathering the leaves. The tea-gatherers were generally seen in small groups, consisting of from eight to twelve persons. One old man was usually at the head of each group, the others being women and children. Each had a small stool formed like a letter T, but broad, of course, at the top, for sitting on while gathering the leaves on the lower sides of the bushes. The foot of the stool being pointed, it was easily forced into the ground in order to render it steady, and as easily drawn out and carried to a different spot. When these tea-gatherers are hired they are not paid by the day, but by the quantity of leaves they bring in to their employers."

Ten years earlier, Robert Fortune had carefully observed and recorded the method used for processing tea leaves: "The Chinese cottages, amongst the tea hills, are simple and rude in their construction. . . . Nevertheless, it is in these poor cottages that a large proportion of the teas, with their high-sounding names, are first prepared. . . .

"The drying pans and furnaces in these places are very simply constructed. The pans, which are of iron and made as thin as possible, are round and shallow. . . . A row of these are built into brickwork and 'chunam'—plaster. . . . The pans become hot very soon after the warm air has begun to circulate in the flue beneath them. A quantity of leaves . . . are now thrown into the pans and turned over, shaken up, and kept in motion by men and women stationed there for that purpose. The leaves are immediately affected by the heat. They begin to crack and become quite moist with the vapour of sap, which they give out on the application of heat. This part of the process lasts about five minutes, in which time the leaves lose their crispness, and become soft and pliable. They are then taken out of the pans and thrown upon a table, the upper part of which is made of split pieces of bamboo. . . . Three or four persons now surround the table, and the heap of tea leaves is divided into as many parcels, each individual taking as many as he can hold in his hands, and the rolling process commences . . . the object being to express the sap and moisture and at the same time to twist the leaves. . . . This part of the process also lasts about five minutes, during which time a large portion of the green juice has been expressed. . . .

"When the rolling process is completed the leaves are removed from the table and shaken out for the last time . . . and are exposed to the action of the air." After this air drying, the process of heating in pans is repeated, the whole being carefully watched to avoid burning. Clearly, to prepare first-class tea required skill, experience, and educated judgment.

Such manual processes of manufacture could serve for tea as originally consumed by Oriental tea drinkers. As, encouraged by a continued barrage of publicity, the tea-drinking habit spread, tea became big business and those early manufacturing processes could no longer suffice. By the time the seeds Robert Fortune was to bring out of China could provide harvestable tea, the increasing consumption of the beverage had encouraged increasing demand, which, in turn, demanded yet greater supplies. There could never be enough Chinese tea workers to fill these soaring demands, and so it became urgent to devise ways for mechanizing the production of salable teas. As this was done, discriminating tea drinkers of the Occident began to try different brands of tea, raised in British India on plantations whose start was largely thanks to seeds a dedicated collector had managed to secure in China.

It was harvest season—October—of 1853 when Fortune undertook to acquire those seeds which were to have been his foremost concern: "Having finished my work at Shanghae, I took my departure for the tea-districts of Chekiang in order to make collections of seeds and plants for the government plantations in the Himalayas.

"When I arrived amongst the tea-hills in that province, I found the seeds of the tea-plant just ripe, and all my old friends employed in collecting them in anticipation of my arrival. . . .

"Having established myself in my old quarters in the temple of Tein-tung, I went to work in Chinese style. It was given out by my people and the priests that I had arrived for the purpose of making purchases of tea-seeds, that I wanted five or six hundred catty"—a total of from 650 to 800 pounds—"and would continue to purchase all that were brought to me, providing they were of good quality, until that quantity was made up. On the day following this announcement, and for many days afterwards, the people began to flock to the temple in great numbers, for the purpose of selling their tea seeds. . . . My time was fully occupied from daylight until dark in examining, settling the price according to quality, and weighing the seeds. In this labour I was greatly assisted by my good friend, the priest . . . who, having a small tea plantation, was an excellent judge of the seed. Many were the little disputes we had as to quality and price, which were always carried on with the most perfect good-humor, and generally referred to the priest for arbitration. He was much respected by the natives themselves, and his word was considered as final."

Tea seeds gathered in China gave the first impetus to what were to become the great and highly profitable tea plantations of Upper Assam and Darjeeling. After disease had ruined the coffee plantations there, Ceylon followed later. Ironically, though, it would not, in the end, be the Chinese varieties but those native to Assam that were to produce the best teas. With the realization of this fact, the Indian tea monopoly was on its way.

The English East India Company, however, had little enthusiasm for the transfer of the tea monopoly to India from China and for reasons that had nothing to do with concern over the welfare of the Chinese. It was the company's welfare they had in mind, for the teas of China had long been furnishing a large part of the funds needed for governing India. A three-cornered trade had provided this—British manufactures exported to India; opium, financed and cultivated in India under the auspices of the company, shipped to China; Chinese teas to Britain. From this trade accrued great profit to British ships and shippers, most of whom, directly or indirectly, were also influential in the company. In the end this commerce led to the opium wars of 1840 and 1858, after the latter of which the China monopolies came to an end, as also did the 258-year-old company.

The Indian tea trade was growing fast. By the year 1896, 120 years after the American Declaration of

Independence, for which the Boston Tea Party had played the overture, the Indian Tea Association was marketing in North America alone nearly nine and a half million pounds of tea from plantations in India and Ceylon. Within another fifty years that figure was to be multiplied by ten. It is one of the ironies of the tea business that by then the English India Company had long since been laid in the grave its own high-handed policies had dug, whereas the independent American colonies were so alive and prospering that their purchases of once interdicted tea were adding materially to the profits of the company's successor in the tea business.

Inevitably, Americans had been trying to grow their own teas. Already in 1795 some tea plants had been set out on a South Carolina plantation where, in 1887, visitors were to be shown a fifteen-foot-high tea tree claimed to be a survivor of that first experiment. By the late 1840s and early 1850s more plantations had been undertaken in South Carolina and Georgia. In 1858 the U.S. Government became sufficiently interested in the tea project to seek the services of Robert Fortune to do for our Southern states what he had done for India. Though he secured seeds and shipped them to our country, the timing was bad. The soon to erupt Civil War could hardly have been encouraging to planters who would have to master new undertakings. Not surprisingly, these were not destined long to outlast that war. Since those days, other sporadic attempts at tea raising have been tried in Southern states—no attempt amounting to much or lasting long. Today *Thea sinensis* is being grown in lands farther to the south, from Mexico to Argentina, though none of these plantations offers a serious threat to Chinese or Indian teas. As far as Argentina is concerned, the native *Yerba maté* has long been more popular as a drink than tea.

A further irony of the great tea business was to be the contribution made by the American ship designers and builders to the transport of teas. The War of 1812 had seen privateers of both Britain and the United States busily pursuing and capturing, as prizes of war, enemy ships of all descriptions. In that kind of undertaking, the old, slow, stately East Indiamen were at a great disadvantage. The ship of the hour (technically a brig) was one of those newly designed Baltimore clippers—two-masted and square-rigged, built so as to run circles around the old-type sailing vessels.

Once the war was over, such vessels came into great demand as packet ships to carry passengers, mail, and cargo on the New York-Liverpool run. So successful did the design prove that, in 1832, a Baltimore merchant was ordering a full-rigged three-masted ship built along the lines of the clipper brigs. Named *Ann McKim* after the merchant's wife, she soon proved to be one of the finest and fastest vessels on the China run—for some time the fastest. Her cargo capacity, however, was not large enough to win over altogether those conservative merchants who were only slowly coming to realize that tea was a commodity whose profits might be considerably bettered by getting it promptly to a waiting market.

It took the knowledgeable eyes of skilled naval architects to appreciate the full potential of a Baltimore clipper. When, in 1841, the *Ann McKim* was undergoing repairs in a New York drydock, two keen young naval architects, Donald McKay and John Willis Griffiths, took the opportunity to study her lines closely. The result of this was the Griffiths-designed clipper ship *Rainbow,* launched in 1845 to create a sensation on the

China run. So amazing did she prove that on her very first run to Canton, she not only paid back her original cost—$45,000—but earned an equal sum above that as profit for her owners. On her second trip to Canton she proved so fast that, outsailing all rivals, she was to bring back to New York the first news of her arrival at Canton.

The English were presently experimenting with clipper-type ships, but after the repeal of the Navigation Laws permitted England-bound cargoes to be carried in bottoms of other nations, American-built clippers were, for a time, carrying much of the tea that reached England. By the time, during the 1850s, when California-bound gold seekers, itching to reach the West Coast as speedily as possible, preempted most of the American clippers, English shipbuilders were designing and building their own "extreme" clippers.

In the tea markets of London, each season, special premiums were paid for the first tea shipments to arrive. In 1861–62 this was rated at 10 shillings per ton. With a cargo amounting to as much as 1,600 tons, this premium could amount to a considerable sum. Of course this led to breakneck competition all along the line, from being the first to load and weigh anchor at Canton to arriving first off the English coast and, therefore, first securing docking facilities at London. There were many such races, the most famous of which, perhaps, was that, in 1866, between the clipper *Ariel* (built in England in 1865) and the *Taeping* (built at Grenock on the Clyde in 1863). Both ships completed their cargoes and left Canton at practically the same moment. Both arrived ninety-nine days later at the Downs, so close together that the news of their sighting so frayed the nerves of their owners in London that they finally agreed to split between themselves the premium which should come to the declared winner. This, by a mere matter of minutes, was decided by the prompt availability of a tug for the final docking.

They were lovely things, those tea clippers, whose end was foreshadowed by the new steam-powered vessels and then by the 1869 opening of the Suez Canal which gave steam-power an edge over sails. The so memorable race between the *Ariel* and the *Taeping* was never to be repeated.

It just could be that tall ships like those memorably swift China clippers could again be of value to an energy-hungry world, had we the men to build and manage them. It would, therefore, be well to take a look at one of those beauties that the American tea trade first called into being—the thousand-ton *Oriental*—which created a sensation in London on her arrival there in 1850. In his book *The Clipper Ship Era,* Arthur H. Clark gives a loving description.

"Every line of her long, black hull indicated power and speed; her tall raking masts and skysail yards towered above the shipping in the docks; her white cotton sails were neatly furled under bunt, quarter, and yardarm gaskets; while her topmast, topgallant, and royal studding-sail booms swung in along her rails, gave an idea of the enormous spread of canvas held in reserve for light and moderate leading winds. . . .

"On deck everything was for use; the spare spars, scraped bright, and varnished, were neatly lashed along the waterways; the inner side of the bulwarks, the rails, and deckhouses were painted white; the hatch combings, skylights, pinrails, and companions were of Spanish mahogany; the narrow planks of her clear pine deck, with the gratings and ladders, were scrubbed and holystoned to the whiteness of cream; the brass capstan heads, bells, belaying pins, gangway stanchions, and brass work about the wheel, binnacle and skylights were of glittering brightness. Throughout she was a triumph of shipwright's and seaman's toil and skill. The ship owners of London were constrained to admit that they had seen nothing to compare with her in speed, beauty of model, rig or construction.

"It is not too much to say that the arrival of this vessel in London with her cargo of tea in this crisis of 1850, aroused as much apprehension and excitement in Great Britain as was created by the memorable Tea Party held in Boston Harbor in 1773.

"The Admiralty obtained permission to take off her lines in dry dock; the *Illustrated London News* published her portrait"—as was not unusual with great ladies— "and the *London Times* honored her arrival by a leader."

A far, far cry indeed—the China tea clipper—from those "grotesque," marginally seaworthy little vessels, such as Magellan's ninety-ton *Victoria,* in which the early navigators and their scurvy-ridden crews groped their slow, painful way to the Spice Islands!

COFFEE

The political situation which, during the 1770s, led to the rejection of tea by the American colonies gave a boost there to other nonintoxicating drinks. One of these—chocolate—was native to the Americas. The other—coffee—was, like tea, from the East, though a not so far East.

Coffea arabica is the name the tree has gone by ever since Linnaeus, the great Swedish botanist of the eighteenth century, undertook the assigning of systematic names to plant families and species. Without that name the drink prepared from the fruit of that plant had already been known to Europeans for the better part of a century, introduced there by one or another of the commercially minded seafaring nations whose survival depended on profitable trade with the East.

Coffee had, perhaps ten centuries earlier, become a habit in Moslem lands, where the preparation and drinking of coffee had assumed almost ritual proportions. Tradition suggests that the drink came first to Yemen, that southwesternmost part of Arabia that confronts Africa across a narrow strait. Yemen's port, Mocha, has given its name to an especially fine coffee. Legend further suggests that coffee was first adopted in Yemen during the later Middle Ages by Sufis— members of a mystically inclined Moslem sect who felt the drink helped them in their religious observances.

By the time, during the 1870s, when the English traveler Charles Doughty was spending years wandering from one Arab camp to another, coffee had become an inalienable part of the Arabs' social life, accepted by all as a gift of Allah. Doughty, ever curious, managed to learn something of the tree whereon coffee grows by talking with men from Galla on the far side of Abyssinia: "Galla men sold into slavery in Arabia related to me that, in their country are trunks of wild [coffee] trees 'as great as oaks'; and very likely those secular stems were living before the first drinking of kahwa in Asia, which from Mecca must soon spread (with every returning pilgrimage) to the whole Mohammedan world. In Galla land, the fallen coffee beans are gathered under the wild trees and roasted in butter; coffee is only drunk by their elders; the younger men, they said, 'would be ashamed' to use, at their years, the caudle drink"—caudle being a kind of thin gruel. Thus reminisced men kidnapped from their distant homes to be sold in the slave markets of Jidda.

By the sixteenth century the coffee habit had become fixed in the Near East. A European, writing during the following century, told that Turkish men— "Turkish" referring to anything of Near Eastern origin—were required, when marrying, to promise they would never let their wives do without coffee. Failure to keep this promise, the writer averred, was considered a legitimate ground for divorce.

By then also coffeehouses were becoming the kind of institution which, as a century later in European lands, began to cause grave concern to rulers. Not only were verses and other literary compositions declaimed there, but conversations bordering on the subversive were carried on. By late 1562 an imperial firman was pointing out to the Cadi of Jerusalem: "Whereas from olden times there was no coffee house in Jerusalem and the local inhabitants were assiduous in their divine worship and pious devotion at the five times of daily prayer, coffee-houses have now been newly established at five places. They are the meeting-place of rascals and ungodly people who day and night do not cease to act wickedly and mischievously, perniciously and refractorily, thus keeping the Muslims from pious devotion and divine worship. It is therefore necessary to remove, eradicate and extirpate the coffee-houses from these venerable places." Not so different from the century-later, short-lived interdiction of King Charles II—and apparently quite as unpopular and ineffective!

Spending time among the nomads, Doughty would come to appreciate the importance of coffee drinking in the lives of people who so generously shared with their foreign visitor the small luxuries they had, when they had any. When they had no few beans of coffee, life was bleak indeed: "The nomads' summer station at el-Eridda was now an uncheerful village . . . the sheyks had spent their slender store of coffee and 'where no coffee is, there is not merry company.' . . . Their coffee hearths now cold, every man sat drooping and dull. . . . Said Zayd, 'This was the life of the old nomads in the days before coffee.'"

Doughty, himself of limited enthusiasm for coffee, wrote of another Bedouin encampment: "When the sun is setting, the Beduins kindle their evening fire. Terky was one of those Arabs, of an infirm complexion, who are abandoned to kahwa, and think it is no day of their lives if they taste not, every third hour, the false refreshment. Had Terky been born in a land of Christians, he had sat every day drunken on his bench in the village alehouse. This Beduwy rode but light; he carried on his long-tasseled white saddle-bags no more than his coffee-roasting pan, his coffee-pot, his box of three cups, his brass pestle and mortar, and a wooden bowl for his own drinking." The three small cups—"fenjeyn" Doughty gave as the Arabic name—were to serve his drinking companions.

The ritual of coffee preparation required the roasting of green beans, then the grinding of them in a mortar. Sometimes no more than a single bean to a person could be spared. Meanwhile, a little pot of water is set over the fire and when it bubbles the Arab "casts in his fine powder . . . and withdraws the pot to simmer a moment. From a knot in his kerchief, he takes then an head of cloves, a piece of cinnamon or other spice. . . . Soon he pours out some hot drops to essay his coffee; if the taste is to his liking, making dexterously a nest of all the coffee cups in his hand, with pleasant clattering, he is ready to pour out for the company"—the order of serving having social significance. A man who received the honor of being served first may demonstrate his courtesy by offering his cup to one below him, who, equally demonstrating courtesy, rejects the honor. Coffee, however, is not publicly served to or by emirs or princes. As Doughty succinctly explained, "In Mohammedan countries, a man's secret death is often in the *fenjeyn kahwa*."

Doughty perceived still further dangers in coffee drinking, notably in the Nejd, the inner highlands of northern Arabia: "The Nejders are coffee-tipplers above all the inhabitants of the East. A coffee-server was my patient, who, in his tastings, between the cups, drank 'sixty' fenjeyns every day. . . . I bade him drink every week ten cups fewer daily and have done with the excess." Amazed and delighted at the "natural wisdom" of his Christian physician, the patient exclaimed happily, "Ye see in this an easy and perfect remedy, and it shall cost a man nothing!"

At exactly what date coffee was first planted and harvested near Mecca no one knows. Presently it was reaching the markets at Jidda, halfway up the eastern shore of the Red Sea. From Jidda cargo vessels bore it to Suez, whence it progressed by camel caravan to Alexandria as, for many centuries, had cargoes of spices. Merchants crowded in alien fonducs must have welcomed the comforting beverage before they secured enough to ship to their home ports.

Which was the first such port we cannot know but we may guess it was either Venice or Marseilles, whence the exotic habit would spread all over Europe. We do know that coffee drinking as a European custom does not seem to antedate the middle of the seventeenth century.

Nevertheless, well before then there must have been men of Near Eastern origins who brought with them their own supplies of coffee to cheer them in the benighted lands where, undoubtedly, the politics of their homelands was forcing them to dwell.

John Evelyn, famous diarist, first recorded his meeting the new drink in 1637, when, as a wide-eyed seventeen-year-old undergraduate at Oxford, he met one of those enforced exiles: "There came in my time to the college one Nathaniel Conopios, out of Greece . . . he was the first person I ever saw drink coffee which custom came not into England until thirty years after." A coffee expert suggests that Evelyn really meant "thirteen years after." Nevertheless, the custom would not be well established until thirty years had passed. Once a custom, it became almost as fixed in England as in Arabia. Life soon threatened to become one long, happy coffee break with the chatter so disturbing to established authority as to suggest to King Charles II his short-lived interdiction of coffee–tea houses in December 1675.

At the time the Greek exile was preparing his own coffee at Oxford there would have been exiles from other far lands doing the same. There may also have been English travelers who brought the habit back with them from their wanderings in Eastern lands. Some of these would have been merchants in what was then called the "Turkey trade." Of these, the ones bearing the most famous name were the Harvey brothers, who were to keep their very famous brother, the physician William Harvey, supplied with the wherewithal to prepare the drink he so enjoyed. Testifying to this is an early engraving of the Harvey home where the doctor is expectantly looking toward a strange contraption that suggests a miscegenation between an armchair and a tea wagon which is being pushed into his presence. On it are displayed a coffeepot and cups. Only a well-ingrained habit could have led to the invention and construction of such an adjunct to the serving of coffee.

Dr. Harvey drank coffee for the pleasure it gave him and, undoubtedly, for the lift it gave his spirits as he saw himself losing patient after patient to the less radical physicians who were pooh-poohing his mad idea that blood, in the animal body, instead of ebbing and flowing like the tides, actually makes full circuit, with the heart serving as pump. Not inclined to conceal knowledge—or, rather, ignorance—in a cloud of verbiage, Dr. Harvey left it to others to proclaim the "Vertue of the Coffee Drink."

Such a one was Pasqua Rosée, no physician but the man who, in 1652, opened the first coffeehouse in London. Using contemporary medical jargon, he announced, "The quality of the Drink is cold and Dry; and though it be a Dryer, yet it neither *heats,* nor *inflames* more than *hot Posset. . . .*

"It suppresseth Fumes exceedingly, and therefore good against the *Head-ach,* and will very much stop any *Defluxions of Rheums,* that distil from the *Head* upon the *Stomack,* and so prevent and help *Consumptions,* and the *Cough of the Lungs.*

"It is excellent to prevent and cure the *Dropsy, Gout,* and *Scurvy. . . .*

"It is very good to prevent *Mis-carryings in Child-bearing Women. . . .*" And so on with a long list of the marvels to be expected by the drinkers of coffee. One legitimate claim stood out among all the others—"It will prevent drowsiness."

Inevitably a battle was joined, with people taking sides for or against coffee and in neither case on perceptibly reasonable grounds. By 1674 this controversy produced a "Women's petition against Coffee, representing to public consideration the grand inconveniences accruing to their sex from the excessive use of the drying and enfeebling liquor," in which women complained that coffee made men "as unfruitful as the deserts where that unhappy berry is said to be bought." Why coffee was accused of producing impotence, whereas tea was presumed to encourage amorousness, no one can now guess. However, one might think that with pregnancy a risky annual business for many women of that age, "unfruitfulness" in men was not to be discouraged. Obviously, the women's problem was not really coffee as much as the coffeehouses where their men were spending altogether too much time.

The idea that coffee caused impotence may have arrived from the East along with the coffee. A story runs that one day the wife of an Oriental dignitary looked out of her casement to see two of her husband's servants struggling to lay a spirited stallion on the ground. When she asked what they were doing, they explained that they had instructions to geld the beast. To this the lady is said to have exclaimed that they might spare themselves the struggle and achieve the same effect by giving the stallion plenty of coffee—as evidenced by what the drinking of much coffee had done to her own husband, their master.

This same belief, entertained in Continental lands, led during the eighteenth century to Johann Sebastian Bach's mini-operetta *The Coffee Cantata*. Here one Schlendrian, a prosy, domineering old father—the very model of an eighteenth-century male chauvinist—tries in every possible way to dissuade his marriageable daughter from indulging in the dangerous coffee vice. He succeeds only temporarily by warning her that he shall arrange no marriage for her. In the end the wayward girl is planning to join her mother and grandmother in a coffee klatsch.

On the other side of the controversy may be quoted these lines:

Do but this Rare ARABIAN Cordial Use,
And thou may'st all the Doctors Slops Refuse.
Hush then, dull QUACKS, your Mountebanking cease,
Coffee's a speedier cure for each Disease.

Whatever the means of persuasion employed and undoubtedly thanks to the publicity engendered by the controversy, coffeehouses had been growing rapidly in number not only in England but in all lands on the Continent. Each coffeehouse was almost a club—St. James Coffee House, for instance, favored by Whigs; Garraways (where tea was first put on sale, too) was preferred by Tories; Button's was for literary lights like Steele, Addison, and, for a time, Alexander Pope. It was at Button's that Pope gathered the gossip that resulted in his "Rape of the Lock" wherein he devoted some lines to extol coffee:

For lo! The board with cups and spoons is crowned;
The berries crackle and the mill turns round; . . .

From silver spouts the grateful liquors glide,
While China's earth receives the smoking tide.
At once they gratify their scent and taste,
And frequent cups prolong the rich repast. . . .

Coffee (which makes the politician wise
And see through all things with his half-shut eyes)
Sent up in vapours to the baron's brain
New stratagems, the radiant lock to gain.

Through all the circumlocutions of the age—"China's earth" for porcelain cups, "smoking tide" for steaming coffee—one thing is clear: Politics and coffee were already wedded.

Wherever that early coffee may have grown and howsoever it reached ports accessible to vessels of Europe, it was becoming an increasingly popular and profitable article of trade. For the Netherlands, whose very survival depended on foreign trade, this growing demand for coffee was to be exploited to the full. Dutch merchants soon perceived that though it might be profitable to carry cargoes from Smyrna, the profits must be far greater could they escape sharing them with Oriental middlemen. Somewhere in the far-flung lands over which they, through the Dutch East India Company, held sway must be areas where coffee plantations could prosper.

By the time Captain Stavorinus was writing in the 1770s, the Dutch had added West Indian Surinam and Curaçao to their dominions. Somewhere, among all their tropical lands, coffee should be made to grow. When the captain was writing, the experiment had already proved a success: "Coffee is likewise a product yielding much profit to Java and a great advantage to the Company. The cultivation of it is performed in the same manner as in the West-India islands. . . . Java, where it is not indigenous, is indebted for this production to Mr. Zwaardekroon, who was governor-general from the year 1718 to 1725, and who procured the coffee plant from Mocha, and after paying a very high price for what was first produced . . . he continued to encourage the cultivation of it by all the means in his power. His endeavours were so well seconded by his successors, that in the year 1753, 1,200,000 pounds

were furnished from Cheribon, at the rate of 2.112
stivers per pound"—that is, about one English penny
per pound—"and full as much from Jaccatra and the
Praeger lands . . . and, in the sequel, the quantity
produced grew so large, that, in the year 1768, the
quantity of 4,465,500 pounds weight of coffee was
delivered to the Company."

If Europe had not already reached the point of
demanding such huge quantities of coffee, the canny
Dutch were likely to do everything possible to encourage coffee drinking in neighboring lands. Nevertheless,
they failed to have included much coffee in the cargoes
they were delivering to New Amsterdam during the
years—1626 to 1664—they held sway there. Nor did
they do better by coffee raising during their far briefer
domination of Pernambuco, Brazil, at about the same
time.

Without a doubt, the first coffee drinker to set foot
on the North American continent was Captain John
Smith (1580–1631), who, in the year 1607, arrived here
as a founder of the Virginia colony. John Smith was a
soldier of fortune, offering his services here and there
as might be needed. While fighting the Turks in the
army of the Holy Roman Emperor, Smith was taken
prisoner—which meant that if no one offered to ransom
him for a considerable sum, he must become a slave of
some Turk. Thus Smith became a household slave
whose duties, in that place and time, certainly included the preparing and serving of coffee with an
occasional coffee tipple allowed for services well performed. Eventually the young English captain made his
escape after killing the master who was brutally mistreat-
ing him. Clearly he could have carried with him on that
hazardous journey of escape no coffee beans, yet he

would not have left behind the acquired taste for coffee.

Another heroic mercenary under another Holy Roman Emperor—the Polish-born Franz Georg Kolschitzky—was, after his military service during the siege of Vienna in 1683, to become actively involved in the future of coffee in his adopted land. Having previously resided for years among the Turks and there having learned their language and habits, he was the only one in the Emperor's finally victorious army to see value in the sacks full of little green beans left behind by fleeing Turks. He received them gladly as part of his booty of war and took them with him to Vienna, where soon he was peddling cups of coffee to the Viennese. Presently he was opening the first coffeehouse there, in which were served cups of coffee and *Kipfel,* those delicious little rolls first shaped in crescent form in 1683 as a sort of defiance to the besieging enemies on whose banners were flaunted the star and crescent.

Germany had long known about coffee through the publication of that famous botanical traveler, by name Leonhard Rauwolf, who visited the Near East in 1573 and described coffee in a book published nine years later, "a very good drink, by them called hot, that is almost black as ink and very good in illness, chiefly those of the stomach." The French were learning about coffee in 1669 through the fascinatingly exotic Soliman Aga, Turkish ambassador to the court of Louis XIV. Of course that would make coffee the rage of Parisian socialites. However, it was to take Louis XIV's successor, Louis XV, to give financial support to the vogue by spending large sums to purchase coffee for his mistress, Madame DuBarry, and incidentally for his daughters. Meanwhile, the coffee vogue had grown among the Parisian public through the agency of a servant of

Soliman Aga who peddled cups of coffee in Parisian streets. In 1672 the first Parisian coffeehouse was established, this soon to be followed by others of varying degrees of elegance, all sharing the common potential of becoming meeting places for the radicals and subversives whose ideas were to bear fruit there a century later.

Though the Turkish ambassador had undoubtedly been responsible for the great and immediate coffee vogue in France, the Dutch influence had also been great, if entirely indirect. When, in May 1692, the English and Dutch fleets were finally joining forces to defeat the French, they were not only to break the extravagant French monarch financially but to seize from him the mastery of the seas. Louis XIV had to find some way of recouping his finances, and since most possible resources had already been exploited, his advisers suggested there might be wealth to be extracted from that new popular drink, coffee.

The means of exploitation was to be the common one of granting a monopoly for a price, farming it out to a private individual who would undertake to handle all of the thus farmed commodity that should come into France. He was to set and collect taxes as he might see fit in order to cover the immediate costs and to repay the initial investment, which, of course, was already comfortably in the king's hands. In return, the king gave his support by way of edict "on the sale and distribution of coffee . . . to derive certain help for carrying on the present war."

The edict runs thus: "His Majesty, after listening to the advice of the Council of State, has granted to Maître François Damame the exclusive privilege, for three years from January 1, 1692, of selling coffee, tea, chocolate and the materials out of which they are made; likewise cocoa and vanilla, in all the provinces, towns and domains of the realm of France.

"His Most Christian Majesty consequently forbids every one to participate in the provision or in the sale by wholesale or retail of the aforesaid commodities without a special permit from Farmer General Damame.

"His Most Christian Majesty ordains that all merchants and shopkeepers who have coffee whether in beans or powdered, or tea or chocolate, in store shall immediately report the amount of the same. In Monsieur's offices, the aforesaid wares will be weighed, investigated, marked, labelled, and sealed. Then the aforesaid wares shall be stored in safe warehouses. Anyone who evades this edict for the reporting of coffee, tea, etc., whether it be the owner or his assistants, will be liable to a fine of 1500 livres [possibly $300]. The unreported stores and the fines will accrue to Farmer General Damame; with the exception that the informer shall receive a third."

M. Damame was to appoint his own staff, which would oversee "the sale and provision of the aforesaid beverages." The edict goes on to limit the permitted ports of entry for the wares, obviously to make the control of smuggling easier. Smugglers and other persons who might presume to carry interdicted shipments in unlicensed boats or wagons were to be fined or punished yet more severely.

The edict ends: "The coffee that is sold may not be mixed with oats, peas or beans, or any other adulterant. The same applies to tea, cocoa, and chocolate, which must be sold pure. Any one who adulterates them becomes liable to flogging and also to a fine of 1500 livres.

"His Most Christian Majesty issues strict instructions to the Councillor General . . . to see to it that this edict shall everywhere be read aloud, published, and posted, and that the action be taken accordingly."

Everything looked rosy for the Farmer General of coffee and of similar drinks. What the edict did not provide for was a way to force a people to continue a recently acquired habit that was suddenly growing costly. By the middle of the same year, Damame was wringing his hands over his mounting losses. Still a year later, the Sun King was following the example of his English cousin nearly a quarter century earlier with the issuance of another edict, graciously stating: "We have recognized that the heavy expenses which Monsieur Damame has incurred in order to make use of his privilege have deprived him of the advantages which might otherwise have accrued to him." So the Farmer General was relieved of his costly privilege and an import duty that should accrue to the Crown imposed. The monopoly was at an end and for the time being coffee consumption again soared.

Royal income, however, did not soar to keep pace with royal expenditures. A quarter century later, when Louis XIV's great-grandson, Louis XV, was on the throne, royal advisers again zeroed in on monopolies. This time the recipient of the coffee monopoly was to be the French Company of the Indies. To avoid the kind of coffee boycott that defeated Louis XIV's hopes for increased income, there was a top limit set on coffee prices.

Punishment for smuggling was to be flogging, branding, banishment. Worst of all, for the rulers who imposed the monopoly as it eventually turned out, was the kind of espionage system that monopoly encouraged: "The agents and inspectors of the West India Company will henceforward be allowed to search all stores, shops, villas, houses and even the residences and palaces of the king, as well as the domiciles of the nobles, monasteries, guild buildings, in a word every place which has hitherto been regarded as privileged. ... We therefore command the administrators of the aforesaid domiciles, including those of the royal palaces, the venerable priors of the monasteries, and the masters of all guild buildings, whatsoever, to open their doors to the aforesaid inspectors whenever these may demand entry. ... In case of resistance, the inspectors are hereby allowed to open the doors with the aid of a locksmith they may bring with them." What better way, one wonders, could have been found to stimulate subversion?

Of course, the edict made no provision for paying salaries of inspectors and wages of locksmiths, let alone defraying the multitude of costs the maintenance of such a system must demand. The monopoly proved to be so costly to the monopolistic Company of the Indies that it was soon abandoned. French coffeehouses, which Louis XIV had tried to turn to profit by a variety of devices, including a licensing fee, were again offering their wares to increasingly articulate philosophers, writers, composers, and, of course, subversives.

One difference there was: Much of the coffee served in Paris was now coming from French West Indian plantations. The king's own drink may have been prepared from berries growing on a plant presented in 1714 by the Burgomaster of Amsterdam. It was undoubtedly the same tree which thrived in the glass house of the Jardin des Plantes, whose offspring started many of the coffee plantations on the far side of the

Atlantic. Its seeds or shoots had to get there first, an undertaking which was to demand imagination, patriotism, and perseverance.

Perfectly equipped for the undertaking was the young captain of infantry, Mathieu Gabriel de Clieu. Stationed in Martinique, he had plenty of spare time to wander over the island in search of possibly profitable crop plants. Having learned that the Dutch had managed to start coffee plantations in Java from seed secured in Mocha and being convinced that what the Dutch could do the French should be able to do better, he had been hoping to start a plantation with coffee plants native to Martinique. His painstaking search revealed no such plants. He must then do it the Dutch way, import seeds or seedlings, since he was absolutely certain Martinique should offer ideal conditions for the growth of coffee trees.

During the early 1720s De Clieu was making a return visit to his native land and, while there, saw among the collections at the Jardin des Plantes the young coffee tree, then well over five feet high, which had come as a gift from the Burgomaster of Amsterdam. Shoots or seeds from this could make his dream a reality, if somehow he could manage to secure some. He contacted and persuaded people of influence in high circles and with their help was able to embark in 1723, carrying with him one precious little seedling, guarded in a box of his contriving and protected from the winds and sea spray by glass covers.

Throughout the voyage, De Clieu watched the plant as he might over a very young and helpless infant, taking it into the sun for daily airings, watering it regularly with fresh water, eying with suspicion everyone who might show too great an interest in it. Years later he was to recount the vicissitudes of that voyage in a communication to *Année Littéraire*: "It is useless to recount in detail the infinite care I was obliged to bestow on this delicate plant during a long voyage and the difficulties I had in saving it from the hands of a man, who, basely jealous of the joy I was about to taste through being of service to my country, and being unable to get this coffee plant away from me, tore off a branch." He was convinced this man must be an enemy Dutchman.

Not only was there this cloak-and-dagger episode, but there were a near encounter with a Tunisian corsair, violent tempests and then the equally to be dreaded calms of the doldrums when water had to be strictly rationed to crew and passengers with nothing set aside for a mere plant.

The young man wrote: "Water was lacking to such an extent, that for more than a month, I was obliged to share the scanty ration of it assigned to me with this my coffee plant upon which my happiest hopes were founded and which was the source of my delight. It needed such succor the more in that it was extremely backward."

Nevertheless, this all but negligible bit of plant life managed to survive, first to be planted in De Clieu's garden in Martinique, presently to become the progenitor of endless rows of coffee trees in plantations all over the tropics of the New World. As its planter told: "Arriving at home my first care was to set out my plant with great attention in the part of my garden most favorable to its growth. Although keeping it in view, I feared many times that it would be taken from me: and I was at last obliged to surround it with three bushes and had to establish a guard about it until it arrived at maturity. . . . This precious plant which had become still more dear to me for the dangers it had run and the cares it had cost me."

De Clieu further recorded the growth of his coffee and the effect on its spread by the disaster of 1727: "Success exceeded my hopes. I gathered about two pounds of seed which I distributed among all those whom I thought most capable of giving the plants the care necessary to their prosperity.

"The first harvest was very abundant; with the second it was possible to extend the cultivation prodigiously, but what favored multiplication most singularly was the fact that two years afterward all the cocoa trees of the country, which were the resource and occupation of the people, were uprooted and totally destroyed by horrible tempests accompanied by an inundation which submerged all the land where those trees were planted, land which was at once made into coffee plantations by the natives. These did marvelously and enabled us to send plants to Santo Domingo, Guadeloupe and other adjacent islands where since that time they have been cultivated with the greatest success."

In 1777, three years after De Clieu's account was published, there were growing on Martinique alone nearly 19 million coffee trees. At the time he brought that carefully guarded seedling from France, De Clieu could not have known that coffee had already been planted on Haiti eight years earlier, actually the same year that coffee cultivation was introduced on Île Bourbon (Réunion) of the Mascarenes. The Dutch were soon raising coffee in Surinam, as Captain Stavorinus had suggested. Jamaican coffee plantations were started by the British a few years later. Everywhere coffee was by way of becoming a highly profitable crop. Yet it did not prove profitable to the man who had so proudly borne the first coffee tree to Martinique. De Clieu, having received no monetary reward and little honor from his king or country, died in conditions of extreme poverty at an advanced age. Even so, he could consider himself more fortunate than the French king, who, by the time of De Clieu's death, had fallen victim to the Revolution which the monopolies sponsored by his forebears had helped to fuel.

Once coffee was thriving in Caribbean lands, it would be largely coffee brought from thence that supplied most of the needs of Colonial America, needs which soared once tea was boycotted. Staunch supporters of the Revolution and the coffee trade were the Browns of Providence, Rhode Island. The Nicholas Brown Company, which included five Brown brothers, was actively engaged in trade with the West Indian Islands, whichever European power claimed sovereignty over the island where desirable cargoes were to be loaded. In 1772 the Browns, although still regarded as British citizens, saw no cogent reason for not trading with the French island of Hispaniola, even though France and England were presumably at war. It took, however, a bit of scheming.

The Browns engaged a man of French birth, Stephen Gregory by name (actually it should have been written Grégoire). He was to resume his original name, claim French citizenship, and acquire temporary ownership of the brig *George*, owned by the Browns, "for the purpose of qualifying you to make said Brig a French Bottom or otherwise get a permit to Trade in said Island." Of course all agreed the ownership was to end with the voyage. In any case, the ruse worked, and in

December 1772 the *George* returned to Providence with a cargo of molasses plus 3,155 pounds of coffee. Equally adroit in outwitting the British customs officials who would be demanding payment of import duty on their coffee, the Browns had it deposited in the custom house at Newport for exportation. It was reloaded on the next vessel out, but it got no farther than a rendezvous with a fleet of smugglers. Whatever this may suggest as to the habits of the Brown brothers, it demonstrates that coffee was already much in demand in the soon to be independent colonies.

Though credit for planting the first coffee trees in the American tropics must be divided between the Dutch and the French, it was certainly the English adventurer Captain John Smith (1580–1631) who was the first coffee drinker to establish himself in North America. Whether he was far too busy getting the Virginia colony started, or possibly because Pocahontas was a distraction, Captain Smith did nothing to stimulate coffee drinking here. With the Dutch having done little to promote coffee in New Amsterdam, it would be the British, who acquired New Amsterdam in 1674 and renamed it New York, who there established the habit of drinking both tea and coffee, the former to go into eclipse by their own acts a century later. By 1683 William Penn, settling in his family's Pennsylvania colony, was sending to New York for a supply of coffee. Soon New York coffeehouses were advertising their wares and, though less influential institutions than their British counterparts, were to become an important part of the American social and political scene.

By 1727 coffee trees from Cayenne were beginning to send their progeny south. Captain-Lieutenant Francisco de Mello Palheta carried coffee seeds from Cayenne to Pará on the Amazon. Soon coffee trees were spreading along the Brazilian bulge, Maranhão, Ceará, and on south until by 1770 coffee was being cultivated in the convent gardens of Rio de Janeiro. Probably the monks, having acquired the coffee habit in Europe, were tending the trees partly to supply their stomachs with the drink, partly to supply their pockets with income.

When coffee began to put down roots in São Paulo, which today is one of the great coffee-growing areas of the world, is not known exactly. However, it must have been about 1790, for in 1797 Captain-General de Lorena, Governor of São Paulo, was writing to his successor: "Much coffee is grown in the village of Santos, and of the best quality." Santos is the port of the state of São Paulo and a very busy shipping center. In 1798, 260 arrobas (about 6,500 pounds) of coffee were being harvested along the coast near Santos. For coffee trees to be bearing by that date there, they must have been planted at least six years earlier, more likely eight. Within a decade or so, small coffee plantations were flourishing near the site of the present city of São Paulo, some miles back from the coast and at a cooler elevation of about 1,000 meters (3,050 feet), which is more favorable to the growth of fine coffee.

Today may be seen the great plantations of that area, miles upon miles of carefully reared and tended trees, guarded insofar as may be possible against natural disasters from fungus or insect pests. Unfortunately there seems to be no guarding against the rare frosts which once every few years can ruin a whole year's crop.

No one who has ever visited a coffee-growing area can forget the breathtaking loveliness of a coffee plantation. The dark-green foliage of the trees is interspersed all along the branches with clusters of white flowers of an unforgettable fragrance. When these disappear, they are succeeded by bunches of shining green berries which finally mature to a lovely red. Then come the pickers, hand or machine, depending on the size of the plantation, the wealth of the owner and his sentiments concerning the desirability of each kind of picking. Hand-picking can add to the picturesqueness, especially in Guatemala, where Indian women in their handwoven village costumes add a colorful touch to the scene.

The coffee berries thus picked have to be relieved of four layers of wrappings before the beans (seeds) are ready to ship. Inside the red skin is a gummy layer sweetish to the taste. Each of the two beans has its own outer two layers, the outer a tough parchment, the inner a delicate silver skin. The removal of these four layers takes place in several steps, some quite time-consuming, all requiring skill. Finally the beans are ready for the cleaning, blending, and roasting that prepares them for the market.

Anyone who has lived in quiet coffee-growing areas of Central America cannot forget the smells and sounds of the daily coffee ritual, the aroma of roasting beans in a home oven, the sound of the coffee mill, and the further aroma as the drink is prepared for the breakfast in which it plays a starring and sometimes an all but solitary role, though a tortilla or two may be washed down with the drink. Anyone who has lived for a while in Brazil will have learned to accept the almost hourly "cafezinha," a demitasse half filled with granulated sugar before very black coffee is poured in. This offering of friendship is not to be rejected without the risk of giving mortal offense, no matter how the visitor may feel about the oversweetened coffee.

CHOCOLATE

Completely unheard of in the Old World until Spanish conquistadors encountered it in the New, cocoa—or, rather, *cacao,* as the plant is referred to—could not spark the kind of internecine struggles for control of a new product that had so long been carried on for cargoes of tea and coffee. Cacao came as a bonus with the newly conquered New World. At first it was not appreciated by stay-at-homes, and its source was soon guarded as a Spanish secret. The drink, chocolate, and the conquistadors had met under highly dramatic circumstances that were to prove good public relations for cacao though tragically otherwise for the Mexican emperor Montezuma, who had his strange banquet guests served chocolate in greed-stimulating golden goblets.

Bernal Diaz del Castillo, conquistador and historian of the conquest, recalled that banquet in every detail many years later when he was an old man living in retirement in Guatemala: "They brought him fruit of every kind there was in the land," he wrote of their host, Montezuma, "of which he ate but little now and then. They brought him in something like goblets of fine gold a certain drink made of cacao. They said it was in order to have success with women and therefore we did not hesitate to partake. Furthermore, I saw them bring in over fifty large pitchers full of froth made from fine cacao and he drank of it, the women serving him with great reverence. And sometimes there were ugly hunch-backed Indians . . . who were clowns . . . and others who sang and danced, because Montezuma was fond of diversions and songs, and to those [who performed] he ordered given the leftovers and pitchers of cacao." The opulent grandeur of the emperor's table did not make the writer forget the reputed cannibalism of the Mexicans. He confessed, however, that he found it impossible to identify, among the so many meat dishes served, any that he thought indubitably of human flesh.

Fifty years later the same suspicions were in the mind of the English traveler John Chilton, who, after living seven years in Spain, was permitted in 1668 to take ship for Spain's New World possessions wherein, for nearly eighteen years, he was to travel extensively as a merchant of indigo and other local products. Of these travels he recorded: 'In all these places, the Indians for the most part goe naked and are wild people. Their common armour is bowes and arrowes, they use to eat up such Christians as they come by. At my return to Mexico, I came along the coast of the South sea . . . into the province of Coloa, where I imploied the silver I had, in a certaine graine, growing like an Almonde, called amongst the Indians Cacao, which in Nova Hispania is currant for money, to buy things of small value, as fruits, etc, for they have no small money there, and in which they also pay the King his tribute. They grinde this graine to a powder, and mingle it with water and so is made both bread and drinke unto them, which is a provision of great profite and good strength."

This drink, according to another chronicler, Oviedo y Valdés, was so valuable that in Nicaragua "none but the rich and noble could afford to drink it, since it was literally drinking money. . . . Cocoa passed current as money among all [Indian] nations; thus a rabbit in Nicaragua sold for ten Cocoa nibs, and one hundred of those seeds would buy a tolerably good slave."

Though Chilton's botany was questionable—no fruit growing less "like an almond" than cacao—he was in general an extraordinarily accurate observer of the lands through which he passed, as anyone who has followed his routes in our day could testify. Of a trip south into the jungle wilderness below the Pacific-facing slopes of Guatemala's mountains, where cacao still grows wild, he wrote: "Leaving Tecoantepec, I went still along by the South sea, about 150 leagues in the desolate province of Soconusco, in which province there groweth Cacao, which the Christians carry from thence into Nova Hispania, for that it will not growe in any colde Countrey. The Indians of this Countrey, paye the King their tribute in Cacao, giving him 400 Cargas, and every Carga is 24,000 Almondes, which Carga is worth in Mexico thirty pieces of rials of plate." Here, "Mexico" refers to the city itself, the capital of New Spain. It is interesting that a tribute of cacao was then as acceptable to the tax collectors of the Spanish king as such had been to those of Montezuma. With a *real* worth perhaps ten cents, this particular tribute must have been of a value of about $1,200—a not inconsiderable amount, especially in view of the high mark-up of the product when sold in Europe.

Covetousness of the new drink can hardly be blamed for the highly questionable treatment received by Montezuma and his family from the Spanish he had so hospitably entertained. Being generally sons of impoverished Spanish nobles, the conquistadors had left their native lands with the purpose of seizing new dominions for their own king and new souls for their Church. That they should line their own pockets on the way, if possible, was accepted usage of the day. For them at first there was no possible compensation to be wrung from the dark little seeds, from which Montezuma's drink was prepared, and had they been offered any, they would have scornfully rejected them as English freebooters were presently to do with the scornful exclamation "Sheep-shit!"

In time the Spanish conquistadors would be conquered by the new, nourishing, delicious drink. Chocolate soon became an obsession of all classes and even made its way into the cloisters, where, though it was already acquiring the usual reputation of being a temptation of the devil and an inflamer of passions, the padres were finding it all but irresistible. In remote, lonely *conventos* scattered in tiny Indian settlements among the mountains and valleys of Mexico and Guatemala, these padres uncomplainingly endured many hardships as they sought to save the Indians' souls by converting those heathen to their own faith. Mastering the strange, guttural Indian tongues was only one of the hardships. Clad in coarse, heavy habits, sometimes barefoot, often shod only in open sandals, they trod the hot, dusty trails from village to village. Water was often hard to find. The sun's rays beat upon them cruelly. Many times they had to rest themselves on burning sands, in the doubtful shade of a bullthorn acacia or spiny cactus. The one special compensation the unkind and alien land might grant them would be a calabash full of delicious, sustaining chocolate at the journey's end.

Cacao brought ever present problems to all *conventos*. A Dominican padre who kept careful record of life in the *conventos* of Guatemala and Chiapas, now part of southern Mexico, mentions cacao again and again. He tells how his order received from their bishop orders to sell all its farmlands so that the padres should no longer be faced with the worldly distractions farming involved. Soon, however, the padres had to repossess the lands, which they then planted with sugar cane and cacao—clearly with an eye to future foaming cups of cocoa.

In another one of those still imposing though earthquake-ruined *conventos* of Antigua Guatemala there was a crypt where dignitaries of the order were laid to final rest. To the novices, this crypt seemed a quiet, safely remote place where they might indulge themselves in frequent, if sinful, cups of chocolate. While thus happily feasting by candlelight, they were confronted by a ghost in the form of their master of novices raising specter-like from behind a tomb. Needless to say, the youths scattered in guilty terror. The chronicler does not claim that they were permanently cured of the sinful habit.

Of all accounts of cacao and chocolate, in and out of *conventos,* the most fascinating are those of the English friar Thomas Gage—Jesuit turned Dominican and later, on his return to England, to embrace the church of that land. Obviously not an overascetic man, Gage enjoyed his chocolate with gusto and enjoyed quite as much the gossip that came to his ears over *jícaras* (little cup-shaped gourds) full of chocolate. His account *New Survey of the West Indies* was published in England in 1648. From it we learn a great deal about the drink that came to fascinate him and, of course, about some of the drinkers.

"The name," Gage explained, "is compounded from *atte,* as some say, or as others, *atle,* which in the Mexican language signifieth 'water,' and from the sound which the water (wherein is put the Chocolate) makes, as *choco, choco, choco,* when it is stirred in a cup by an instrument called a 'molinet' or 'molinillo,' until it bubble and rise unto a froath." Whether Friar Gage's derivation is correct or not, certainly he knew whereof he wrote when he described the early reactions of other nations toward the strange beans: "Our English and Hollanders make little use of it when they take a prize at sea, not knowing the secret virtue and quality of it for the good of the stomack, of whom I have heard the Spaniards say that when we"—the English, that is—"have taken a good prize, a ship laden with Cocoa, in anger and wrath we have hurled overboard this good commodity, not regarding the worth of it."

"Like its name," Gage wrote, "so the confection or drink is composed of various ingredients, according to the different temperaments of those who use it. But the chief ingredient, without which it could not be made, is cacao, which is a kind of bean or rather a large rounded almond which grows on a tree, called cacao, enclosed in a shell which at times containes up to thirty or forty of these beans . . . it contains a kind of butter with which I have seen natives rub their faces to make the skin more smooth."

Unlike the fruit of most trees, the large coconut-size cacao pods do not develop on the ends of small branches but directly on the main trunk. "The tree which bears the fruit," Gage noted, "is so delicate and the region where it grows so warm that, to protect it from the sun, they plant other trees which they call mother-cacao, and when these have grown sufficiently to shade cacao trees, they plant the cacaotales [cacao plantations]. Its fruit does not grow bare but covered with a sheath, and each bean has another coat, white and full of water, which covers it. This the women suck with much delight since it refreshes as it dissolves in the mouth."

The Spanish were to encounter such cacao plantations from southern Mexico to northern Peru, the varieties varying in appearance and excellence as the pod color varied from yellow through red to a brownish purple. Viewed from within, such a plantation is a delight to the eye, as one visitor described it: "the vista is like a miniature forest hung with thousands of golden lamps—anything more lovely cannot be imagined. . . . The many walks were wide and clean, and so effectually roofed in by the broad tops of the cacao-madre that one might almost imagine oneself within the spacious aisles of some grand natural temple." The "clean" walks—that is, the absence of a heavy leaf carpet—is characteristic of tropical forests where insects quickly devour most fallen leaves. The fifty- or sixty-foot-tall cacao-madre trees are *Erythrina* species, in general, which further add to the beauty of plantations after they drop their leaves in March and burst into bloom with gorgeous clusters of bright crimson flowers.

Friar Gage and his fellow padres were not instantaneously won to chocolate drinking. When they first arrived at Veracruz to set foot in the New World, they were served in the *convento* there a drink they found "unpalatable." Soon they were appreciating the new beverage, and by the time he was recording his adventures Friar Gage was a total convert to chocolate. He had noted the multitudinous ways in which native populations might prepare it. First, of course, came the cacao beans, then: "As for the other ingredients of chocolate, there are great differences in composition. Some add black pepper . . . but generally instead of pepper they add the native peppers they call *chiles* which burn the mouth. . . .

"Also added to chocolate may be white sugar, cinnamon, cloves, anise, almonds, hazelnuts . . . citrus

juice, achiote. . . . Furthermore the amounts of such
ingredients fit the variety of temperaments of the users.
Antonio Colmenera" (a physician of those days) "usually
prescribes to each hundred beans, two chiles, a handful
of anise and . . . with two rope flowers or vanilla, unless
it is desired to replace the vanilla with six roses of
Alexandria, powdered, and adding to all this two
drachmas" (about a quarter ounce) "of cinnamon, a
dozen almonds, a half pound of white sugar, and
enough achiote to give color. This writer is not in favor
of mixing cloves, musk or perfumes, things much used
in the Indies.

"Some add corn . . . but only because of stinginess
or greed, for it increases the quantity and doubles the
profit. . . . Cinnamon is the best of all ingredients and
no one omits it. . . .

"Commonly all the mentioned ingredients are used,
but in greater or lesser quantity . . . which results in a
chocolate that may be adapted to any stomach, when
used in moderation.

"Before grinding, all the ingredients, with the excep-
tion of the achiote, are well dried over the fire so that
they may more easily be reduced to powder, but stirring
constantly so as not to burn or toast them too much; for
when they are dried too much, they become bitter and
lose their strength. . . .

"It's best to crush all ingredients separately, then
place them in a container where the cacao already is,
mix well with a spoon, transferring the paste to a
mortar, under which are a few embers to keep the stone
just warm, but no more, for too hot a fire consumes the
fatty part. . . .

"When all is well ground and mixed, which one
recognizes by the thickness of the mass, a part of the

paste, which is almost liquid, is taken up with a spoon to make little cakes or else it is thrown into some little boxes for hardening as it cools.

"To give it the form of bricks, a spoonful is put on a sheet of paper. The Indians use a palm leaf and put it in the shade to harden because the heat of the sun melts the chocolate. When it is all dry, the little brick separates easily from the palm leaf. . . .

"Ways of taking chocolate vary: because some, as in Mexico, take it hot with corn meal (atole), dissolving a pastille in boiling water and beating it in the cup in which it is served, with a molinillo, and when the cup is filled with foam, filling the cup with hot atole, then sipping it; others dissolve the chocolate in cold water, beating it with a molinillo, removing the foam which they put in a cup, heating the remainder with sugar and when it is quite hot, add it to the foam which they removed, and take it thus.

"But the most common way is to heat the water well, fill a jicara or cup half full, dissolve in it one or two cakes of chocolate until the liquid thickens, when it is well beaten with a molinillo until covered with foam, fill the container with hot water, add the needed sugar and dunk some sweet cakes or marzipan in the chocolate."

Similarly elaborate recipes for the preparation of chocolate were soon current in Spain and England, though how long they persisted is hard to say. In any case, the many and elaborate ways of preparing the drink and the large number of ingredients which might or might not be added show that chocolate as a drink was of very old, much valued status long before the Spaniards set foot in lands where cacao grew native. If these were not enough proof, there is the fact that cacao, which grew wild, though scattered in the jungles, had been cultivated in plantations which Cortés and Bernal Diaz del Castillo told of encountering in southern Mexico, Guatemala, and Honduras. Had the native appetite for chocolate not already outrun that to be easily gathered from trees scattered, like all jungle growth, among many other species, it is hardly to be thought that they would have undertaken the setting out of cacao trees in plantations.

The yield of such plantations, exacted as tribute by Montezuma's tax collectors, was what supplied his tables with the numberless cups of chocolate described by the chronicler. In a very short time the tribute was transferred to the Spanish monarch as the conquistadors learned to value the drink which, in contrast to tea and coffee, supplied nourishment as well as refreshment.

In Mexico City, even the padres were swiftly acquiring the habit of eating frequent and heavy meals washed down by chocolate. Gage wrote of his sojourn there: "We found that two or three hours after a good meal of three or four dishes of mutton, veal, beef, kid, turkeys or other fowles, our stomackes would be ready to faint, and so wee were fain to support them with a cup of Chocolatte, &c., which was allowed in great abundance." Friar Gage, one would imagine, would soon be rivaling the legendary Friar Tuck in size. Nevertheless, he managed to travel widely at a time when traveling meant either going afoot or riding astride a beast of burden, neither being exercises for the obese.

Of the multitude of possible ways he had listed for preparing the drink, Friar Gage found cinnamon the "best of all ingredients," in addition, of course, to the basic cacao. Cinnamon still rates high with many people. And, despite the friar's scornful rejection of maize, there is still to be had, in parts of Costa Rica, a most pleasant drink called "pinolillo," which is compounded of chocolate, a bit of sugar, and maize that has been toasted and ground.

As for the drink's effect on the passions, the imputation seems to be no better founded on medical fact than that made against tea. Nevertheless, Gage's account of his stay in a *convento* of Chiapas, in southern Mexico, reveals that chocolate could become an inflamer of passionate discords.

Described by Gage, Chiapas is "the most remarkable place in a way . . . here are also two cloisters of nuns which are talked of far and near, not for their religious practices, but for their skill in making drinkes which are used in those parts, the one called Chocolatte, another Atolle. Chocolatte is also made up in boxes and sent not only to Mexico, but much of it is yearly transported into Spain. . . .

"The gentlemen of Chiapa are a by-word all about that country, of great birth, pharisticke pride, joyned with simplicity, ignorance, and penury. One hundred fighting soldiers would easily lay low these Chiapa Dons, and gain the whole city, which lyeth so open to the fields that the mules and asses come in to graze. . . . The women of that city, it seems, pretend much weakness and squeamishness of stomack, which they say is so great, that they are not able to continue in church while the mass is briefly hurried over, much lesse while a solemn, high mass is sung and a sermon preached, unless they drink a cup of hot Chocolatte, and eat a bit of sweetmeats to strengthen their stomackes. For this purpose it was much used by them to make their maids bring them to church, in the middle of mass or sermon, a cup of Chocolatte, which could not be done to all without a great confusion and interrupting both masse and sermon. The Bishop, perceiving this abuse, and having given faire warning for the omitting of it, but all without amendment, thought fit to fix in writing on the church doors an excommunication against all such as should presume at the time of service to eate or drinke within the church.

"This excommunication was taken by all, but especially by the gentlewomen, much to heart, who protested, if they might not eate or drinke in church, they could not continue in it to hear what otherwise they were bound unto. . . . But none of these reasons would move the Bishop. . . . The women seeing him so hard to be entreated, began to slight him with scornefull and reproachfull words; others sleighted his excommunication, drinking in iniquity in the church, as the fish doth water, which caused one day such an uproar in the Cathedrall that many swords were drawne against the Priests, who attempted to take away from the maids the cups of Chocolatte which they brought unto their mistresses, who, at last seeing that neither faire nor foule means would prevail with the Bishop, resolved to forsake the Cathedrall; and so from that time most of the city betooke themselves to the Cloister Churches, where by the nuns and Fryers they were not troubled.

"The Bishop fell dangerously sick. . . . Physicians were sent for far and neare, who all with a joynt opinion agreed that the Bishop was poisoned.

"A gentlewoman, with whom I was well acquainted, was commonly censured to have prescribed such a cup of Chocolatte to be ministered by the Page, which poisoned him who so rigorously had forbidden Chocolatte to be drunk in Church. Myself heard this gentlewoman say that the women had no reason to grieve for him, and that she judged, he being such an enemy to Chocolatte in the Church, that which he had drunk in his house had not agreed with his body. And it became afterwards a Proverbe in that country, 'Beware the Chocolatte of Chiapa!' "

Even the easygoing, life-loving friar was shocked, the more so when he began to receive advances from the lady thus suspected and realized the possible price of rejecting them. She had, as he wrote, "often used to send me boxes of Chocolatte, which I willingly received of her, judging it to be a kind of gratuity for the paines I took in teaching her son Latin; until one day she sent mee a faire plaintin, wrapped up in a handkerchief buried in sweet jasmines and roses; and looking further upon it, I found worked up on it with a knife the fashion of a heart with two blind Cupid's arrows sticking in it, discovering unto my heart the thoughts of the poisoner that sent it. I thought it a good warning to be wary of receiving such presents or chocolatte, from such hands, and returned unto her again her plaintin with this short rhyme cut out with a knife upon the skinne, *'Fruta tan fria, amor no cria.'* as much as to say 'Fruit so cold, takes no hold.'

"I remembered the Bishop's Chocolatte and so was wary, and staid not long in that poisoning and wicked city, which truly deserves no better relation than what I have given of the simple Dons and chocolate-confectioning Dorenas."

In the *convento* of his order in Antigua Guatemala, Friar Gage might have found refuge from the dangers of Chiapas but correspondingly sterner rules of conduct for the inmates. One rule of conduct he would have found even less acceptable than most of the other padres: No one under sixty years of age was to be permitted to drink chocolate. The chronicler who reported this interdiction did not explain the reasons—whether the older ones were supposed to need the nourishment chocolate might supply, while their age should put them beyond the dangers that accompany inflamed passions, or whether their years of devoted service had earned for them this particular indulgence. Of course, as the writer admitted, the interdiction only made the younger ones crave the drink the more. It is hard to imagine Friar Gage remaining in that *convento* any longer than he had to.

How much influence the recipes that friar offered may have had on the European public in general we cannot know for certain, though the printed accounts dated within two decades after Gage's book was available suggest that many were tried. Chocolate, by those accounts, was being prepared, both in Spain and in England, with much the same number and variety of strange ingredients as the chocolate of the Indies. The usual strange medical verbiage prevails. For "cold constitutions" are recommended several spices, whereas "in hot consumptive tempers" almonds, pistachios, and such may be added. Finally, rhubarb stalk is recommended for "green young ladies."

Chocolate was at the beginning added to the items available in coffeehouses, as witness the 1657 announcement in the London *Public Adviser:* "In Bishopsgate Street, in Queen's Mead Alley, at a Frenchman's House, is an excellent West India drink called Chocolate to be sold, where you may have it ready at any time and also unmade at reasonable rates." "Reasonable rates," by modern reckoning, would mean about five dollars a pound.

Eventually chocolate was to graduate from coffeehouses and acquire houses of its own, though it was not thereby to be excluded from coffeehouses. Of it D'Israeli wrote that, after receiving it from the Indies, the Spanish, "liking its nourishment, improved it into a richer compound with sugar, vanilla and other aromatics. We had Chocolate Houses in London long after coffee-houses; they seemed to associate something more elegant and refined in the new term when the other became common." D'Israeli, apparently, had not heard of the many and weird additives in vogue in the Indies.

To patronize a chocolate house then was to suggest aristocratic leanings and a more fashionable taste than attained by frequenters of mere coffeehouses. During the reigns of Queen Anne and George I, while chocolate was "so highly esteemed by courtiers, by lords and ladies, and fine gentlemen in the polite world, learned physicians extolled its medicinal virtues"—all that was needed to demonstrate that chocolate had made it on the social scene. To further demonstrate its importance came government regulations of the sale and preparation of solid chocolate with customs duties, to supply increasing support to the government, a final proof. By the year 1950 these would have soared to a noteworthy amount, with Britain importing in that year over 292 million pounds of raw cacao, estimated to be worth in the neighborhood of $130,000,000. A considerable portion of these imports were raised on English-owned cacao plantations in Africa.

France had first heard of the drink in 1600. Probably long before that, French monks had been introduced to chocolate by brothers returning from overseas and, when they could secure the ingredients, were preparing and drinking it privately in their monasteries. However, the drink was not to become fashionable in that land before 1660 when the Spanish princess María Teresa married Louis XIV, bringing with her to Paris her Spanish retainers and their Spanish customs. María Teresa's ancestress, Isabel la Católica, would have been amazed at the status then attained by those despised little black beans brought back from America by a navigator who hoped that somehow she might find in them partial compensation for the Oriental treasures he had failed to find.

Eighteenth-century American shipmasters trading in Caribbean ports would bring home a variety of tropical products, including cacao beans. Consumers roasted and ground these, probably with mortar and pestle, into the powder they used for preparing their own chocolate drinks. Progressive, money-conscious importers were not long in perceiving they might enhance their profits by roasting and grinding the beans before sale. Obadiah Brown, a resourceful businessman of Providence, Rhode Island, was writing to a Newport correspondent in 1752: "I have been at considerable charge to git a chocklit mill going by water which have now completed. . . . I shall be glad to supply you with all you have occasion for at ye cheapest rate you can have it at Newport or any whair else."

Mills "going by water" lined the streams of New England, the most essential being gristmills and sawmills. When two chocolate mills were noted on a single stream—as was done by Yale President (1795 to 1817) Timothy Dwight in the course of his travels—it was a sign that chocolate had long been there a more than passing fancy. It had also offered housewives a welcome alternative when, in the 1770s, the political situation made the buying and drinking of tea a subversive act. The forehanded Browns of Providence had profited by that.

Linnaeus had named it *Theobroma cacao*—"food for the gods"—that chocolate-producing tree which, like scrub apples to be found on every New England hillside, has sprung up wild throughout tropical lands wherever someone may have dropped a seed. You may come upon a cacao tree in almost any Central American jungle clearing. Its foliage is varicolored according to the age of the leaf, from pinkish brown for the newly unfolded leaves, through dark green to a mottled yellow for the oldest leaves that hang limply on the boughs or briefly litter the ground beneath until consumed by the teeming insect life of the forest floor. The almost black surface of the trunk and main branches is studded with surprisingly dainty pink blossoms on very short stems or with the maturing fruit that may be as large as a canteloupe and, when yellow, give that so admired effect of golden lanterns.

Today cacao plantations may be found all over tropical lands—Asia, East Indies, West Indies, the American continent, Africa—moved from the original central American home by ambitious agriculturalists of various nations and ages. Who first deliberately set out a cacao tree we can never know. Nor can we guess when, before that, cacao as a food first became appreciated. All we can be sure of is that, by ancestry at least, it is 100 percent American. It's still an American favorite. From the half million tons of cacao entering the young United States in 1790, the import, by 1950, had soared to 700 million tons annually—a far from negligible item in the economics and politics of nations. In the burgeoning plantations, such plants were soon issuing irresistible invitations to plant enemies, insects of one kind or another and microscopic plants that parasitized the larger ones. These enemies had had to struggle for survival when the plants which played unwitting hosts were growing widely separated among the numberless and varied trees of a tropical jungle. Crowded plantations offered them a field day.

4

Plant Enemies

Every living organism has its own select enemies, visible and invisible. That is the price of living, which is a constant struggle to survive lethal attacks and to destroy the attacking enemy, a struggle whose outcome may grow increasingly doubtful if people interfere with previously established patterns of growth. If plants of economic importance are crowded together in plantations where few other plants are allowed to grow, old plant enemies may take advantage of the new environment to intensify their attacks on so easily available plants. Men, for whom that particular plant has acquired importance, must seek and find the enemies, then seek and hope to find means of control.

The wheat rust that has, since Biblical days, periodically and disastrously lowered grain yields is a case in point. Long ago, observant farmers noticed that where barberry bushes grew, something seemed to blast their grain. Nineteenth-century traveler Timothy Dwight reported about 1810: "A farmer on Long Island sowed a particular piece of ground with wheat every second year for nearly twenty years. On the southern limit of this field grew a single barberry bush. The southern winds prevailing at the season in which this bush was in bloom carried the effluvia, and afterwards the decayed blossoms over a small breadth of this field to a considerable distance; and wherever they fell, the wheat was blasted, while throughout the remainder of the field it was sound."

This apparent hostility between wheat and barberry bushes had long since been noticed and long puzzled observers. As early as 1642 Massachusetts passed a law requiring the eradication of barberry bushes in the vicinity of wheatfields. Clearly there was some "effluvium" borne from bushes to grain. It was natural to blame it on the visible flowers rather than on the invisible organism which was not identified until much, much later. In fact, the twentieth century had already begun before plant scientists worked out the fact that an organism which they named *Puccinia graminis* was the real enemy and that, for it to fulfill its own life cycle, it must grow alternately on wheat and on barberry bushes. To control the disease on wheat, the alternate host must be eliminated and thus the extinction of barberry bushes in proximity to wheatfields was the correct means of control, though it was a long time before anybody knew why.

Many plant diseases are not so simply controlled, the least controllable, perhaps, being those of the moist tropics which offer so favorable an environment for the growth of microscopic plant enemies. Thus, as long as a plant or tree was left growing in some remote native habitat whither native people went to garner the crop, no one noticed or cared very much whether a particular tree sickened and died. Always there were others.

As, however, native crops came to represent greater and greater wealth, the situation was bound to change. If a single tree could represent some wealth, how much more valuable could be a great plantation with trees set out in rows where the crop might be so much more easily harvested than in a jungle environment where no single species predominates. For men who understood nothing of diseases, plant or human, the idea was irresistibly alluring. Living in times when epidemics were generally believed to be divine punishment for sinful men, people knew nothing about how illness spreads or that crowding people into tenements or plants into man-made plantations must be an invitation to disaster.

By now men have learned the hard way to recognize the menace to themselves and to their nations of plant diseases—bacterial, fungous, viral—and of the more mobile plant enemies: worms, for instance, and insects in all sizes and shapes. A century ago the grim possibilities were being drastically brought home to the coffee planters of Ceylon. In 1869 their plantations were being devastated with a leaf rust. It was not the unsightliness of such great brown spots that most disturbed the planters but what those spots were meaning in terms of the survival of trees set out and tended with so much care and expense.

Rust damage to leaves limits a plant's respiration, which takes place only through the leaves and is a process as essential to plants as it is to people. Moreover, as the green chlorophyll is destroyed, so also is destroyed the plant's power of photosynthesis—of taking from the air carbon dioxide and water vapor and with those building blocks constructing carbohydrates, as sugars, starches and the cellulose which supplies the structural element of plants. Lacking sufficient effective leaf surface, a plant cannot survive. And though men may survive a few such plant deaths, the death of hundreds and thousands of plants soon brings disaster to people.

In that never forgotten year 1869, all that Ceylon coffee planters could do was to uproot their totally diseased plantations and try tea instead, praying that the tea bush would escape the fate of the coffee trees. Since they knew practically nothing of what was causing the disease, still less about the life-styles of the many kinds of microscopic plants that, as we have since learned, delight to feed on highly visible ones, they would have been unaware of the fact that most microscopic organisms are very selective as to the genera and species of higher plants on which they will establish themselves. Only a rare microorganism infects more than a single plant genus save in the case where two distinct species—"alternate hosts," we call them—are required for the organism to complete its life cycle. For people, this is a fortunate situation, since less choosy organisms must long since have spelled total disaster for both plants and people.

Thus, the tea bush newly planted on Ceylon in 1869 was not menaced by the coffee rust, and today Ceylon tea is famous. Losses from plant epidemics may vary considerably from the totality of the Ceylon coffee epidemic. Though statistics on such losses are hard to come by, we do have some from an expert on cacao diseases that underline the grim potential. Before 1915 Ecuador was a leader in world production of cacao. Seven years later a *Monilia* disease had reduced the previous high annual production of 50,000 tons to an annual 30,000 tons. By 1925, with a witches' broom complicating the picture, the yield had dropped to

20,000 tons, and Ecuador had permanently lost her lead.

While the *Monilia* "watery pod rot" seemed to be confined to New World cacao, a cousin of the potato blight fungus named *Phytophthora palmivora* was invading plantations in other parts of the tropical world. This "black pod disease" is caused by an unfortunately less choosy organism which can also grow on bananas and palms, so that its control, even more its elimination, is practically impossible. Such a disease has reduced by half cacao production in western Africa, with statistics for losses in the Solomon Islands Protectorate running between 2 and 50 percent.

In 1869 it was that same reverend gentleman, Miles Joseph Berkeley, who had fifteen years earlier pinpointed the potato blight fungus, who spotted the *Hemileia vastatrix* that ruined the coffee on Ceylon. Assigning a name to an infecting organism does not, of course, kill it. Yet until the enemy is recognized little can be done to fight it. About twenty years more were to pass before chance, acting in partnership with what Louis Pasteur once called "the mind prepared," should reveal the effectiveness of that leaf spray, Bordeaux mixture. Even more important than the mixture itself was to be the impetus its discovery gave to the entirely new plant science first called "Vegetable Pathology." Later, it would receive the more dignified name "Phytopathology," which is just a more formal way of saying "Plant Pathology." By any name, it is a science which concerns itself with the nature and causes of disease.

As one of that new breed of scientists was to reminisce later, this good, safe, inexpensive fungicide, Bordeaux mixture, did more than any other single thing to influence and shape the development of plant pathology for many decades to come. The very year 1885 in which the new fungicide was discovered saw the establishment of the Section of Mycology of the Botanical Division of the U.S. Department of Agriculture. The brilliant scientists first appointed to the new division, together with others working in every state and territory, were soon producing an amazing amount of highly significant work, both from the theoretical and the practical point of view.

The scientists had plenty to study. Potatoes alone, for instance, may have to cope with one or more of forty-six recognized fungous diseases, six bacterial, eighteen viral, plus five nematodes (worms) and a miscellany of other visible enemies such as beetles, aphids, grubs, moths, plant lice, what-would-yous, some of which, already known or as yet unrecognized, may suddenly make their appearance out of the blue.

Of the latter self-propelling plant enemies, the story of the now too familiar brown and yellow striped Colorado potato beetle is a case in point. Unknown to potato planters of North America before 1855, the beetles had long been feeding happily on the leaves of the potato's cousins, the native wild *Solanums*. By 1855, however, the frontier of potato raising had progressed westward to where the *Solanums* grew wild. Finding cultivated species more luscious than the wild, the beetles forsook their wild provender and began moving eastward across the newly available potato plantings. By 1864 the enterprising beetles had arrived at the Mississippi River. Ten years later they had made it to the Atlantic seaboard, there to remain as a permanent threat to the crop plants that fed them.

When and how the beetles managed to take passage across the ocean is not known, but presently they were proving as great a nuisance in Europe as in America. Actually, during World War II, when Germany was desperately in need of potatoes to supply both food for people and a base for the manufacture of industrial alcohol needed by war industries, impartial American beetles were devastating potato crops there. Nazis presently were accusing our planes of showering their land with bomb loads of potato beetles—which, whether true or not, suggests the extensive damage such beetles can achieve.

The idea is fantastic, yet its implications should not be laughed off. If a plant enemy as small as a beetle which a man can crush between his fingers can threaten crop damage sufficiently severe to elicit such hysterical accusations against a human enemy already known to possess huge lethal, though nonreproductive, weapons, then the potential of such beetles clearly may not be ignored as a factor in history. As with the potato blight of a century before, a tiny plant enemy, if uncontrolled, can bring disaster to people, most of whom understand very little about plants, still less about plant enemies which inevitably must also be their own.

Civilizations that could not have developed without flourishing crops to support them have sunk into oblivion when such crops failed. Nations that have risen to heights of wealth and power through special crops over which they had seized control lost much of that power when they lost control over the sustaining crop. People may fail to acknowledge their total dependence, direct or indirect, on plants, while burgeoning populations whose burgeoning demands for the products only plants can adequately supply must strain to the limit the crop potentials of many lands. Yet unless people study the lessons of plant dependence that only the past can teach and thereby learn to shape thought and action toward a yet more demanding future, their civilization could well go the way of many that now are long since forgotten.

Plants, people, and their politics are, whether we like it or not, inextricably bound one to the other.

5

Plants on People's Side

THE FEVER BARK TREE

Of more personal importance to the peoples of this world, present as well as past, than the fortunes and political power once to be achieved through commercial exploitation of exotic plants have been other kinds of plant potentials, many of which have called into being a new type of adventurer—the botanical collector. The search in the valley of the Amazon for high-yield rubber trees, the gathering of their seeds for the starting of plantations elsewhere forms a fascinating example. Equally fascinating and even more frustrating has been the search for plants reputed to produce remedies for some of the most intractable illnesses that people have fallen heir to. For though, in the case of rubber, no one doubted the utility of the product or the identity of the tree thus sought, both the curative powers of a plant and the identity of that plant might long remain in question. Failure is an expected part of such a search, while the occasional success may have justified not only the costly years of mounting frustration and dimming hopes but have encouraged other men to follow other dim and winding trails, to everybody's eventual profit.

Three typical searches—those leading to the increased availability of quinine, chaulmoogra oil, curare, and of their eventually improved derivatives—will give a feeling for all such. Each product was used long ago by relatively uncivilized peoples. Each had a long, hard struggle to find its place among those accepted by men who thought themselves civilized.

Each such natural product must start with an elaborate plant synthesis of a kind and efficiency that long remained the despair of early scientists who called themselves natural philosophers. The relatively simple tasks performed by nitrogen-fixing bacteria have, in higher plants, become infinitely expanded, as varied as they are infinite, as mysterious as they are varied. Sometimes an identity of achievement can be still more puzzling. How did a tree in the forests of Abyssinian highlands come to manufacture the same alkaloid—caffeine—as an unrelated bush native to remote China? What induced the garden pink to synthesize the same essential oil as the clove tree of the Moluccas? What combination of genes and environment work together to produce any known end product? Without concerning itself with such theoretical considerations, folk medicine has long coveted a variety of end products, sometimes foolishly, sometimes with a wisdom that time has revealed, as in the case of the foxglove-derived digitalis.

The study of botany, which deals with the plants themselves, is one of the most ancient of sciences if one may dignify by the word "science" anything as empirical as, for centuries, botany long remained. Everyone had a stake in plants—for food, for clothing, for shelter, for profit. Yet for hundreds of years no awareness of this stimulated natural philosophers to undertake a systematic study of all plants.

What was to provide the needed stimulus was medicine where it could prove of vital importance to distinguish a valuable drug plant from a lethal one. Thus, the study of plants long remained closely allied to medicine. Many prominent botanists of the nineteenth century and earlier had received their academic training in schools of medicine where botany, under the guise of Materia Medica, held an honorable place in the curriculum.

Many an ancient philosopher, medical or nonmedical, had written about plants, yet because such a treatise could then be produced only by limited and time-consuming hand copying, none but the most dedicated of natural philosophers managed to secure copies for their personal libraries. The lore incorporated in such volumes was to remain for centuries the guiding wisdom of their philosophic readers who rarely indulged in the luxury of independent thought. Then in the mid-fifteenth century was born the art of printing, which was to have as fundamental an effect on the lives of people, by enlarging the communication of facts and ideas, as did radio and television in the twentieth century.

Among the earliest of printed books were herbals, those compendia of plants and their "vertues," one of the most imposing of these being published in London in 1597, authored by "John Gerarde, Master in Chirurgerie." This practicing barber-surgeon owned a private apothecary garden and also functioned as superintendent of the gardens of Queen Elizabeth I's chief minister, William Cecil, Lord Burghley, to whom Gerard dedicated his herbal. A book on such a subject dedicated to so prominent a patron had every chance of becoming a best seller.

By 1633 a new edition was in order, this being undertaken by "Thomas Johnson, Apothecarye," who added about 800 plants to the approximately two thousand listed by Gerard, while correcting some of Gerard's most obvious errors. He also added, addressed to the "Courteous Reader," a lengthy introduction of his own wherein he expressed his personal convictions as to the value of a knowledge of plants.

"Give me leave onely to tell you," he wrote, "that God, in his infinite Goodnesse and bountie, hath by the medium of plants, bestowed almost all food, clothing, and medicine upon man. And to this off-spring we also owe (for the most part) our houses, shipping, and infinite other things, though some of them, Proteus-like, have run through divers shapes, as this paper whereon I write."

It was natural for sixteenth-century surgeons and apothecaries like Gerard and Johnson to show special interest in the medicinal uses to which special plants might justly be put. What seems more than a little overdone is the universal assigning to every plant listed an amazing number of "vertues," though this, too, may have been natural in an age when medicine was even more empirical than botany. Not original with the authors of the herbal, most of the hoary and unquestioned wisdom recorded there had been accumulating since the days of revered ancients like Galen, of the second century A.D., and Dioscorides, a century earlier than Galen.

A few random examples taken from the herbal may suggest the general attitude: "Raw Wheat, saith Dioscorides, being eaten, breedeth wormes in the belly;

being chewed and applied, it doth cure the biting of mad dogs." Or, for St. John's wort (*Hypericum*): "The same Author saith, That, being taken in wine, it taketh away the Tertian and Quartan agues." Another authority is responsible for a different way of dealing with the same illness: "Onions sliced and dipped in the Juice of Sorrell, and given unto the sicke of a tertian Ague to eate, take away the fit in once or twice taking them."

Did the writers believe all they recorded or were they drowning men reaching for any straw of hope? Certainly one fact to be gathered from the herbal is the prevalence of serious illnesses such as those so frequently referred to as agues. The variety of weird treatments so solemnly offered suggests the desperation and helplessness of people thus threatened and, though of course not mentioned, of their physicians.

Agues—alternating chills and fever—are among the most ancient and debilitating of human ills. Classified according to the frequency of the wretched seizures, the tertian return every three days, the quartan every fourth, with quotidian, apparently a combination of the first two, involving daily seizures. The social and political impact of such a disease throughout the ages is beyond measuring, for no infusion of St. John's wort, no slice of raw onion could modify the inroads of that all but universal enemy or alter its impact on men and nations.

When, in 1803, Thomas Jefferson's envoys negotiated the Louisiana Purchase, the President's political enemies were quick to point out that he was throwing the citizens' money away on a dismal swamp unfit for human habitation. Even several decades later, a traveler was writing back east from Illinois, "But of all the other epidemics, the 'fever and ague' is the scourge of the

West. . . . When severe and protracted, it completely shatters the constitution, and the victim ever after bears about him a living death." In the valleys of the Mississippi and its tributaries, this fever had caused men to abandon fertile lands, leave behind all their investments of time and money, all their cherished dreams, to return to healthier if more crowded lands in the East.

Another name for this fever, assigned in 1740, was malaria—literally "bad air"—which suggested what men had long since guessed, that the illness was due to some lethal miasma emanating from swamps, particularly at night. The observation, as far as it went, was as correct as had been the one that perceived the disastrous relationship between wheat and barberries. Like that observation, it did not go far enough, though as with the wheat rust, the disease could not spread without its alternate hosts—in this case, men and mosquitoes.

"The requirements for the spread of malaria," a textbook of tropical medicine states succinctly, "are (1) human beings who have . . . malarial parasites in their peripheral circulation; (2) efficient anopheline [mosquito] hosts; (3) a sustained atmospheric temperature above 60°F. (16°C.). Whatever favors the presence and increase of efficient anopheline mosquito hosts and the access of these malaria infected insects to human beings favors the spread of malaria." The same textbook points out that there are over eighty known species of the worldwide genus *Anopheles* and that of these about three-fourths might be classed as "efficient." Clearly, the total elimination of either alternate host is not to be expected.

An English physician who, at the turn of the century, was studying malaria in numerous British-controlled tropical lands expressed the frustration of fellow physicians and colonial administrators alike: "Malarial fever is important not only because of the misery it inflicts upon mankind, but also because of the serious opposition it has always given to the march of civilization. . . . No wild deserts, no savage races, no geographical difficulties have proved so inimical to civilization as this disease."

Inimical to any kind of human endeavor in the lands where it held sway, malaria was bound to be a potent political force, its ravages able to change a critical balance of power as, some medical historians conclude, it did in the year 701 B.C. when Sennacherib's army was encamped before Jerusalem: "Then the angel of the Lord went forth, and smote in the camp of the Assyrians a hundred and four score and five thousand: and when they arose early in the morning, behold, they were all dead corpses. So Sennacherib, king of Assyria, departed and went and returned." Making allowance for the exaggeration in numbers dead to be expected of an enemy chronicler, recent archaeologists believe they may have found some basis for this account in piles of charred bones of young men, datable to about 700 B.C. Medical historians suggest that the winged vector of death was no hovering angel but tiny insects that some time before had delivered their lethal burdens to the soldiers who, in the vicinity of Jerusalem, were finding the kind of environmental conditions to bring out their malaria in its most swiftly lethal form.

Alexander the Great, young and triumphant world conqueror of the fourth century before Christ, was finally vanquished in India by this disease. He died there, wracked by alternating chills and fever, shaking as miserably as the least of his soldiers. Had he escaped the infection or known a way to control it, there is no telling how the world of his era and of subsequent ones might have been affected. More important, had there throughout the ages been any way to control such infections, the history of the whole world must have been changed.

Almost to a man, the early explorers and exploiters of tropical lands were to carry the malarial parasite *Plasmodium* in their bloodstreams, to suffer themselves and to provide infecting material wherever they might go. Men who left their European homes to pursue fortune in far lands could hardly expect to escape periodic attacks of illness, the survival records of colonial administrators being grim indeed. In Batavia (Djakarta), all but one of the company of Captain James Cook's *Endeavour*, forced to remain in that port for three months—October to December 1770—while their vessel underwent essential repairs, were to sicken of malaria. Some were to die of it there, others on the voyage home; others would live on with health permanently impaired.

Captain Stavorinus, who served as master of ships of the Dutch East India Company during the eighteenth century, gives a chilling picture of conditions in hot, steamy, swamp-surrounded Batavia, which, with his unfailing frankness, he condemned as "one of the most unwholesome spots upon the face of the globe" where "the destructive unhealthiness of the climate is carried to the very pinnacle of corruption." Statistics he cited for the five years following 1733 reveal that "the deaths amounted annually to more than two thousand among the free merchants, and full fifteen hundred slaves besides," with a possible third more remaining unrecorded to avoid payment of a funeral tax. By 1769, he noted, "the proportion of the dead to the living, is, at Batavia, as twelve to twenty-seven." This meant that of every nine people alive at the beginning of the year, four would have died by the time of another new year. Even with deaths in the "out-settlements" reaching a less shocking total, the company was destined to lose one-sixth part of its servants each year. Such were the risks hopeful travelers took in exchange for a chance to accumulate fortunes, each one, of course, believing that somehow he was to escape the almost universal doom.

Of course, cures for the so debilitating diseases of the tropics were sought and tried, though the best was generally little more effective than the raw onion recommended by Dioscorides. The worst would have been the then universal panacea—bleeding a patient whose blood was already tragically depleted by the inroads of the *Plasmodium.* If he survived that treatment, the patient could expect little remission in the typically intermittent seizures.

The Newe Founde Worlde was to afford the first really effective means of control, though a century too late for Nicolas de Monardes to extol its virtues. It was in 1633 that the Augustinian monk Father Calancha brought the substance to the attention of contemporaries in a brief note recorded in the *Chronicle of St. Augustine*: "A tree grows in the vicinity of Loxa"—today's Loja in the mountains of southern Ecuador—"whose bark, of the color of cinnamon, made into powder of the weight of two small silver coins and given as a beverage, cures the fevers and tertians; it has produced miraculous results in Lima."

Whoever experienced those miraculous results, it could hardly have been a person of influence in the sophisticated viceregal society of that day, which almost to a man rebelled at the very thought of being dosed with a dark powder made from the bark of a tree

growing somewhere in the wild mountains. Worst of all
to such a society was the fact that it was recommended
by heathen Indian practitioners. Few Spaniards had
anything good to say of it; fewer still were willing to risk
life and their immortal souls in thus dosing themselves.

If the fever bark had a cool reception in Lima, it was
to encounter positive hostility in a Europe that no
longer had an ear for that kind of "joyfull newes."
Perhaps chills and fever had so long been an accepted
part of human existence that medical men, finding
themselves impotent in the matter of real cures, were
bound to scorn a treatment sponsored by witch doctors
untrained in acceptable schools of medicine. The break-
through was to be made by a similarly uneducated
European practitioner whom medical men of his day
were to denounce as a quack.

Legend long insisted that, in the early seventeenth
century, the Countess of Chinchón, wife of the Viceroy of
Peru, was so dramatically cured of her fever by taking
the native remedy that ever after the Count remained
an active sponsor of the bark both in Peru and Spain.
Probably untrue—since the Countess appears to have
died in Colombia in 1639, leaving behind a recently
discovered diary which reveals her as a, for her day,
almost uniquely healthy woman. The tale, however,
acquired sufficient force for the eighteenth-century
botanist Carl Linnaeus to name the tree after her—
Cinchona.

Ten years after the lady's death, Juan Cardinal de
Lugo, a Jesuit padre of great energy and wisdom, was
finding it incredible that no physician of his day had so
much as tried to investigate the potential of the bark.
The Cardinal presently was to become such an active
promoter of the bark, even to the point of dosing the

young French Dauphin who was destined to reign as Louis XIV, that it became known as "The Cardinal's Bark" or "The Jesuit's Bark." Nevertheless, despite such sponsorship, even Catholics who should have been desperate enough to give any remedy a trial continued to shake with the ague, be bled white in the name of respectable medicine, and die long before their time. As for Protestants, a Jesuit bark was bound to be worse than a folk remedy.

What noblemen and churchmen had failed to accomplish was to be achieved within a couple of decades by an Englishman whom all the medical profession agreed to be a quack. Imagine the nerve of a man pretending to practice medicine who refused to bleed his patients, who dosed them neither with violent purges nor emetics but simply saw to it that they partook regularly of his secret remedy. Had those patients died under his care, physicians would quickly have brought the quack to justice as a murderer. They found it still more unforgivable that his patients appeared to recover.

Least forgivable of all, perhaps, was that the quack, Robert Talbor by name, numbered among his patients many members of the reigning houses of Europe, including Charles II of England. By way of reward the quack was finally knighted and died in 1682 as Sir Robert Talbor, with only a very few people having guessed the secret of his remedy. This may have been just as well in times when to dose an English monarch, head of the Church of England, with a bark sponsored by a Jesuit cardinal could easily be called treason, especially if, during the course of his treatments, the king had died from any cause whatsoever. Fortunately for himself, Sir Robert, the quack, was a man of courage, imagination, and luck. Fortunately for those who came after, he confided his secret to a friend to whom also he gave permission to reveal it after Sir Robert's death. The curative properties of the bark, finally recognized as having long received royal approval, were no longer to be totally rejected by people newly aware of their need for it.

Though tropical climates have always favored the devastating effects of malaria, the disease has in no way been confined to tropical lands. Chills and fever have in the past been reported in northern lands such as Scandinavia and Holland and in Vermont along the marshy shores of Lake Champlain. It has since disappeared in many such regions, but whether because of changing climate or diminished swamp areas or because the particular anopheline vector no longer thrives in those regions is not now to be settled with certainty. In states farther to the south, the disease has been even more prevalent and devastating, soldiers of our Revolution having to add that to their other burdens. George Washington, while campaigning in New Jersey, is said to have dosed himself with fever bark. Throughout the Civil War, malaria was actively fighting against both North and South. For every man wounded during the Spanish-American War, four sickened with malaria. It was malaria that during World War I immobilized troops in Greece and Macedonia. With the fighting of World War II extending to so many lands where malaria is endemic, hundreds of thousands of soldiers had that universal enemy to contend with. Supplies of *Cinchona* bark and its derivative quinine being cut off by advancing troops, malaria added materially to the misery of people confined to the Bataan Peninsula and Corregidor. The time had long since come for the world to make certain of adequate supplies of the needed drug, adequate stands of the drug tree that could produce it.

The fever bark tree—where exactly did it grow? What did it look like? How might it be distinguished from trees of other plant families? Some barks were known to yield a lot of quinine, others very little. How were the barks to be assayed once the right tree had been located somewhere beyond Loja, where not even most of the people who proclaimed the bark's wonderful power had ever seen a living fever bark tree?

By the eighteenth century, with the systematic study of plants gaining momentum and an awareness of the importance of that particular tree growing, there also grew a determination to seek out and study in remote areas of the world plants that might turn out to be of general as well as botanical importance. This was to be no task for a swashbuckling adventurer of the kind who had first sailed Far Eastern seas in pursuit of spices. Here there could be no promise of sudden riches to spur the new breed of explorers on. With no certainty as to just what they might be looking for, they had yet a compensating scientific curiosity and the certainty of adding many newly encountered plants to the lists of those already known to science. And for those who believed that the source of an efficacious drug to control malaria might be located, there could also be the satisfaction of having contributed a bit toward the lessening of human suffering. These two motives— science and benevolence—were in general to supply the sum total of rewards for that new breed of explorer, the brave and determined plant hunters who otherwise and for the most part were to end their lives in poverty.

Their debut was to be delayed by the fact that Spain,

like other colonial lands, long kept the ports of its overseas possessions carefully closed to foreigners, and it happened to be foreigners, not Spaniards, who first felt the drive to go plant hunting in far lands. Somehow, though, in 1735, Spanish authorities were persuaded to grant permission for a group of French scientists to visit South America with the avowed purpose of measuring the length of the earth's meridian at the equator near Quito, in today's Ecuador. The three principal members of the group were, of course, primarily geographers, though no scientist of that century learned enough to have been elected to the French Academy would dream of confining his interests to one narrow field. Attached to the mission in a minor capacity was Joseph Jussieu, whose main interest was botany.

Though the expedition originally planned to remain in South America no more than three years, seven had passed before the first member of the group returned to France. Thirty-six years later the last member—Joseph Jussieu—would arrive back in France a raving lunatic. Compared with an elaborate expedition of our day, it was a strangely disorganized affair. Before their time was up, various members had to sell personal belongings to help finance their stay. They got into controversies with the natives. As a consequence, the expedition's surgeon was killed. While natives, both Spanish and Indian, watched with disdain, expedition members disagreed violently and the expedition split up.

Though, to judge by the bickerings of those French scientists, they would not have been above deserting one another, the botanist, at least, remained in South America because he wished to. Joseph Jussieu had decided that before returning home he would make a complete study of the fever bark tree. It was an ambitious scheme whose difficulties he could not possibly foresee. He intended to view these trees in the remote mountain fastnesses where they grew, make careful records of their variants, test their barks for potency, leave absolutely nothing in doubt. It was to be the botanical masterpiece of the century and should assure him eventual membership in the French Academy—or so he dreamed.

Since Jussieu knew no one whom he might interest in helping finance the undertaking, he financed it himself. He earned money as needed by teaching botany, practicing medicine or engineering, designing bridges, dams and roads and supervising their construction. The years went by, and he grew from youth to middle age and beyond. Yet he never swerved from his purpose of accumulating all possible information on the fever bark tree. This he kept stored in great boxes that accompanied him wherever he might go.

Joseph Jussieu's native servant, looking at those boxes, wondered what special treasure the strange master might be hoarding there. The master foolishly kept them locked, forgetting that none but he could care a bit about the manuscripts and maps and dried plant specimens inside. Had the servant seen them, he might have thought his master as mad as he was later to become. Denied a glance inside, the servant concluded his master must be hoarding golden riches. Someday, he hoped, that master might grow careless and give him the opportunity of helping himself to some of the chests' contents, at least.

Then, one day, it was borne in upon that servant that his master was preparing to leave for his far-distant home, taking his riches with him. Not able to bear the thought of losing the riches he had so long promised himself, he swiftly fled into the trackless jungle, taking the boxes with him. When, at a safe distance, he pried the boxes open to find only dry plants and brittle papers, he surely cursed the master who, he felt, had bitterly deceived him. Certainly he was unable to see in the disappointing contents of those boxes twenty-five irreplaceable years of another man's life, years which had made him sick and old and given him nothing save the dreams which can make a lonely life endurable.

With those plants and papers, Jussieu lost everything that had given his life meaning. For ten years he disappeared from sight, no one knowing where he had gone or what he might be doing all that time. We can imagine him following, hopefully and agonizingly, one dimming jungle trail after another, always believing himself to be on the point of catching up with the faithless servant and with the papers which, long before those years were up, must have rotted away.

In 1771, Joseph Jussieu arrived back in France so completely deranged that no one was ever able to get from him an account of those ten lost years. Nor was anyone ever to be the wiser for his long, painstaking, tragically futile years of study of the fever bark tree. Only from another member of the original expedition—one who had no pretensions to botanical eminence, Charles Marie de la Condamine—was to come a brief description of the tree. This would enable the great Linnaeus to give it a place in botanical classification and a name—*Cinchona*.

In 1761, the same year that the no longer young Jussieu was making ready to transport his precious boxes back to France, an enthusiastic young man came out from Spain to the "New Kingdom of Granada"—today the Republic of Colombia—full of his own dreams of botanical exploration. The youth, José Celestino Mutis, had, typically, studied in a medical school. He had no interest in practicing medicine unless it might bring him closer to the realization of his botanically oriented dreams.

From Cadiz, the Spanish port where Mutis grew up, great galleons were constantly setting out for the fabulous New World while town boys sat on the quays and watched them come and go. Mutis was among these, watching every cargo that was unloaded, keeping his ears tuned to sailors' talk of the strange and wonderful world beyond the seas. Thither, the lad decided, he must go.

As he grew to manhood, Mutis realized that he had scant chance of reaching American shores without money or influence. Without personal fortune or influential friends, Mutis took an alternate route that he believed might end in his being able to set himself up as a botanist. This was the one that detoured via medicine. Without any enthusiasm for practicing medicine, though strangely with considerable ability in that direction, he accepted a post as personal physician to the Viceroy of the New Kingdom of Granada who wanted a personal physician enough to assure the reluctant youth that he should have plenty of time to pursue his botanical studies. Once having the young doctor settled in the viceregal seat of Santa Fé de Bogotá, the viceroy promptly forgot his promises.

Knowing that residence in Bogotá involved risks to his own health, the viceroy had no slightest idea of letting his personal physician wander far afield on trips of botanical exploration. He saw to it that the foolish, though able, young doctor was kept busy in the capital with a rapidly expanding medical practice. To another physician the wealthy and fashionable clientele of the viceregal court might have been all that a medical heart could desire. Not so, however, with a man who wanted only to write an exhaustive and immortal, if unprofitable, treatise on the plants of the New World.

Mutis was in a difficult position. To resign his post would leave him without any means of support. To continue in it must prevent him from doing the work he had dedicated himself to. In 1763 he tried to solve this problem by petitioning the king, Charles III of Spain, for support of his projected study. "America," the petition ran in part, "is not only rich in gold, silver, precious stones and other treasures, but also in natural products of the greatest value. . . . There is quinine, a priceless possession of which Your Majesty is the only owner and which divine Providence has bestowed upon you for the good of mankind. It is indispensable to study the cinchona tree so that only the best kind will be sold to the public at the lowest cost."

That last sentence was, undoubtedly, a mistake. To sell the best quinine at the lowest price to a general public could not seem very important to a king at a time when even the boldest of his subjects must hesitate to question the divine right of kings to rule and, hence, do as they might wish to. Perhaps the king found a disquieting hint of republicanism in Mutis' further suggestion that if he failed to finance a study of quinine, he might later be haunted by shades of those who had died of fever when, by royal foresight, they might have been saved. Naturally Mutis received no help from that quarter.

Possibly if Charles III could have foreseen that an ever increasing demand for fever bark would presently strip his Spanish dominions of their most accessible supplies and of the income they produced, he might not have turned so deaf an ear to Mutis' petition. Mutis' plan included more than just a systematic study of the tree *Cinchona*. With this made, the best varieties could be determined and from these cinchona plantations started in more accessible places. Self-interest might have moved the king had he been able to perceive that control of fever bark production was presently to pass out of Spanish hands.

Meanwhile, José Mutis kept doggedly on, taking every moment he could spare from his practice in searching for the cinchona tree where it had never previously been reported—in the vicinity of Bogotá. Should he find it, he would have achieved more than a mere botanical triumph, for with trees growing in New Granada the product could be shipped direct to Europe from Caribbean ports instead of having to make the long voyage north from Peru to Panama, thence to be transhipped by mule train across the isthmus and loaded on ships plying the Atlantic.

Finally, Mutis fled from his medical practice to a remote silver-mining town where, in 1782, he was located by a new viceroy, the churchman and scholar Archbishop Antonio Caballero y Góngora. Recognizing the exceptional talents of the now fifty-year-old Mutis, Caballero persuaded him to return to Bogotá by assuring him he need not again undertake medical practice. The archbishop went further and induced the king to pay Mutis' debts, purchase for him whatever books and instruments he might need, grant him a salary, and even finance an expedition for the purpose of studying the cinchona tree in its native haunts. At last it seemed that this naturalist was to realize the dreams of his youth.

In the newly founded Botanical Institute of New Granada, Mutis could pursue his studies without interruption or distraction, save by the young men who came to work there and receive instruction from him. The focal point of all this work was the fever bark tree. The quantity and complexity of the information assembled, the numbers of carefully drawn and hand-colored plates, the unceasing study should have made the work the masterpiece of Mutis' youthful dreams. But Mutis, the perfectionist, never could quite bring himself to call the work finished. Always there was another important item of information to be collected, another plate to be drawn. Finally, with the work still unfinished, Mutis grew blind and ill. In 1808 he died, leaving the completion of his life's work to one of his devoted students, Francisco José de Caldas.

Politics now intervened as, in 1808, Spain's American colonies began to break away, one by one, from the mother country. Students and scientists were, as in later times, leaders in revolt, and in the forefront of these leaders, sad to relate, was Francisco de Caldas. Thus when, in 1816, Spanish Imperial forces temporarily gained the upper hand in New Granada, Caldas was a marked man, seized, and executed as a traitor.

With Caldas' death ended all hope of finishing the work on the fever bark tree as envisioned by Mutis. Caldas had begged his captors to allow a few months' reprieve while he put the finishing touches on the work. He would work with chains about his ankles, just so the cinchona study might be brought to completion. The Spanish commander, perhaps aware that a delayed execution might, under the circumstances, be no execution at all, refused. Soon Spanish forces, leaving New Granada for good, were packing up all the contents of the Botanical Institute—instruments, drawings, papers, maps—and shipping them back to Spain, where, for many decades, the boxes remained undisturbed and unopened under thickening coats of dust.

Ill-fated studies of the fever bark tree remained unfinished, use of the bark itself limited, physicians generally regarding it as of doubtful value. At this point the young science of chemistry was to take a hand. In 1820 two French chemists, Caventou and Pelletier by name, managed to isolate from cinchona bark two powerful alkaloids—"quinine" and "cinchonine" they called them—which could be shown to be the active principles of the bark. It was to be many decades before other chemists could pinpoint the structure as well as the composition of those molecules, still many more before the molecules could be synthesized in chemical laboratories. Yet never have men learned to rival the efficiency and economy of alkaloid production by the fever bark tree itself.

Though the preparation of a pure crystalline compound should have made the drug more acceptable—a compact pill to be swallowed at one gulp being far more attractive than a bitter dirty brown powder—physicians had already passed final judgment on the bark and its derivatives, or so most of them thought. They continued to dose their patients with powerful emetics, purge them with cathartics, and to bleed them in the name of medicine.

Fortunately there were a few of independent mind who were willing to grant that the new crystalline drug might be worth an honest try. By substituting the new pills for the dark powder that so frequently disagreed with their patients' digestion, the physicians could also regulate dosage more effectively, as pointed out by Dr.

John Sappington of Missouri in his book *The Theory and Treatment of Fevers,* published by him after a long and successful practice in the treatment of fevers, notably those that so long had been the "scourge of the west."

"The names of Caventou and Pelletier," Sappington wrote, "who first separated the pure alkaline salt, called *quina,* from the bulky and inert mass in which nature had placed it, deserve to be remembered with gratitude by all mankind.

"Since that fortunate era in medicine, I have been enabled to administer the bark at any stage and in any quantities that I might think advisable. . . . The discovery has not only afforded me heartfelt gratification—for the reason that it enabled me to give more prompt and certain relief to the sick—but it has been instrumental in giving me a character and standing in my profession, well calculated to excite the envy of the physicians around me. But this I desired not; for I did not conceal from them, in our consultations, my views on either the theory or practice which gave me such superior success. It seemed that the most melancholy experience was not sufficient to convince them of their errors, and they still, from the mere force of education, considered my practice as empirical."

If the shade of Sir Robert Talbor ever wandered so far from his lifetime haunts as to reach the western banks of the Mississippi, it must have smiled in sympathy and amusement to see Dr. John Sappington selling his remedy as "Sappington's Anti-Fever Pills" and, to use the doctor's own words, "concealing their composition that they might acquire a reputation upon their own intrinsic worth."

In 1849, four years after the publication of Dr. Sappington's book, a French botanist named Weddell finally produced the much needed systematic study of *Cinchona*, bringing back from his jungle travels seeds of that tree to be planted in greenhouses of England and France and thus to give people of those lands some idea of the long-ignored tree.

The time for starting truly large plantations was definitely at hand. As the drug began to acquire medical respectability, with more and more physicians prescribing it for the ague, the uncertain supply and high cost of wild cinchona caused increasing alarm. And whose the responsibility to cope with this need? Not Spain's, for she no longer wielded power in lands where the fever tree grew wild. The new young American republics were too preoccupied with other more immediately pressing concerns to become involved in the pursuit of that tree. Thus it became the concern of outsiders—of the British, who needed to control the fevers of India, and of the Dutch, who had the same needs in Java. Besides, cinchona just might prove a profitable crop plant in those other tropical lands.

In all this, no one consulted the Indians of the Andean highlands where cinchona grew. The lands and all the fruits thereof had always belonged to their ancestors and, as far as they were concerned, now belonged to them as they would to the next generation of Indians. They were, of course, willing to sell dead cinchona bark for profit, all the bark gatherers—*cascarilleros*—being Indians and knowing the market value of this product. Being shrewd and intelligent, they also knew what might happen to that market should they sell either trees or seed to outsiders.

In the Amazon basin, the botanical collector Richard Spruce was discovering that similarly alert Indians might steal seeds he had collected, boil them, then put them back so that not for months would he learn his collections were valueless. In the Bolivian highlands where the best cinchona grew, Indians were even more determined to hold inviolate what they claimed as their own heritage.

Few civilized men knew enough to take seriously the unlettered savage's unwillingness to part with such possessions. A shinier mirror, these outsiders think, a brighter length of trade goods, and the bargain will be closed. So believed Justus Karl Hasskarl, director of the Botanical Gardens in Java, where he hoped to start cinchona plantations. When, both in Bolivia and adjoining Peru, he found his hopes frustrated, he approached a shady local character named Henríquez, who agreed to deliver the desired plants for a large sum of money.

In 1854 Henríquez delivered the required number of seedlings to Hasskarl, who paid him off, then set out promptly for Java. It really could be none of his business that natives of the regions whence the stolen plants had come promised to cut the thief's feet off should they ever get their hands on him. Now with enough money to live quite comfortably, Henríquez had no intention of returning to the jungles. The Dutchman, as it turned out, held the bag, for he had purchased inferior and sickly plants that could bring nothing of value to his garden in Java.

The British were the next to try their luck, and for help they turned to that dedicated English scientist and plant hunter Richard Spruce. Born in York in 1817, Spruce had always cherished a dream of becoming a plant hunter. Failing to secure any financial backing, Spruce nevertheless, in 1849, set out for the jungles of the Amazon and the adjoining Rio Negro, determined to pay his own way by selling dried specimens of the plants he hoped to collect there. In the 1850s there were, throughout Europe and America, plenty of private herbaria and public natural-history museums eager to acquire representative collections of plants from all over the world, willing to buy such specimens at so much per specimen. This uncertain and irregular income, plus the few months' government pay he drew while collecting cinchona seedlings, was all Richard Spruce had to live on during the fifteen years he spent in South America. He had even less when, his health broken, he returned to his native land.

For eight years, mostly accompanied only by native guides and servants, Richard Spruce had penetrated areas of the Amazon basin where no man of science had ever before set foot. His observant naturalist's eye, quick to spy out interesting plants, was equally alert to the human scene about him. In his carefully kept journal, as in his plant collections, he lives again today.

He moved along the Amazon and its tributaries from one primitive settlement to another. Sometimes he had to cope with violent storms and raging floods. At other times—many times—he found his native help incompetent. Yet only once did he record any serious personal trouble with those poor, remote natives who well might have been tempted to slaughter this Englishman, alone in their midst, for the small articles of civilized manufacture and the trade goods he carried with him. Most of the Indians liked and trusted the odd foreigner who was not above enjoying himself at their festivals and who really tried to talk to them in their own tongues.

If any foreigner could succeed in the ticklish business of getting seeds and seedlings out of the jungles which the Indians regarded as their own, it would be

Richard Spruce. So, at least, reasoned the director of Kew Gardens, who may not have understood too well the difference between the natives of the Amazon lowlands and the Indians of upland Bolivia and Ecuador where the desired red cinchona grew. Even the latter quickly perceived that Spruce was no sly, cheating Henríquez and that, moreover, he could do his own plant exploring and collecting. Not even he, they were confident, would be likely to stumble upon their most remote and valuable stands of cinchona.

In any case, whatever the Indians of upland Ecuador may have thought of Spruce, they did not pursue him with active violence. Perhaps they expected their ancestral gods to assume responsibility for his punishment. If so, they were right, for Richard Spruce, his health already undermined by eight years in steaming lowland jungles, endured sheer misery in the penetrating cold of those high slopes of the extinct volcano Chimborazo where the red cinchona grew. His health never quite recovered from the effects of his residence there.

Though he was assigned two fellow Englishmen— one a resident of Ecuador and the other a gardener from Kew—to aid him, the ultimate responsibility was Spruce's. His first problem was to locate an area where fine red cinchona could be secured. This turned out to be in the vicinity of a place named Limón, where "existed formerly the finest manchón of Red Bark ever seen. It was all cut down many years ago, but I was informed that shoots from the old roots had already grown to be stout little trees large enough to bear flowers and fruit." The tragic end of a crop that destroyed the tree which produced it was here becoming all too evident. Natives who guarded their natural productions so jealously did not hesitate to strip the trees of their bark and thus kill them. Plantations of the fever bark-bearing tree were being planned none too soon.

Having located the stand of red cinchona, Spruce and Dr. Taylor, the Englishman residing in Ecuador, next had to approach the men who held title to the land. "With these two gentlemen," Spruce wrote in his report, "I had, therefore, to treat for permission to take from the bark woods the seeds and plants I wanted. At first they were unwilling to grant me it at any price, but, after a good deal of parley, I succeeded in making a treaty with them whereby, on the payment of 400 dollars, I was allowed to take as many seeds and plants as I liked, so long as I did not touch the bark."

Labor, which the Ecuadorian owners of the land were to help him secure, was largely made up of half-breed squatters of doubtful value. Moreover, the whole land was in a state of civil war where any able-bodied man might be conscripted by one side or the other, depending on which came upon him first. Worse still, light-fingered soldiery was constantly passing and repassing the Englishmen's camp. Small articles were constantly disappearing. Pack mules, which Spruce had assembled for the purpose of transporting cinchona seedlings to the coast, were also conscripted. The outlook for the hoped-for cinchona plantations in India seemed as cold and depressing as the forests around Limón.

Somehow, Spruce managed to collect the seedlings, get them to the little river port called Aguacatal, and then transship to a raft he had had constructed for the purpose of carrying them farther—to the ocean port of Guayaquil. "Some difficulty," Spruce wrote mildly of his troubles, "had been experienced in procuring the requisite number of beasts of burden, and the making of cylindrical baskets to contain the plants had proved a tedious task; besides that, the tying up each plant in wet moss, and the packing them in baskets were delicate operations which Mr. Cross [the gardener] could trust to no hands but his own. There had been not a few falls on the way, and some of the baskets had got partially crushed by the wilfulness of the bulls in running through the bush; but the greater part of the plants turned out wonderfully fresh. . . . As we might expect some rough treatment on the descent to Guaya-quil, we did not put on the glasses, but in their stead stretched moistened strips of calico over the cases, which seemed to answer admirably." At the river port the plants had been moved from their baskets to wooden cases in preparation for the long ocean voyage ahead.

The raft trip held its own dangers for both plants and men. "The river had risen to its winter level and . . . is narrowed in some places to 30 yards, and the navigable channel is further straitened by the trees which hang far over the water. Add to this that the river ran like a sluice, and that the turns were frequent and abrupt, and it will be seen how difficult it was to maintain our clumsy craft always in the mid-stream. . . . At length at a sharp turn, the raft went dead on, and through a mass of branches and twiners that hung over the middle of the river. The effect was tremendous: the heavy cases were hoisted up and dashed against each other, the roof of our cabin smashed in, and the old pilot was for some moments so completely involved in the branches and the wreck of the roof, that I expected nothing but that he had been carried away; he held on, however, and at last emerged, panting and perspiring, but with no further injury than a smart flogging from the twigs, which indeed none of us entirely escaped. . . .

"Our deck now presented a lamentable sight, but we had little time for ascertaining the amount of damage, as at every turn a similar peril awaited us. . . . The plants, thanks to Mr. Cross' tender care of them, bore scarcely any traces of the rough treatment they had undergone in their descent from Limón and in their late voyage from Aguacatal, and the only thing against them was that they were growing too rapidly, owing to the increased temperature to which they had lately been subjected."

Two days later, Richard Spruce saw his plants stowed aboard a freighter. "[I] then took leave of Mr. Cross and the plants, satisfied that as long as they were under his care they were likely to go on prosperously, and having done all I could on my part to conduct the enterprise to a successful issue." By 1860, cinchona plantations were finally started in India, in Ceylon, and, through a gift of young trees to the Dutch government, in Java. Richard Spruce, briefly financed to that end by his government, returned to his lonely, self-supported plant collecting.

"*Cinchona succirubra*," Spruce recorded in his journal, "is a very handsome tree and, in looking over the forest, I could never see any other tree at all comparable to it in beauty."

It was not beauty but quinine content that was to matter here, and, as it turned out, that was less than hoped for in the species collected by Spruce. In the end it was not a botanist but a trader, Charles Ledger, who would secure viable seeds of the best cinchona species, eventually to be known in his honor, *Cinchona ledgeriana*.

Yet Ledger himself would have been the first to say he had secured those seeds at too high a price.

Charles Ledger went out to South America in 1836 with the hope of making money by trading in articles in demand at home, among them the cinchona bark. A kind man, of wisdom and integrity, he won the respect of the Indians who knew him well and were sufficiently devoted to him to make for him the ultimate sacrifice.

Ledger made his home in the town of Puno at the Peruvian end of the high bleak Lake Titicaca. Upon the huge body of water and upon the incongruous little steamer that today makes regular trips between the Bolivian end and Puno, the snow-clad, towering Andean peaks look down with cool, distant aloofness. The Indians who make their homes along the rush-lined shores of the lake care very little just where the line runs that divides Bolivia from Peru. As far as they are concerned, the land is all theirs, as it has been their ancestors' since time immemorial.

Of these Indians, the ones called Aymaras are said to be the most fanatically devoted to their land and its fruits. It is said they would sooner sell their own children than part with ancestral acres. Always reserved, they might serve foreign masters for money, yet withhold their first loyalty. Personal devotion to a man like Charles Ledger could bring only tragedy to an Aymara, for it involved a conflict of deep-rooted loyalties. So it proved with Ledger's servant Manuel, who had lived long in the foreigner's house and grown to love him.

Manuel's people could find nothing to object to in Manuel's serving an outsider for money, nor even in his helping Ledger purchase highest-yielding barks. But when Ledger tried to discover where these fine barks were gathered, tried to secure seeds and seedlings of the trees which produced them, Manuel knew well enough he must make the bitter choice: the master whom he had served for eighteen years, whose fortune he had helped make, who trusted him in everything, or his own people and their inviolable traditions. Either he must lead his master to the desired cinchona trees or he must leave him.

So, after those years of living in the foreigner's house, Manuel returned to his own people to take up work there as an independent *cascarillero* in the cinchona forests. Now more a stranger to his own people than to Ledger, he yearned for the good man, still wishing to prove his undying devotion. Four years later he returned alone across eight hundred miles of bleak Andean highlands where travelers resting by the wayside might freeze into seated statues. Concealed in his long hair, Manuel brought a packet of seeds for the man he loved. They came, the Indian said, from an especially fine stand of cinchona trees he had encountered in the course of his bark collecting. Then he took his departure to return across the frozen miles to his people, who, should they learn of his act, would certainly execute him as a traitor.

The betrayal, as Manuel had anticipated, was discovered and punished. Years later his son, who had also lived long in Ledger's house, told of his father's death, then offered to collect more seeds for the Englishman, should he still wish them. Touched by the devotion, horrified to learn what it had brought to the youth's father, Ledger promptly refused the offer.

Actually, it was no longer a matter of such great importance. For the cinchona seeds collected at such cost and, which, in the 1860s, the British government showed no interest in acquiring, were sold in London by Ledger's brother. Part went to an English planter in India, part to the Dutch, who acquired a pound for a mere twenty dollars. They have since through their plantations reaped great profit from that purchase, for the *Cinchona ledgeriana* yields as much as 13 percent quinine when mature as against from 3 to 5 percent for its nearest rival.

What of the fever bark today? Purchased with so much personal suffering, it now provides the means of relieving the sufferings of millions. The drug quinine, still prepared from the bark extract, being more costly than a mixed alkaloid extract called "totaquine," is less widely used than the latter, which, at about one-seventh the cost of pure quinine, serves large populations in the underdeveloped countries as it has for armies struggling in malarial lands. People, whose science and ingenuity have showed them how to synthesize quinine, have never found out how to perform that synthesis as efficiently and cheaply as the plant which first taught them the drug's value.

THE KALAW TREE

Malaria might bring great suffering, but for the man sick with malaria there has always been understanding and care. With millions living in areas of high malarial incidence, people had grown to expect that sooner or later everyone would be afflicted. It was almost a routine hazard of living.

Not so with another disease which has long prevailed in much the same lands where malaria has been rampant. From ancient Biblical times, leprosy set its sufferers apart from their world, as witnessed by the long passage in Leviticus which, in part, runs as follows: "And the leper in whom the plague is, his clothes shall be rent, and his head bare, he shall put a covering on his upper lip, and shall cry Unclean, unclean.

"All the days wherein the plague of leprosy shall be in him, he shall be defiled; he is unclean; he shall dwell alone; without the camp shall his habitation be."

Such isolation of lepers extended into medieval times and beyond. Once the plague of leprosy was in a man, all he could look forward to was a miserable existence ending only in death. As far as nonleprous humans were concerned, he was already dead, for once unsightly skin lesions made their appearance and, correctly or not, were diagnosed as leprous, the Church performed a burial service over him, thereby washing its hands of future responsibility for the person and soul of the living corpse he was thereby doomed to become. The law required he wear a special dress, use a clapper to warn off other folk if he walked in a public place, speak to no one in a loud voice, drink nothing from a public fountain, eat in no company save that of fellow lepers. Dwelling, by edict, in a hut set in an open field, he became for all a symbol of misery and rejection, the disease a horror beyond description.

The irony of it was, as we know today, that before men had any way of pinpointing the causative organism, many a sufferer from other kinds of skin diseases was thrust apart as a leper. Certainly present in northern Europe by the fifth or sixth century of our era, true leprosy was to show a dramatic increase there during the eleventh century, after Crusaders began to arrive home from their Near East adventures, many already unwittingly bearing with them the seeds of that very slow-incubating disease. The first leper asylum recorded for England was founded in Canterbury in 1096. By the thirteenth century Europe had some 19,000 of these "lazar houses"—a name applied two centuries later—with two thousand in France alone.

It may have been the cruel isolation of the ill that helped gradually to reduce the number of new cases of a disease that generally seems to make its appearance in a new victim only after prolonged contact with a leper. By the mid-twentieth century, a medical writer was still forced to admit, "Nothing definite is known of the method of transmission. This question is complicated on account of the long incubation period of the disease," which, according to another medical authority, "is ordinarily as long as 5–10 years and may be as long as 20 years." Obviously, then, it is extremely difficult for an epidemiologist to gather relevant information as to the when, where, and whom of the disease source. Add to that the fact that the organism, first recognized about a century ago by the Norwegian scientist Gerhard Armauer Hansen, grows on practically no laboratory animal, and the complete study of leprosy has remained a real problem.

Leprosy remains a problem today. Despite improved precautions and a general medical feeling that isolation of lepers is as ineffective as it is unkind, leprosy is not yet a disappearing disease. The World Health Organization reported for 1974 a total of 151 newly recognized cases in Europe, with, for the same period, upward of 14,000 cases in the whole world, about two-thirds of these in Africa, one-quarter in Asia.

Whether the figures quoted are totally accurate or not—cases reported from remote areas possibly being diagnosed without positive identification of Hansen's bacillus in tissues—they show that leprosy is still a menace, notably in Africa and Asia. Europeans who, during the last century, had probably never seen a case of real leprosy at home, were, on taking up residence in far lands, becoming well acquainted with its ravages, a few through contracting the disease personally. European-trained physicians could do little for them, having nothing among their usual remedies that could, by one jot or tittle, alter the course of the disease.

Desperation can make people try anything. The special stigma attached to leprosy was bound to make anyone who found himself a leper listen with more than passing interest to the tales of cures vouched for by local legend only. The presumed curative agent was called "chaulmoogra oil" and was said to be pressed from the seeds of a "kalaw" tree growing in the hills of remote Burma. The legend which assigned to this oil remarkable curative powers might be pure fantasy, yet might just contain some grain of truth and, therefore, some grain of hope.

Once upon a time—so ran the Indian legend—there lived in Benares a king named Rana whom neither power nor wealth could protect from infection with leprosy. He might, for a little time, conceal from others the typical lesions—lumps under the skin, areas where he could feel no pain when cut or burned—but as the nodules increased in number and became open sores with flesh and tissues underneath beginning to wear away, there was no hiding the true state of affairs from anyone. In dread, he saw himself becoming noseless, faceless, fingerless like other lepers.

Soon his courtiers were seeing it too and, having guessed the worst, were finding excuses for leaving the court. No royal favors, no lavish gifts could persuade them to risk becoming lepers. Seeing this and knowing that his son, too, might be infected from him, Rana finally abdicated in his son's favor and went forth to dwell alone in the jungle.

The hollow of a great tree became the king's only shelter, his food made up of roots and herbs and, especially, the fruit of a tree called by natives "kalaw." Presently Rana was finding the disease leaving him until, finally cured, he was feeling better than ever he had while dwelling amidst the luxuries of his Benares palace.

In a cave not far from the hollow tree lived the once beautiful Piya, princess of a neighboring kingdom. Deserted in the jungle by brothers and sisters who had discovered she was a leper, she, like Rana, was having to fend for herself, also keeping alive on roots and herbs but somehow overlooking the wonderful kalaw. One day, stalked by a tiger into her cave, she screamed so loudly that Rana, who just happened to be passing by, penetrated the hidden cave mouth and saved the princess from the ravening beast. He also rescued her from her leprosy by teaching her to eat of the kalaw. Piya, of course, soon regained her former beauty and the dazzled ex-king married her. They lived happily ever after in the jungle kingdom the two shared, raising sixteen pairs of twin sons which, in due time, Piya bore her lord.

A charming legend! Yet might it contain some grain of truth, might Rana and Piya be real persons, afflicted once with leprosy yet miraculously cured? Had not, perhaps, someone less exalted experienced a seemingly miraculous cure and then woven around it the fabric of a romantic tale? Was there really a curative kalaw tree and, if so, what manner of tree might it be?

Vendors in the Calcutta bazaars sold something they

called chaulmoogra oil, derived, so they claimed, from the kalaw tree. Dirty, ill-smelling, and nauseating, it yet brought high prices, willingly paid by folk to whom leprosy must prove costlier still. It seemed, so physicians would presently note, that for some lepers, at least, it worked. If even this slight hope should prove valid, then the chaulmoogra oil and the kalaw tree whence it came must be scientifically investigated.

For this, it would not do to work only on a product too frequently sold by shifty native vendors. Seeds must be secured, carefully controlled tests made—tests which must demand considerably more oil than was to be purchased in the markets. Meanwhile, just in case the oil proved to have some virtue, some seeds must be used immediately to start plantations. Eight years, at the very least, must pass while the planted trees grew to maturity and began to produce seeds, and hence oil, on their own. While they grew, men would undertake to investigate such oil as they might secure in local markets.

What, though, was a true kalaw seed? What was the tree that produced it like? Where was it to be sought? For so lengthy a project the word-of-mouth tradition could not be relied on exclusively. Yet in the 1840s, when development of kalaw plantations was first proposed, people in India had no slightest idea as to what kind of tree they were looking for. All the bazaar vendors could say was that the oil they sold came from seeds gathered under trees that grew somewhere in northeastern India or Assam or Burma or, even, Siam. They had only the word of illiterate tribesmen that the seeds were from the kalaw trees.

"Kalaw," of course, was no scientific name like the botanical one which classifies a plant first in its larger group or genus, then by the species name, the second part. So it was with *Cinchona succirubra* and *Cinchona ledgeriana,* both being cinchonas, each recognizably distinct. Until it might thus be identified with precision, there could be no assurance that a tree grown from a bazaar-purchased seed would produce the much desired oil.

Nevertheless, since that seemed the only way to start, such seeds were purchased and planted, the shoots carefully tended. When, years later, the fruit was collected, the seeds removed and their oil pressed out, men hoped they might be nearing their goal. Now, with a controlled, fresh supply of kalaw seeds, the beginning of large-scale treatments and tests was possible. Men were wise enough not to expect miraculous or even immediate results, for a slow-developing disease was not to be cleared up in days or weeks.

Yet as months and years went by without any conspicuous improvement, ever skeptical physicians began to pooh-pooh the so-called wonderful native cure. Witches' tales—nothing more—just what they'd expected! Others would not give up so easily. Perhaps plantation-grown trees did not have the vigor to produce the curative oil; perhaps there was something hurtful in the plantation soils. Perhaps the oil had not been properly expressed. Or might it not be that the patients they had selected for test treatments had too deep-seated infections? On the other hand, the skeptics might be right. All those reputed cures of the past might not be cures of the genuine Hansen's disease but of some other skin infection.

Whatever the cause of failure, it led to a growing disrepute of chaulmoogra oil among Western physicians. The trouble, as it turned out, was in the name. The kalaw seeds purchased had come from another tree natives called kalaw, not from the one producing the curative oil. Those first plantations—the years of careful tending, the money so hopefully expended—were a total waste.

Only some fifty years later was the actual source of chaulmoogra oil to be identified botanically. In the year 1890 Colonel Prain, then director of a botanical survey in India, wrote enthusiastically to one of his colleagues, "Your 14421 from Chittagong is a great find. These are the real chaulmoogra seeds of the Calcutta bazaars and of the Paris and London drug dealers." By exactly what paths a botanist had arrived at such certainty is not exactly clear, but what is clear is that at long last the kalaw tree—the special one desired—had been tracked to one of its lairs in Chittagong or, at least, close enough to that trading center for it to have originated in Assam or Burma.

About twenty years later another man, a plant hunter by profession, could still write of the elusive kalaw tree: "Dealers in chaulmoogra oil have never seen the tree in its wild state. Even the native Bengal dealers in Chittagong had not been in the forests of the Chittagong Hill tracts. All depend on jungle people . . . who are more or less indolent. Moreover . . . at least 50 percent of the crop is lost every year. The Burmese name kalaw is applied to more than one species, and these species resemble one another so closely that the jungle people make no distinction between them. . . . [These trees] do not bear a regular crop but . . . sometimes are without fruit for two years or more. The natives stated that the fruit is collected by them every three years.

"The remoteness from civilized centers of the forests where these trees occur, the dangers and difficulties encountered in collecting the seeds . . . point to the necessity of starting plantations of *Taraktogenos kurzii*, which is known to yield true chaulmoogra oil, and also of such species . . . as yield oils of similar composition. . . . It has been stated . . . that owing to the very encouraging work carried out in Hawaii and the great success achieved in the treatment of leprosy with chaulmoogra oil derivatives, the lowest yearly demand will be for 1,000,000 litres [264,170 gallons] of oil. . . . With this in view, the expedition was undertaken . . . for the purpose of securing viable seeds of as many species as possible."

The man who wrote those lines—Joseph F. C. Rock—was extraordinarily well fitted to undertake such an expedition. Born in Vienna, Austria, in 1884, he early developed an absorbing interest in botany and a talent for mastering foreign languages, including the very difficult Chinese. In 1907 he received an appointment to teach in the University of Hawaii, where he gave instruction both in the Chinese language and in botany. Up to 1920, when he resigned his university post, Rock was making a botanical name for himself through his unusually fine collections of Hawaiian plants. In later years he would make similarly fine collections in China and Tibet. Herbarium specimens labeled "Collector: Joseph F. C. Rock" may today be found in most herbaria where plants from the Pacific area are preserved.

Naturalized an American citizen in 1913, Rock joined the Plant Introduction Service of the United States Department of Agriculture in 1920. This Service was then becoming increasingly conscious of the desirability of searching previously unexplored areas of the world for as yet unfamiliar plants that might be grown in

American flower or vegetable gardens or in orchards. Joseph Rock, botanist and linguist combined, was just the kind of man the Service needed.

A man who traveled fast and who could take care of himself in out-of-the-way spots, he had a determination to let no obstacles come between him and whatever plants he set out to secure. Definitely, he was the man to track *Taraktogenos kurzii* to its native haunts. Since the medical value of chaulmoogra oil had by then been demonstrated, the plant hunter was in pursuit of something more substantial than a legend. Yet as the plant he sought continued to elude him again and again, he must have begun to wonder about its reality. Characteristically, Rock traveled light and moved swiftly, either unaccompanied or with native companions. Tedious and difficult as his journey was at times, the names of the places through which he passed read—to Western ears, at least—like the stuff of which real legends are made.

Disembarking from his steamer at the port of Singapore, Joseph Rock first faced a rail journey of 1,018 miles to Bangkok, Thailand (then Siam). Such a rail journey may not sound much like adventure, yet a slow train running sluggishly through lowland tropical jungles, stopping each night at some small remote settlement, does not sound unadventurous either. Each night passengers found what accommodation they could in hot, crowded, comfortless rest houses.

After six days' such travel, Rock had reached Bangkok, yet found himself seemingly no nearer the object of his quest. No one there could tell him where the kalaw tree might be found. He traveled on, asking questions everywhere of everyone until, in the upcountry town of Chiengmai, the viceroy's wife recalled that she had heard people say the tree was plentiful near her girlhood home in Korat. To Korat Joseph Rock set out at once. Yes, the people there agreed, the tree did grow in nearby jungles. Just where? Now, that would be hard to say. A tree that provided such excellent firewood was usually cut down before it could get very big. Sometimes it was very hard to find. And as for any trees big enough and mature enough to bear seeds—well, that was hardly to be expected.

Back in Chiengmai in early December and still empty-handed, the plant hunter chartered a houseboat for a ten days' journey down the Meh Ping River to Raheng. Starlit nights were cold with a heavy soaking dew that might become a thick shroud of fog by morning. When, as day progressed, the fog lifted off the surface of the water, he could feast his eyes upon extraordinarily beautiful scenery—narrow, steep-walled gorges, perhaps, or the gentler distant hills forested with mighty bamboos and silk-cotton trees. In the space of those ten days, the houseboat had to negotiate forty-one rapids. Nights, when they remained moored and fogbound, had their own terrors. An elephant herd might go rampaging through the bamboos, trampling upon larger ones, crushing the hollow sections with a noise as deafening as machine-gun fire and perhaps, coming as it did through the stillness of a jungle night, even more terrifying.

Raheng, the end of that journey, still produced no kalaw trees. So Joseph Rock decided to head across the thickly forested mountain ranges to Moulmein. Amid these giant trees, some soaring to more than 150 feet, he encountered a few kalaw trees, but these bore no fruit and hence were valueless to him. Each night the little party camped in the jungle, whose wild animals—

leopards, tigers, snakes—left him unperturbed. Christmas Eve found him in Moulmein, where he took a day off in the company of missionaries resident there.

The day following Christmas, Rock set off once more, this time for the Martaban Hills in Burma. With him went an interpreter, a cook, and a houseboy, though there was to be no house. In fact, the party actively avoided houses and villages where swarming ticks and mangy dogs made the less certain menace of attack by wild animals a preferable risk. In the Martaban Hills, Rock actually encountered a single kalaw tree in fruit and carefully collected the precious seeds—170 in all—to send back to the Department of Agriculture. So many miles, so much hardship, so many dangers, for a few plant seeds that might never sprout!

"Much of the seed is lost," wrote the collector, "as native collectors do not take the fruits from the trees when ripe, but wait until they drop, a much less troublesome way to collect them. However monkeys are fond of the fruit flesh and attack the fruits on the trees, dropping the seeds to the ground: and many of the seeds are lost in the crevices between the innumerable rocks and boulders. Porcupines also devour the seeds and the result is that in all probability about 50 percent of the crop is lost."

People were still the tree's worst enemy, cutting it for firewood or destroying it in a more long-drawn-out manner by gradually removing the bark. The natives considered that a tea brewed from this bark could serve to treat intestinal disorders and skin diseases. Living kalaw trees were marked by tying strings around the trunks. Then, as medicine might be needed, they would send children to the jungle to cut out enough bark for the doses they thought they should take. Soon large areas of bark would be removed from the living medicine chests. Even if the now defenseless jungle giant had not been killed by girdling, white ants and termites would get to work and settle the matter.

The 170 seeds from a single tree were in no way sufficient, even should all sprout. All having the same inheritance, no latitude for selection was allowed. So Joseph Rock, listening to rumors that he might find trees in the upper Chindwin district of Burma, set out again, his first destination Rangoon. Though by now it seemed that kalaw trees must always be growing where he was not, Rock could not afford to overlook any lead. Arrived in Rangoon, he took the train through a semi-desert region to "dirty, dirty Monya," on the upper Chindwin River.

The dust in Monya was several feet thick and in it mange-ridden dogs fought noisily, sending clouds into the air. Squatting women chewed constantly on betel nuts and spat as constantly into the dust. Piles of rotting fruits and vegetables added the final revolting touch to the market. Without a shade of regret, the explorer set forth from Monya the next day on the stern-wheeler *Shillong*, bound for Mawlaik.

By eleven o'clock, when they were happily clear of the town, the fog lifted to reveal a pleasing view of boats in midstream and people in colorful costumes along the banks. At Mawlaik, Joseph Rock paused briefly, not to collect kalaw seeds, for he knew the trees to be still several days' journey beyond, but to secure a letter of introduction, written in Burmese by a local government official.

This, which he called his "magic letter," turned out to be of great value. If he just showed it to the headman of a town, there would be conjured up almost at once all the coolies he might need to carry his baggage out and his plant collections back. Of course there was a consideration of two cents per mile per man, but money without the magic letter was powerless to secure those coolies. The first part of the further journey was by dugout canoe, this being followed by two days' march afoot, in the course of which the river was crossed and recrossed times without number. Finally they arrived at their destination, Khoung Kyew.

There, at last, Rock came upon his first genuine chaulmoogra tree, the earlier ones having been only closely related species which also produced curative oils but were not the long-sought *Taraktogenos kurzii* he had been sent to find. It would have been too much to expect a good crop of seeds in the first village visited, but, at last weary of eluding so determined a pursuer, a good stand of trees bearing mature fruit was encountered in the next village, where a she-bear and her cub were already at work making collections of their own. When the natives raised a loud shout, she fled, leaving behind both seeds and cub.

Finally loaded down with seeds, they started back to the village along the path they had followed on their way out. Fresh tiger tracks brought to them the chilling realization that they, too, had been hunted. Perhaps the tiger had decided the departing bear might make easier as well as tastier game.

It may have been that same tiger which later in the night attacked one of the nearby villages, killing three women and a little girl as they huddled, fearful and helpless, in their flimsy shelters. While coolies joined the villagers in an organized tiger hunt, the plant collector waited through additional terrors. A fearful storm came up; lightning flashed almost continuously. Frightened by the storm, a herd of elephants went rampaging through the town, trampling huts, ruining the crops in the fields, devouring stored grain, bellowing noisily all the while. The tiger was caught and killed; quiet and peace returned to the town, which, in a single night, had been ruined.

With this dramatic climax, the long quest came to an end. Rock had now enough seeds to start plantations in various places—in Washington greenhouses, outside in Hawaii and the Philippines. Enough had been learned along the way about the growing habits of the kalaw trees to make these plantations successful—to provide quantities of seeds from which might be pressed the precious oil so needed by desperate folk. Just seeds they were—those small brown lumps that, with care and luck, might eventually produce replicas of the trees that had produced them. Yet they were far, far more. They were months out of a plant hunter's life, frustrations endured, dangers overcome, victory snatched from defeat. They were, still more important for millions the world over, an ancient legend realized, new hopes stimulated.

Though today, as recent statistics have revealed, leprosy is far from totally vanquished, there is now something that can be done about it. Chaulmoogra oil, once the only refuge of the few lepers who might be fortunate enough to find the true oil in purchasable quantity, is now more generally available. Treatment which combines such oil with an antibiotic produced by a microscopic plant called *Streptomyces orchidaceus* can be quite effective, especially if sufficiently prolonged, even for as much as five years. Yet the mere fact that prolonged remissions, possibly total cures, have been effected encourages sick and well alike, especially in lands where leprosy is still not an uncommon threat.

Meanwhile, though Hansen's bacillus has in the past generally compounded the problem of study by refusing to produce recognizably leprous lesions in any laboratory animals so far tried, it has now been found that it can be grown on the footpads of mice, where it affords a place for bactericidal testing outside of human sufferers. For many thousands of these, the seeds of the kalaw tree still provide the only available and effective treatment. Best of all, they provide hope for the previously hopeless.

LIFE FROM THE FLYING DEATH

It was nothing more exalted than the curiosity of an alert and inquiring mind that set men in pursuit of the flying death—that arrow poison which so fascinated the soldier in Sir Walter Raleigh as to make him devote some space to it in his book *The Discoverie of the Large and Bewtiful Empire of Guiana Performed in the Year 1595.*

Of the people encountered there, Sir Walter wrote: "These are valiant, or rather desperate people, and have the most strong poyson on their arrowes, and most dangerous to all nations; of which poyson I will speak somewhat, being a digression not unnecessary. There was nothing of which I was more curious than to find out the true remedie of these poysoned arrowes; For, beside the mortalitie of the wound they make, the partie indureth the most insufferable torments in the wound. . . . And it is more strange to know that in all this time there never was a Spaniard, either by gift or torment, that could attain to the true knowledge of the cure, although that they have martured and put to invented torture I know not how many of them. But every one of these Indians know it not, no, not one among thousands; but their soothsayers and priests who do conceal it, and only teach it but from father to son."

This, one of the first accounts of the flying death written by an Englishman, shows clearly how Sir Walter was fascinated by it. Something that might make the slightest scratch fatal could render less than useless heavy armor like that he and his men, as well as the Spaniards before them, bore so wearily through the oppressive tropical heat of Guiana. The frail, slender, poison-tipped arrows, soundlessly flying through jungle fastnesses, filled him with a horror that made him exaggerate the torment of the death they inflicted. Centuries later, it would appear that the real horror was in the painless suffocation induced by the arrow poison that has borne many names—"urare," "woorali," "curare," among them.

The soldier in Sir Walter must have made him consider the value of such poison if applied to his own arms. Yet without the knowledge of some antidote, this chemical warfare could prove too risky. Otherwise it might well have become the great secret weapon of the seventeenth century—that is, if it were not also so extremely hard to get and the plants of which it was compounded not even to be guessed at.

The soothsayers, those witch doctors of the jungle tribes which the Spanish called "*brujos*," guarded their secrets well. They couldn't care less if the annoying outsiders planned to use the curare against each other. But the *brujos* cared a great deal about holding on to their personal power, and they knew that their knowledge of drugs and poisons and the elaborate rituals of magic which surrounded them were what kept their own power and influence among their tribesmen. Naturally they agreed wholeheartedly with the ancient tribal tradition that decreed that only with other witch doctors might such priceless knowledge be shared.

Throughout the centuries since Sir Walter's day, outsiders have again and again sought the secret formula, offering generous pay. Yet today, when purified and standardized curare is available in sterile ampules to physicians and surgeons of the outside world, that rule of sharing still holds. In all the intervening years, there are only three or four records of any jungle native sharing with uninitiated *brujos* even part of their secret of curare preparation.

One of these outsiders was an Englishman named Edward Bancroft, who in 1769 gave a list of the ingredients he had been told went into arrow poison: six parts of the root of "Woorara," two parts of the bark of "Warracobba coura," one part each of "Couranapi, Baketi, and Hatchybaly." But what plants were designated by such names, no one could discover. They might turn out to be anything to any man. And, yet again, they might turn out to be no more than confusing words.

Some thirty-five years later the naturalist Alexander von Humboldt gave an eyewitness account of the preparation of curare as seen in the town of Esmeralda in "Guiana": "We were fortunate enough to find an old Indian less drunk than the others and who was occupied with the preparation of curare poison from the freshly collected plants. This was the local chemist. . . . He had the impassive air and pedantic tone formerly found in the European pharmacist.

" 'I know,' said he, 'that the whites have the secret for making soap and this black powder which if it misses has a fault of making a loud noise which scares away the animal. Curare which we prepare is far superior to that which you make over there, beyond the seas. It is the juice of a plant which kills quietly without one knowing whence the blow came.' "

Obviously sophisticated beyond the usual practitioner of witchcraft, this curare maker let von Humboldt watch him prepare the poison brew, giving his guest a sample of the final product. Yet he did not reveal what plants went into the brew, where they were collected, and just how to repeat the process of manufacture.

Some thirty years later, in the 1830s, the brothers Robert and Richard Schomburgk made the next recorded observation of curare preparation. Born in Prussia, these brothers spent most of their lives in England and in British overseas territory. Robert was finally knighted for his services to the land of his adoption. It was he who wrote of his own first attempts to discover, in Guiana, the plant source of curare.

"After I had engaged some guides," his account runs, "I started in the morning of the 25th of December, in search of the mysterious plant. Our way led first to the south, over pathless savannahs [plains], until we met with a place in the Rupununi [River] where we could ford it. . . .

"At last, after we had walked more than five miles . . . the ascent commenced. It was by no means an easy matter; the path, Indian-like, quite narrow, led over fallen trees, between boulders of granite, and was often so steep that we had to use hands and feet. . . .

"At three o'clock in the afternoon, after a most fatiguing march of eight hours and a half, we reached a few huts on Mount Mamesua, inhabited by Wapisianas, and learned from our host Oronappi, an old acquaintance, whom we had met a few weeks ago in the valley, that he himself knew how to prepare the poison, and that he would willingly accompany our guide and bring the plant for our inspection.

"This proposal did not agree with my plans. I was anxious to see the plant in its native growth, and when we gave him to understand that it was our intention to accompany him, he attempted by signs to make us desist from going with him. He told us that the path was very bad, and that it was so far that we could not reach the place till afternoon, and that we would have to sleep on the road; he repeated the same story in the morning, and as he observed that we were determined to insist on our first plan, he made a sour face and did not speak for a length of time. Whether he thought that we were not able to stand the fatigues, or whether he wished us not to learn the place where the plant grew, I know not . . . the path was wretched; all traces of it were frequently lost, and an Indian only could have guided us; and he directed his course mostly by broken branches, or marks cut in the trees, sometimes standing for a few moments to consider in which direction to turn.

"Our path was over 'hill and dale.' . . . It became every moment wilder: we had to cross several mountain-streams which flowed in deep beds . . . underbrush became scarce; it appeared as if Nature here delighted only in gigantic forms . . . as we arrived at a stream that ran rapidly over sloping ground, our guides stopped, and pointing to a ligneous twiner which wound itself snakelike from tree to tree, they called out 'Urari', the name of the plant in the tongue of our guides.

"My wish was thus realized; and the plant which

Baron de Humboldt was prevented from seeing, I now saw before me."

The plant was not in flower, which was a disappointment since it is flower characters that help fix the botanical place of a plant, yet Schomburgk was gratified to find fruit, at least—"and their inspection assured me that, as von Humboldt suspected, the plant belongs to the genus *Strychnos*." He was not, however, to be permitted to witness the preparation of the arrow poison from that plant at that time. He must try again.

Later, on another expedition into the interior of Guiana, Robert Schomburgk "found opportunity to revisit the regions which, in consequence of the arrow poison, had been previously of interest to me. . . . During our stay in Pirara, a Macusi village on the classical site of Raleigh and Keymis' El Dorado, I ascertained that an Indian lived in the vicinity, who was far-famed for the preparation of Urari poison. I induced him by presents of some consideration to prepare it in my presence and he promised to do so."

Still cherishing the hope of being able to collect the plants in flower, Schomburgk accompanied this Indian, too, as he went to gather the ingredients of the "Urari" poison. Again they encountered no flowers. However, three baskets were filled with the necessary materials and brought back to the village. Preparation could not start at once, for the jungle chemist knew his brew must turn out worthless unless he fasted rigidly for several days before undertaking it. Meanwhile, an influential Macusi chief arrived on the scene and persuaded the poison maker to retract his promise.

So all was to come to nothing, though, fortunately for Schomburgk: "The bark was in my keeping, and as I had paid for it, I considered myself to have a full right to it; and although he demanded it back, it was my turn to refuse him . . . and with the pure bark in my possession, we departed."

A brave man, Schomburgk, to turn his back on an angry Indian whose silent arrows were tipped with curare, who knew how to place those arrows in his long, slim, reed-lined blowgun, who knew how to aim the blowgun and how to fill his lungs, then empty them so that the force of his breath could drive the arrow straight to its mark! Fortunately for the botanist, it was animals and not men that Indians were accustomed to slaying with their arrows. The foreigner, they undoubtedly told themselves, was hardly worth the trouble of ambushing. For, since he could not know the solemn Indian rituals needed for the preparation of "Urari," the barks he bore away could serve no useful purpose.

Those Indians would never know that in a safely distant spot, the strange visitor would extract the bark with water, boil the extract to concentrate it, then test the product upon chickens, which died within a half hour in a manner typical of death by arrow poison. Definitely not so strong as the jungle-made curare, the preparation convinced Schomburgk that he really had in his hands one source, at least, of the true arrow poison.

It was to be his brother Richard who, in the 1840s, was to have the privilege of being perhaps the first white man to view the whole process of curare preparation. And while he could not manage to ascertain the botanical names of all plant ingredients, he recorded the ones he could determine, with the Indian names of the others, together with the weight of each component that went into the brew. The account, published in 1849 when Richard Schomburgk was director of the Botanical

Garden in Adelaide, Australia, gives his observations in detail: "At last my long cherished wish to witness the preparation of *urari*, of which many fables had been told (as there always will be about anything enveloped in a certain mystery), was to be fulfilled, and I found the process, except a few unimportant ceremonies, as simple as possible."

When he examined the collected ingredients, he was told that they grew "far, far away in the mountains; it would take him five days to get there." With due ceremony, the poison maker arranged the deep earthenware pot for extracting the curare and the shallow vessels for evaporating the extract. Then he pounded the various ingredients to pulp in a wooden mortar.

"The *urari* maker, after having arranged everything, built a hearth with three stones and laid the wood ready to light the fire though there was a large fire burning close by us, but which was of no use, being lighted by profane hands. Neither dare he use any water except that brought in the pot to be used for the operation; in fact, no other implement could be used but such as has been made by the cook; neither would he have assistance from any of the inhabitants. Any transgression of the sacred rules would nullify the operation of the poison. . . . As soon as the water began to boil the Indian added at certain intervals a handful of the other ingredients except the Maramu root. In doing so, he bent his head over the pot, strongly blowing into the mixture, which he said afterwards was adding considerably to the strength of the poison. . . .

"Within the next twenty-four hours, the old man left the fire only for one moment, keeping the mixture at equal heat."

In that time, the mixture had become somewhat

concentrated. The old man then filtered it and set it out in flat pots for the sun's heat to accomplish further evaporation. Finally he added the Muramu root which gave it the consistency of heavy molasses. By the third day, the poison was ready for testing on animals. Cold-blooded animals—lizards—were used for this, because with them the test would be more sensitive. If a lizard died in one minute, as it did, then warm-blooded animals would be dead in half the time.

Thus, though still only in part, was the mystery of the arrow poison cleared up. With each group of South American Indians having its own secret formula, the pinpointing of ingredients could be no simple task. Plant constituents of samples of such poisons from different tribes might be practically identical or might vary considerably. The plants had yet to be collected and studied, though, in a hundred years of trying, no one had managed to identify all the ingredients in just one sample of curare.

Meanwhile, explorers of the laboratory were becoming actively interested in the mysterious substance. Though chemists of the 1850s were fascinated by the chemical identity of curare, their science had not yet reached the stage that could enable them to study and reproduce the molecules to which curare owed its special character.

Biologists did not have to know this chemical structure to study the physiological effects of the molasseslike material put up in crude jungle containers such as calabashes or sections of hollow bamboo stems. How, they wished to know, did curare kill? What functions of that intricate mechanism which is the human body does curare so interfere with that life must cease? Bit by bit they narrowed the possibilities. Death resulted from a muscular relaxation so complete that vital functions like breathing came to an end. Was this action of the drug directly on muscle tissues or on the nerves which supplied impulses to the muscles? That question could be answered in only one way—by watching what curare did to animals.

In 1814 an eccentric Englishman named Charles Waterton, who had traveled widely in Guiana and had brought home a gourd of the "real, original Wourali-poison," obtained directly from Indians there, tested the product on several asses, reporting his experiments in detail.

"Several experiments were made with the wourali poison," he wrote. "A she-ass received the wourali poison in the shoulder and died apparently in ten minutes. An incision was then made in its windpipe and through it the lungs were regularly inflated for two hours with a pair of bellows. Suspended animation returned. The ass held up her head and looked around; but the inflating being discontinued, she sunk once more in apparent death. The artificial breathing was immediately recommenced, and continued without intermission for two hours. This saved the ass from final dissolution; she rose up, and walked about; she seemed neither in agitation nor pain. The wound, through which the poison entered, was healed without difficulty. . . . She looked lean and sickly for above a year, but began to mend the spring after, and by summer became fat and frisky.

"The kind-hearted reader will rejoice on learning that Earl Percy, pitying her misfortunes, sent her down from London to Walton Hall, near Wakefield. There she goes by the name of Wouralia. Wouralia shall be sheltered from the wintry storm; and when summer comes she shall feed in the finest pasture. No burden shall be placed upon her and she shall end her days in peace."

Wouralia did end her days in fine pastures nearly twenty-five years later, a footnote records. Perhaps the other asses, incapable of comprehending her great contribution to science, envied her her favored position. Unknowing and unasked, she had risked her life to show men how curare acts and, incidentally, that if respiration be maintained, the effects of the poison may pass off and the victim survive little the worse for the experience.

When the true nature of curare's action became evident, it occurred to physicians that here might be a means of counteracting the terrible muscle spasms that make tetanus infections (lockjaw) so painful and so fatal. As early as 1811, a Dr. Brodie of England suggested this application. Yet it was not until 1858, long after Wouralia had gone to her grave, that, after testing curare on horses infected with tetanus, it was tried on similarly infected humans. Though not always effective, curare was yet effective enough to offer the first real hope of saving the otherwise doomed victims of tetanus.

Today, more than a century later, are still to be found in medical journals case histories of treatment of "severe systemic tetanus" by means of a purified curare alkaloid. This same alkaloid is also used in the treatment of spastic paralysis, in shock therapy to lessen the intensity of the bone-breaking spasms which so often accompany it, and in anesthesia. Combined with a noninflammable, inhaled anesthetic like nitrous oxide, it can help give a satisfactory anesthesia for throat surgery where inflammable mixtures constitute a special danger. The cautery so often required in such operations can supply the spark to ignite them. What future lifesaving purposes our modern standardized curare can serve we cannot even guess.

Why, some may ask, did a century have to pass before curare became a respectable drug? Partly, of course, this was because it was first approached not as a drug but as a curiosity and partly because of the difficulties in finding and identifying the ingredients of the ancient arrow poison, then in securing them in quantities sufficient to permit tests which could not be performed convincingly until the thick brown mess had been purified.

Here there was no native lore to guide, for curare was a poison, not a native remedy like quinine or chaulmoogra oil. Yet time was running out. As civilization has encroached, the art of brewing arrow poisons has been disappearing. To find witch doctors who still performed the ancient ritual of brewing arrow poisons required ever longer and more dangerous trips into the untouched jungle.

It was a personal need for curare as a drug—a realization that it might be the only one that could bring relief from the spastic paralysis that had long kept him bedridden—which was to send the ultimately successful plant hunter on his quest. Curare just might help him, his physician guessed, if only it was available in some purified, standardized form. It was something that South American Indians used to poison their arrows, but it also had remarkable life-giving properties if used right.

Other sufferers must have heard those same not very encouraging words, but this time they fell on the ears of a man able to do something about it. The man was Richard C. Gill, who owned a ranch in eastern

Ecuador on the very edge of the wilderness whose rivers drain into the Amazon basin. The trail that passed his remote dwelling bore, like a river, a continuous stream of jungle humanity—Indian visitors curious to set eyes on the strange white man and woman and their stranger house. Shyly, apologetically they would approach the patron and beg permission to camp on his land. So he'd had chances to talk with them and watch their manner of living even as they watched his. Gradually there had grown up an odd friendship between the modern couple and these people of the Stone Age.

Then one bright day the patron's horse reared at the sight of a quivering leaf, and the patron wrenched his back so badly as to result in a spastic paralysis. As he lay in misery in his home in Washington, D.C., Richard Gill asked himself if ever again he should see his Ecuadorian ranch, ride his horse, visit his Indian friends. The most skilled physicians could promise him nothing—nothing, that is, without a drug that could not be had. A dangerous drug if not properly handled, a powerful drug, as the few who had handled it knew. There were also interesting records in the medical literature. If only there were enough available and it was pure enough— but no use talking, for it was a secret of the Indians of the Amazonian jungles, closely guarded by their witch doctors.

As his physician talked on, the bedridden patient, homesick for his remote Ecuadorian ranch, pricked up his ears. A witch doctor! Why could he himself not qualify? His Indian friends, to whom he had demonstrated some modern man's tricks, already regarded him as something of a *brujo*. Surely he, if anyone, could persuade the Indian *brujos* to reveal their secrets. It wouldn't be easy, yet it must be tried because of the thousands of other sufferers who might profit from the drug.

As the slow months of recovery dragged by, Richard Gill began to make plans for an expedition into the jungle fastnesses. It must, at one and the same time, be well equipped and well staffed, yet small enough not to overtax available transportation by canoe or whatever rudimentary shelter they might find or build. His companions must be knowledgeable, courageous, and diplomatic, aware that a social blunder might have to be expiated with arrow poison. There would be great expense, great risks, and, just possibly, great rewards medically if not financially.

In 1938, almost exactly a hundred years after the Schomburgk brothers had first witnessed a portion of the curare ritual in Guiana, the Gill–Merrill Ecuadorian Expedition set out from New York. They went from Guayaquil, on the Pacific coast, into the city of the high sierras where they put in three weeks completing their equipment with small local purchases and packing all their baggage in large tins so that each might make a manload and two could be balanced nicely over a mule's pack saddle. This completed, they set out for the ranch whence the jungle trek was to start.

After a three days' journey thence, the mule trail came to an end and the Indians shouldered the loads while the mules returned to the ranch. Ahead lay only narrow, dim, winding jungle trails where mud sucked at the men's feet and where lianas trailing down from jungle giants clawed at the intruders. It was a treadmill where the scenery never altered and they seemed to make no progress at all.

Many days later they came to the banks of a river where, as arranged in advance, waited six dugout canoes with their boatmen—*bogas*—to take the party to its destination farther down the river. They could now move but more dangerously. The river had come a long way from the Andean snowfields. Between stretches of quiet water it was still rushing along at headlong speed, boiling violently in rapids that foamed white across the boulder-strewn streambed, roaring so deafeningly that, as Richard Spruce had once noted for other rivers of that region, they could be heard an hour before they were reached.

To take loaded boats through such waters requires the most skilled of *bogas*. Alerted by the sound of rapids ahead, they watch keenly for the first line of foam, when the leading boatman shouts a warning to those who follow. He drops his now useless paddle and, in one swift gesture, picks up the pole he will use to hold the canoe away from rocks, visible and invisible. The *boga* knows the channel, knows the risks, and knows his own skill. He remains calm as the canoe shoots ahead, tilts crazily, buries its nose in the waves and ships water to a degree alarming to his passengers. Sharp granite boulders reach greedily for the boat's sides. Undisturbed, the *boga* gets the canoe through to still water, where, for a brief triumphant moment, he pauses to rest and to watch his fellows bring their own canoes through to safety.

Again and again this experience is repeated. Days are counted not in hours but in rapids passed. And each time, as the explorer watches his boatmen bending skillfully with each twist and turn of the canoes, he wonders how he dare hope his luck will hold. Even the fittest and most experienced of canoemen must tire under the constant strain and make some small fatal mistake.

What, he asks himself while considering this, can he spare from all the equipment? If given a choice, which canoe would he sacrifice to the greedy god of the river? Mentally running through the inventory, he shakes his head sadly. Because he has planned well and there is nothing superfluous on his list, there is nothing expendable. Fuel, lamps, stoves, firearms, foodstuffs, clothes, trade goods, medicines, scientific equipment—if any of these remain in the river the expedition must fail.

None of them did. At long last they arrived safely at their destination: a jungle village situated not too far from the banks of the river, with a white beach close by and a charming promontory above and overlooking the river. Here, if he could get permission from the elders of the neighboring village, the director hoped to make the expedition camp. Boats could be tied up at the protected beach where, also, baths might be taken. The encampment, of course, must be on the promontory. The frightening flood potential of the rivers of the Amazon basin has in no way changed since Richard Spruce described them so graphically a century earlier.

"We had barely resigned ourselves to sleep," he wrote of the early experience which taught him an unforgettable lesson, "when the storm burst over us and the river almost simultaneously began to rise. Speedily the beach was overflowed, the Indians leaped into the canoes; the waters continued to rise with great rapidity, coming in on us every few minutes with a roaring surge which broke under the canoes in whirlpools, and dashed them against each other. . . . We held on, the Indians using all their efforts to prevent the canoes from being smashed by blows from each other or from the floating trees which now began to career past like mad bulls. So dense was the gloom that we could see nothing, while we were deafened by the pelting rain, the roaring floods, and the crashing of the branches of the floating trees, as they rolled over or dashed against each other; but each lightning-flash revealed to us all the horrors of our position. Assuredly I had slight hopes of living to see the day . . . the rise during the night had been eighteen feet."

Gill knew enough not to take immediate possession of the promontory without consulting the Indians who dwelt nearby. Indians had always sought the patron's permission to camp on his land and now, when the tables were turned, he must follow the pattern. He approached the *curaca* of the village and, by means of appropriate words and alluring trade goods, persuaded him not only to consent to the encampment but to cooperate in the construction of the camp. At the *curaca*'s command, the men and women of his village cleared about one acre of land from its heaviest growth and built the palm-thatched, split-bamboo-floored shelters which were to be the expedition's headquarters.

The most difficult part was yet to come. It would take a great deal more than respectful words and desirable trade goods to secure the desired secret formula. In the jungle, as in less remote parts of the world, negotiation takes time, though here time seems to be a valueless commodity. With no sense of hurry, the jungle dwellers subject the strangers to wary and thorough examination which the examined must accept without protest. In due time, if the Indians conclude the visitors are harmless, if altogether inexplicable, a cautious exchange of views may begin and this, eventually, may lead to a discussion of more important matters.

Sufficiently impressed with the alien white witch doctor's chemical sleight of hand and his earnest respect for their own powers, the jungle witch doctors came to accept him as one of their privileged guild. To him, then, might be revealed even the secret of curare preparation, including the plants used, of which he might be permitted to make collections of his own. They would share with him even the details of preparing the brew from such plants.

Every detail of the jungle ritual must, Gill knew, be treated with deadly seriousness. He must carefully learn the prescribed fasts, the things a *brujo* might do, the gestures he must make, the words he must or must not say while the witch doctor's cauldron is bubbling. Not only did the future of curare as a drug depend on how skillfully he conducted himself; the future of every member of the expedition might here be at stake. Anything less than the deepest respect shown to the experienced *brujos* could spell death to them all, possibly by means of the *brujo*'s own brew.

Necessary ingredients were gathered—the roots of one plant, the bark of others, notably of a woody liana, now bearing the botanical name *Chondrodendron*. His collections complete, the *brujo* returns to some spot nearer home, yet sufficiently remote from the habitations of his tribe so that he may keep an uninterrupted vigil while the brew—the *jambi*—boils in the pots and over the firewood already set out.

The *brujo* is aware that all these—the right ingredients, the right pots, the right firewood, and the right methods of boiling—can yet fail to secure a strong curare if he forgets for one moment any of the elaborate ritual his father taught him. The food he eats, the liquid he drinks, the people he looks upon or who look upon him in the course of this ritual—all these matter as much as in the Schomburgks' day and for eons before.

The *brujo* must, during the time of preparation, keep away from home and family. The presence of women can ruin everything. For several days before starting the ritual, he must have abstained from salt, from fermented liquor, and from the hot pepper he loves. During the very last day he must take no food at all. If he fails in any of this, his curare will be weak and worthless.

The first day's work consists of beating the collected ingredients, placing each on a flat stone and pounding it with a wooden mallet. Then, still fasting, he retires to his lean-to, specially prepared for the occasion, and rests briefly. Early in the morning he builds his fires, sets his pots in place, pours in just the right amount of water, and adds the ingredients according to custom, which had comfortably decreed each step.

Custom, however, could not forecast for him what the presence of a white-skinned colleague might do to the *jambi*. The colleague knew this, too, and knew that even on the verge of fulfilling the promise to initiate him into the secret the Indian *brujo* would try to find some not dishonorable way out of his commitment. Gill was all too aware of this as the expected *brujo* turned up, face long with worry, and seated himself silently before his would-be colleague.

Finally, after a long period, the young man murmured gravely, "My heart burns low, but I can make no *jambi* for you. I cannot continue the sacrifice or do the cooking until six moons have gone across the hills." His woman, he went on to explain, had just given birth to a fine, strong man-child. To make the *jambi* now could cause his child to sicken and die. Everyone knew a father must wait six months or the magic of the *jambi* would enter his child. With a girl-child now, he might have taken the risks. But a man-child and his first . . . He shook his head sadly.

The apprentice *brujo* listened respectfully, then,

offering Yasacama, the young *brujo*, a cigarette, spoke quietly in speech such as an Indian understands. He reminded the young man how long he had been living among Yasacama's people and they should know him well. Had he not always spoken true words to them? Had he not always given them merchandise of the best quality? The knives they had from him did not bend at the first cut. The cloth their women had from him wore well. Most of all, they knew his "thought magic" to be true.

Yasacama listened in grave silence, then spat several times between his fingers—a sign that he understood and agreed.

Gravely, Gill handed him a peppermint Life-Saver, telling the young *brujo* that if he would but hold that in his mouth while he lit his cooking fires, no harm could come to his man-child from the *jambi*. Yasacama studied the strange round white object for a while, clearly trying to decide whether he should use the magic thus put into his hand. Finally he promised to start cooking the *jambi* early the next morning in his friend's presence. Before parting for the night he warned, "But, friend, it will not be good for you if my man-child travels in the death canoe."

So, sucking on the Life-Saver, Yasacama lit his cooking fires and began the preparation of the *jambi* while his white colleague sat close by, weighing each of the ingredients before it went into the pot, keeping a record of every detail.

While the pot was boiling, one of Yasacama's brothers slipped silently into the little clearing, whispered a few words to Yasacama, then departed as silently as he had come. Yasacama looked Richard Gill in the eye and told him somberly the news his brother had brought. His man-child had sickened. He stared at his visitor darkly, telling him that the magic of *jambi* was working against his child who had been well and strong before his cooking fires were lit. Then, admitting he had the taste of his visitor's magic still in his mouth, he said he would continue to make the promised arrow poison but "It will not be good for you if my man-child dies."

Three days later the curare came to its "point," and Yasacama poured it into the gourd that had been prepared to receive it. At that very moment his brother returned to the clearing and whispered again, departing as quickly and silently as he had come, not glancing at the stranger.

Yasacama looked at that visitor wonderingly while he handed him the gourd of curare, still hot from the cooking. At last he was free to speak and did so, puzzlement revealed in his voice and eyes. His child was no longer ill and would live. But, he insisted, it was not as his fathers had believed—that any magic could possibly be stronger than that of the *jambi*. He had learned a new thing. His visitor's words and magic were good, also "I like the taste of your magic in my mouth."

The news spread up and down the jungle trails. Here, believe it or not, was a man with a magic actually more powerful than any the Old Ones had ever known! Such a man was to be helped in every way, a colleague whom native *brujos* might introduce to the most secret bits of their jungle lore. This they did, and Richard Gill was able to take home with him the botanical specimens needed to identify with certainty the plants that went into that particular kind of arrow poison. Further, he secured more kinds of curare than anyone on the outside had ever dreamed might exist. And all because he had the courage and will power to stake so much on the frail life of a jungle baby.

Today, we have not just the crude arrow poisons,

with their history of romance and adventure and terror, but purified chemical derivatives, of which one called d-tubocurarine was the first but assuredly not the last. Of that tubocurarine, the *Physicians' Desk Reference* to pharmaceutical specialties states unromantically: "Recommended to provide muscular relaxation and reduce the amount of anesthetic agent during anesthesia for most general and specialized surgical procedures. Depending on the length of the procedure, Tubocurarine will provide effective relaxation for orthopedic manipulations and for bronchoscopy and gastroscopy." Romantic it is, nevertheless, for its discovery and use may be laid to the *jambi* of an ignorant *brujo* of remote Amazon jungles—literally a life-saving material from the ancient flying death.

6

Plants
Divine
and
Otherwise

When there is no known plant to cure primitive man's illnesses, he may be lucky enough to stumble upon one to lessen the suffering—which, to him, would mean the same thing. In desperation, nibbling at this or that, he could have found a wonder plant that made him insensible to pain, hunger, drowsiness, exhaustion. If that did not mean his illness was cured, he would have been none the wiser. The more hostile the environment in which circumstances forced him to live, the more eagerly would he seek refuge in a euphoria thus found to be within his reach. Through the ages many such plants in many lands have been providing relief from human suffering. We will here zero in on just two, of totally unrelated plant families, native to widely separated continents and cultures, whose discovery was a boon to man, whose overuse has become a disaster.

No one will ever know exactly where, when, or why some Indian of the Andean altiplano, visiting some warmer mountain valley, first put the leaf of a common native shrub into his mouth and, finding it gave him an unusual sense of well-being, repeated the experiment, plucking some leaves to take with him to the higher, colder altitudes where he dwelt. It is not hard to understand why such a plant, whose leaves, fresh or dried, can lessen the stress and strain of life at bleak altitudes, became an object of frequent use until it should become a part of the Indians' rites of worship to the point where no ceremony from birth to marriage to burial could be regarded as complete unless leaves of that yard-high shrub, coca, played a role.

When, in the twelfth century, the Incas rose to power, they assumed—or tried to assume—total control over the coca crop, for by then it was a zealously cultivated plant which thus became "the divine plant of the Incas." They set guards about their coca plantations, distributing judiciously to their laborers the dried leaves whose use could stimulate them to perform tasks otherwise beyond their strength.

Chewing those leaves with powdered slaked lime brings about a slow release of the active principle, which speeds up circulation, stimulates breathing—important at high altitudes where oxygen content of the air is low—and lessens feelings of drowsiness and hunger without, unfortunately, supplying any of the nourishment an active worker needs to maintain body weight or of the accessory foodstuffs like vitamins. Habitual coca users, though unaware of their lacks, will presently come to suffer from the effects of overwork and undernourishment. The ruling Incas carefully rationed the precious coca leaf to their workers but allowed unrestricted use to priests, whom the plant could put into a state of intoxication whereby they came to believe they were making direct contact with the gods they worshipped as well as the demons they undertook to exorcize from the sick.

Coca—now botanically baptized *Erythroxylum coca*—came to the notice of Spanish conquistadors as soon as they climbed out of coastal lands into the highlands where Andean civilizations with their considerable cities had long flourished and where coca, a crop in the somewhat lower, warmer valleys, was in regular use. By the 1570s, when Nicolas de Monardes was broadcasting his *Joyfull Newes*, coca's use was generally recognized by the conquerors, who, one suspects, may have occasionally found it helpful during their long, arduous marches of conquest. Strangely, however, even the 1633 revised edition of Gerard's *Herball* does not acknowledge the existence of that plant.

We may safely assume that a sample of the coca plant was included in the little "Paket" sent Monardes by soldier Pedro de Osma—"a small Cheste made of a little peece of Corke, of a good thicknesse together, which was worthie to be seen, and in the holownesse of it came the hearbes." Of the plant itself Monardes wrote: "I was desirous to see that hearbe, so celebrated of the Indians, so many yeres past, whiche they doe call the Coca, whiche they do sow and till with muche care, and diligence, for because they doe use it for their pleasures, which we will speake of. The Coca is an hearbe of the height of a yerd, little more or lesse. . . .

"The use of it amongest the Indians is a thing generall, for many thinges, for when they doe travaill by the waie, thei use it in this forme. Thei take Cokles or Oisters, in their shelles, and they doe burne them and grinde them, and after they are burned they remaine like Lyme, verie small grounde, and they take the Leves of the Coca, and they chawe them in their Mouthes, and as they go chawyng, they goe mingling with it that pouder made of the shelles in suche sorte, that they make it like to a Paste, taking lesse of the Pouder then of the Hearbe, and of this Paste they make certaine Bawles rounde, and they put them to drie, and when they will use of them, they take a little Ball in their mouthe, and they chaw hym: passing hym from one parte to an other, procuring to conserve him all that they can, and that beyng doen, they doe retourne to take an other, and so they goe, using of it all the tyme that they have neede, whiche is when they travaill by the waie, and especially if it be by waies where there is no meate, or lacke of water. For the use of these little Bawles doe take the hunger and thurste from them, and they say that they doe receive substaunce, as though that they did eate. At other times thei use of them for their pleasure, although that they labour not by the waie, and thei doe use the same Coca alone, chawing it and bringing it in their mouthes, from one side to another untill there be no vertue remainyng in it, and then they take an other.

"When thei will make them selves dronke, and bee out of judgemente, thei mingle with the Coca the leaves of the Tabaco, and thei doe chewe them all together, and thei goe as they were out of their wittes, like as if thei were dronke whiche is a thyng that dooeth give them great contentment to bee in that sorte. Surely it is a thyng of great consideration, to see how the Indians are so desirous to be deprived of their wittes, and to be without understandyng, seying that thei doe this of the Coca with the Tabaco, and thei use of the Tabaco, for that thei would bee without understandyng, and to have their wittes taken from them"—an interesting early description of what today is called "synergism," whereby the effect of two drugs taken jointly may turn out to be more than the sum of their individual effects.

Whether the Incas succeeded in holding a monopoly of the product of a plant that grew wild in their empire we cannot know. Certainly it was small concern of theirs, or of most of the Spanish conquistadors of that empire who had been awarded *encomiendas* (grants of land together with the Indians on it) whether their Indians had "wittes" as long as they retained the power and the will to work without demanding great quantities of costly foodstuffs. For this, coca served well the masters and still serves employers of such Indians. Accounts written by travelers throughout the centuries mention the constant chewing of coca and lime. Thereby enabled to do heavy work without flagging and on the most scanty of diets, such Indians were slaves whatever their official social status and served well the ends of profit-conscious *encomienda* grantees as well as managers of mines in high, cold regions where the most valuable metal deposits were to be mined and where snow might pile up almost any month of the year.

Whether they actively wished it or not, Spaniards connected with mining operations, as near the silver-mining city of Potosí at an elevation of about 13,500 feet, would personally become involved in the coca habit. In the late seventeenth century Bartolomé Arzáns de Orsúa y Vela, chronicler of that famous city whose population once reached 150,000, wrote engagingly of his visit to a nearby mine when a boy of ten: "Wishing one day to take part in the work, I was prevented by the Indians who said I might not enter without taking into my mouth that herb, I refused but they persisted until a Spanish miner warned me of the superstition of the Indians that no one should enter without chewing the herb, that otherwise the richness of the metal would be destroyed. I took it to satisfy the proprietor who assigned me to watch a screen where there was part of the precious metal, so that the Indians should not steal any.

"When I put two leaves into my mouth, my tongue seemed to swell so as not to fit in my mouth, and felt so harsh and burning that, not being able to endure it, I told the miner that I thought it impossible to enter considering the effects of the coca. He made fun of me and gave me a small black tablet saying that they called it 'sugar' and, on taking it together with the coca, the bad effects of the coca could be overcome. When I understood it to be what he said, I took it and I can assert that never in my life have I experienced anything more bitter. I vomited up the sugar together with the herbs and after that would have vomited my guts." The so-called sugar would have been the burnt "Cokle and oister shells" Monardes wrote of. When finally the lad's insides calmed down, he washed out his mouth, then took a piece of bread and with that in his mouth "entered the mine without causing the mineral to lose the richness God had placed in it."

Even though few Spaniards may have been totally hooked on the coca habit, the herb corrupted them in other ways. Pedro Cieza de León, one of the first crop of conquistadors and a chronicler of the Spanish conquest of Peru, complained in the 1550s: "There are in Spain men who have grown wealthy through the value this coca has acquired, buying it to resell at high prices in the markets of Potosí where it can not be grown." Though neither Cieza nor Arzáns seemed to approve of such profiteering, Arzáns found a yet greater vice to rouse his antagonism to the coca plant.

He wrote: "But human wickedness has corrupted it [the coca] so that the devil (Inventor of vices) reaps a notable crop of souls through it, for there are many women who have taken and take it for participation in the sin of sorcery, invoking the devil and attracting him. . . .

"Since the principal intention of the devil is to corrupt our Holy Catholic faith and the women are so deceived by evil, it is they who most often succumb to the temptation of this sin . . . and in this kingdom [of Peru] the herb coca has shown its evil power through the invocations they make and their sin of sorcery. And even when they do not take it to cast spells, there are many wicked people who place it in their mouths and thus are lost, men as well as women, and they become beggars and whatever alms they receive goes only to maintain this infernal vice."

How to end this vice? The writer's remedy has a quite modern sound—extirpate the offending plant wherever it grows: "Could not our king order the uprooting of this noxious herb wherever it grows and not permit even a memory of it to exist, even though the interests of *hacendados* [hacienda owners] and of the proprietors of those lands be damaged. It is worse that so many people should obstinately continue to invoke and make pacts with the devil." Citing several instances of the practice of witchcraft by people acting under the influence of coca, the writer shows equal naïveté in believing it is really possible to extirpate totally a plant that was native to the land before men reached it.

Neither coca nor the coca habit was to be extirpated. The habit still persists, and it is estimated that today, in the Andean regions alone, there are some fifteen million users. In the remoter areas, particularly, coca still plays an essential part in rites which our seventeenth-century chronicler must have looked upon with a jaundiced eye. How he would have looked upon

the further fact that coca growing and using has spread
to lands like India, Java, Sri Lanka can only be imagined.

Like so many plants of strictly New World origin,
coca was soon introduced into Europe as a botanical
curiosity to be grown in herb, medicinal, and botanical
gardens. Three centuries later it was by way of becoming much more than a mere curiosity when, in 1860, the
German organic chemist Albert Neimann isolated the
active principle of coca and gave it the name "cocaine."
A small crystal of this purified cocaine, when placed on
the tip of the tongue, revealed what was soon to be
recognized as its almost magical power as a local
anesthetic, though use was not actually realized until
1884 when the Austrian physician Carl Koller used it in
eye surgery—a dramatic first. Exact determination of the
chemical structure of cocaine and, ultimately, the laboratory synthesis of that compound was not to be
achieved until the turn of the twentieth century by the
gifted German organic chemist Willstätter (1872–1942).
Nevertheless, the yard-high shrub of the Andes can still
do that job more economically.

Ironically, the nineteenth-century development of
organic chemistry—analytic as well as structural and
synthetic—received its greatest impulse through the
mounting need to find some means of disposing profitably, if possible, of the accumulating piles of coal-tar
residues produced by the gaslight industry that had
been born with the century. As the wonderful new
gaslights came to replace lamps and candles inside
homes and out, men truly believed that the day of the
footpad who haunted dark streets was bound to end.
Men optimistically rated the new lights in terms of
police service thus rendered superfluous by discourag-

ing the kind of criminal whom cocaine addiction was to make more criminal than ever.

Fortunately for those in need of local anesthesia, the organic chemists have not only synthesized cocaine but have learned to modify it by adding or changing a small group here or there on the complex molecule. Novocaine, so familiar to anyone who has had to have a tooth pulled, is one of these, as are many others, practically all boasting the same origin and the same word ending— -caine—all valuable if used wisely and well.

Papaver somniferum—which means, the "sleep-giving poppy"—is as common almost everywhere as the coca shrub is uncommon. There seems to be nothing sinister about those garden flowers, their lovely scarlet or pink or white blossoms swaying on long furry stems. And yet the poppy, through the opium man has prepared from it, has a dark history brightened only by its effectiveness, throughout the ages, in making endurable painful illnesses doctors cannot cure. Yet even that merciful use has its sinister side, some opium users succumbing to the habit to the point where they end as hopeless addicts to one or another of the drugs to be derived from the poppy—codeine, morphine, heroin, and others.

Throughout recorded history opium has been known and used—the Sumerians of 4000 B.C. referring to it as the "joy plant." Greeks and Romans knew it—which is hardly surprising, since the plant is believed to have been native to Mediterranean regions. To produce a profitable crop, poppies require soil conditions such as are found especially in some parts of India, Iran, Turkey, Greece, and Yugoslavia. The climate should be hot and very wet during the growing season and until the seed-bearing capsule forms, very dry thereafter. In such regions, Arab traders purchased the opium they would distribute as far east as China, thereby starting a chain of events which was to lead, during the last century, to two wars.

Stavorinus, that frequent visitor to and collector of information about the Far East, recorded at length what he was told about the cultivation of opium in India: "Opium is a very important production, both for the inland trade and that which is carried on by sea . . . all that is exported comes down the Ganges [from Bahar] through Bengal. More than one hundred thousand pounds weight of the drug is annually shipped by our [Dutch East India] Company's vessels, and is consumed in *Java* and the *Moluccas*, and other places in the eastern part of Asia. The natives of all these countries are very fond of it, chewing it together with their tobacco, or chewing it unmixed.

"The mode in which it is collected is as follows: the seed is sown in the month of October, in a soil which has been specially prepared for the purpose, without much trouble.

"A fortnight or three weeks afterwards, some of the seeds are dug up, in order to see whether they have already germinated and struck root; if this be the case, they begin to water the fields, which are all cut through with furrows, conveying the moisture to every part.

"When the bulbous capsule of the plant begins to arrive at maturity, which only happens after the petals of the flowers have fallen, the planter daily examines one of the poorest bulbs, to see whether they are ripe enough for collecting the sap; for this purpose, he makes use of a little sharp knife, with which, in the morning, he makes an incision in the bulb, and if he find, in the evening, that a gummy sap, the opium, have exuded from it, it is a sign that the capsules are sufficiently ripe. Hereupon, men, women, and children, for an incredible number of people are employed in this work, resort to the opium fields, in order to open the bulbs. They take them in the hollow of the hand, holding them fast by the stalk between the fingers, and make an incision, yet with great precaution, that the inner membrane be not wounded, for then the capsule dies instantly. And after having thus cut open the bulbs in the evening, they all return early the next morning to the field, each with a little pot and gently scrape off with a little shell, the congealed sap, which has extilled from the bulb, into the pot, giving another cut in the capsule, the produce of which they again collect in the evening.

"If the bulbs be fine and large, the incision can be repeated three or four times.

"The sap, which is collected both morning and evening, is delivered to the proprietor of the field, upon return of the labourers; and it is then put all together into large tubs, where it purifies itself by fermentation.

"The collection of the Opium takes place in the months of January and February. A piece of land ten rood square [a rood = ¼ acre] is generally estimated to yield five or six pounds weight of opium, and affords great profit to the planter. . . ."

"A gentleman who had resided many years at *Patna*, and from whom I obtained the above particulars, told me, that the quantity of this drug collected annually in *Bahar*, amounted to sixteen thousand maunds, which make upwards of one million pounds; the largest part of which is employed in the inland trade, and is conveyed by land-carriage from *Indostan* to almost every part of Asia."

Of the Dutch interest in the opium trade, Stavorinus wrote: "A society was established at *Batavia* during the government of Baron Van Imhof, for the opium trade, which is still in existence. . . .

"Every chest of opium stands the [Dutch East India] Company in two hundred and fifty, and sometimes three hundred rixdollars, and is delivered to the society for five hundred, and sometimes more. On the other hand, the Company is bound to sell this drug to no other. The retail of it produces large profits, as the society make eight or nine hundred rixdollars, and more, of every chest. [A chest contains about 133 pounds.] The gain would be more considerable, if this monopoly could be strictly enforced, for the whole quantity of opium, consumed in the eastern parts of India . . . but those who engage in this illicit trade, take too many precautions, to run any danger of detection. The smuggling trade which the English carry on, in this article, in the eastern islands, and by way of *Malacca*, is also extremely detrimental to the society."

It was the detriment to that Dutch society, not to the people thus encouraged in the use of opium, that worried men of the late eighteenth century. Within a half century England—or Englishmen, at least—were to be severely embarrassed by two wars fought essentially to maintain their Chinese opium market.

Crude opium contains several alkaloids, among them 10 to 18 percent morphine, 2.5 to 10 percent narcotine, with codeine to a lesser percentage and still others to still lesser percentages. All mentioned have their place in the pharmacopoeia as potent drugs to relieve pain. All are habit-forming if improperly used, the morphine derivative, heroin, being the worst of all. Isolated in pure crystals just after the turn of the nineteenth century, morphine was frequently used as a painkiller by the 1830s. Only after good hypodermic needles were being manufactured, some twenty years later, did the combination of rapid pain relief and addiction raise some doubts as to the propriety of its general use. So widely used was it during both the Franco-Prussian and the American Civil wars to lessen the miseries of the wounded that morphine addiction was to become known as the "soldier's disease."

There were other, less obvious ways in which such an addiction might get started, notably that of the overuse of morphine or codeine in medicines available to an unknowing public. Even a now so innocent drink as Coca-Cola—its name telling of the source of one of. its ingredients—was, until the coca part was interdicted in 1904, creating its own set of addicts. More serious were the patent medicines which flourished especially in the late nineteenth and early twentieth centuries which the public came to rely on. Ladies suffering from that malady referred to as "vapors" were, generally without being aware of it, becoming addicts. So were the fretful teething babies to whom "teething syrup" was being given. Codeine in cough syrups and in medicines like paregoric to relieve diarrhea and dysentery might prove an equal menace, though taken with restraint they could prove a boon. Doctors, harassed by patients suffering real, perhaps incurable or psychosomatic illnesses, contributed to the formation of drug habits by overprescribing opiates. A survey conducted as early as 1888 revealed that perhaps 15 percent of all prescriptions first filled contained one or another opium derivative. Still more suggestive of addiction is the fact that the percentage soared to 78 percent for prescriptions that were refilled. By the time our century dawned, possibly one out of every four hundred Americans had been hooked by the habit.

How many Europeans of earlier centuries acquired the habit is now hard to guess. No one seems quite certain as to when opium first made its appearance in the western lands of that continent. One legend suggests that the first active medical use of opium derivatives there was due to a picturesque sixteenth-century physician born during the years when Columbus was on his first voyage of discovery. Self-baptized in part at least, he gave his name as Philippus Aureolus Paracelsus Theophrastus Bombastus von Hohenheim and acquired fame of a kind throughout contemporary Europe and immortality through the addition of the word "bombast" to language generally. His fame was of two kinds—among scholars for unconventional ways, contentiousness, and arrogance; among suffering human beings for an almost miraculous ability to lessen miseries other physicians seemed unable to do anything about. Both attributes were probably as exaggerated by the ignorant and the envious as are those of any popular figure upon whom attention is focused.

Paracelsus' cures, it is thought, were largely due to his use of a drug he is said to have picked up during wanderings in the Near East. He called it simply "laudanum"—the Latin for "praiseworthy"—and kept its source secret. It was, of course, some form of opium. In any case, there was little likelihood that any serious addiction could result in the Europe of Paracelsus' day where opium would have been too rare and too costly to lend itself to addiction.

By the early decades of the nineteenth century opium was no longer rare. Some quite famous people succumbed to the habit—among them Thomas De Quincey, known especially for his *Confessions of an Opium Eater*, and the poets Elizabeth Barrett Browning and Samuel Taylor Coleridge, who thereby enhanced their flights of fancy.

It was not, however, the eating of opium in England but the smoking of opium in China that was to lead to war between those two lands. Once introduced into China, that vice spread so rapidly among Chinese that officials became alarmed and issued edicts designed to control the vice by limiting the availability of the drug. In 1796 there came an official Chinese interdiction of the importation of opium, which then came almost wholly from India, where the British East India Company had expended large sums in raising it and was exporting it to an annual amount of over four thousand chests, or well over a quarter of a million pounds. So ineffectual was this interdiction that within forty years importation into China had increased tenfold to about two and a half million pounds each year. Clearly, this was a trade in which the huge monetary profits to be made encouraged merchants and smugglers. The greatest profits, of course, would accrue to the East India Company, which owned the poppy fields, and to clipper captains, both English and American, whose vessels were transporting it from India to China. Corruptible Chinese officials in the ports were eagerly taking their share of the profits.

By 1838, alarmed by the devastating effect of opium smoking on the people of his land, the Chinese emperor appointed a viceroy of amazing incorruptibility who took the edicts literally. He ordered seized and destroyed all opium to be found hidden on ships in the river leading to Canton, as well as that which had been accumulating illegally in the warehouses, the total amounting to the equivalent of one year's importation. This, for men whose money was invested in the high-priced drug thus destroyed, aroused howls of protest.

By 1840 war had broken out, a war which has caused many embarrassed Englishmen, then and later, to ascribe its inception to all kinds of peripheral causes. At the time, the young and rising politician William Gladstone pulled no punches when speaking before the House of Commons: "A war more unjust in its origin, a war more calculated to cover this country with permanent disgrace, I do not know and have not read of. The British flag is hoisted to protect an infamous traffic; and if it never was hoisted but as it is now hoisted on the coast of China, we should all recoil in horror."

Gladstone's biographer, Lord Morley, wrote of the affair no less condemningly and with a longer perspective: "There was no pretence that China was in the wrong, for, in fact, the British Government had sent out orders that opium smugglers should not be shielded; but the orders arrived too late, and, war having broken out, Great Britain felt compelled to see it through."

The war ended with Britain triumphant. By the Treaty of Nanking (August 1842) the Chinese were forced to pay an indemnity of six hundred thousand pounds for the opium they had seized from British citizens and destroyed. Four treaty ports were to be opened under consular supervision, and, as a special goody, Britain was awarded Hong Kong, which her troops had been occupying for about a year. Curiously, the treaty did not define the status of the opium trade, so that almost at once Hong Kong was becoming a base for smuggling operations. The production of opium in India continued to increase until, by 1858, nearly 75,000 chests (about a million pounds) of opium were being exported each year from India, destined for the China trade.

Meanwhile, efforts were continued to persuade China to agree to the importation of opium. In 1843 Lord Palmerston was instructing a British representative there "to endeavour to make some arrangement with the Chinese Government for the admission of opium into China as an article of lawful commerce." It was to be impressed upon that government how profitable such a trade might be made to be for the Chinese. The Chinese emperor was adamant, replying sadly, "It is true that I cannot prevent the introduction of the poison; gainseeking and corrupt men will, for profit or sensuality, defeat my wishes; but nothing will induce me to derive a revenue from the vice and misery of my people."

As smuggling continued to grow, Chinese officials saw their continued opposition plunging them into another, yet more disastrous war (1856–1858). Of the Treaty of Tientsin, drawn up in 1858, an official British report commented baldly: "China still retains her objection to the use on moral grounds, but the present generation of smokers, at all events, must and will have opium. To deter the uninitiated from becoming smokers, China would propose a very high duty, but, as opposition was naturally to be expected from us in that case, it should be made as moderate as possible." Finally that "poison," so long and disastrously an object of international struggle, gained entry into a still reluctant China "at less duty than the English levied on Chinese teas and silks." In 1871 a distinguished witness before the House of Commons would state: "We forced the Chinese Government to enter into a treaty to allow their subjects to take opium"—a state of affairs which British historians still struggle valiantly not to believe.

Fifty years were to pass before China succeeded in

persuading an increasingly shamefaced Britain to agree to a gradual reduction in opium importation until, when ten years should have passed, it was to be reduced to zero. To the amazement of all foreigners resident there, that agreement, further reinforced in 1911, was fulfilled to the letter by China so that by 1917 she was substantially freed from the curse of opium.

Needless to say, the remainder of the world has never been thus freed from the curse of habit-forming drugs which destroy some people for the enrichment of others. Extirpating the plants will never serve, for plants spring up wherever seeds may have been dropped. It is well so, since the drugs have valuable legitimate uses. In the last analysis it is people, not the drugs they take, who must be controlled, and to control people effectively all the world must make up its mind, as did the Chinese emperor of a century past, to forego political and financial profit, even against the great odds posed by a flourishing drug trade whose customers believe it is their right to destroy themselves by any means they may choose.

Though in our day people seem to have forgotten, plants have always played a crucial role in the world men think they dominate. All kinds of plant "vertues" have been involved. All kinds of people—the adventurous, the greedy, the ambitious, the imaginative, the self-seeking, and the self-sacrificing—have, by exploiting those virtues, determined not only their own future but also the course of world history.

People should realize that now, as in the past, somewhere out there among the seemingly endless plant species, they might stumble on the best and least costly answers to problems that have been plaguing them—that is, if any out there remains to be explored.

This possibility can justify the sometimes overstrained efforts to protect species people see as endangered. Admittedly, it is true that had the long-extinct dinosaurs remained on earth to multiply and exploit their own right to survival, there could now be neither food nor place for people. Equally true is it that if people do not place a proper value on plants, no political system can save them from the doom of the dinosaurs.

BIBLIOGRAPHY

Acosta, José de, *Historia natural y moral de las Indias,* ed. Ed O'Gorman. Fondo de Cultura Económica, Mexico, 1940 (first published 1585).

Alboquerque, Alfonso d', *The commentaries of the great D'Alboquerque, second viceroy of India.* Hakluyt Society, 1875, reissued Burt Franklin, New York.

Arzáns de Orsúa y Vela, Bartolomé, *Historia de la villa imperial de Potosí.* Providence: Brown University Press, 1965.

Boxer, C.R., ed., *South China in the sixteenth century, being the narratives of Galeote Pereira, Fr. Gaspar da Cruz and Fr. Martin da Rada O.E.S.A.* (1550–1575). London: printed for the Hakluyt Society, 1953.

Bradford, Ernle, *Southward the Caravels: the story of Henry the Navigator.* London: Hutchinson, 1961.

Buller, A. H. Reginald, *Essays on wheat.* New York: Macmillan, 1919.

Cameron, Ian, *Magellan and the first circumnavigation of the world.* New York: Saturday Review Press, 1973.

NOTE: The Arzáns book is in Spanish, from which brief excerpts have been translated by B. S. Dodge.

Caporael, Linda R., *Ergotism: the Satan loosed in Salem?* in *Science*, 192:21–26, 1976.

Cavendish (Candish), Thomas, in *Hakluyt's Principall navigations* (letter to Lord Chamberlain, followed by account signed "n.H."), pp. 808–815.

Chilton, John, *A notable discourse . . . touching the . . . memorable things of the West Indies seen . . . in the space of 17 or 18 yeares,* in *Hakluyt's Principall navigations,* pp. 587–594.

Clark, Arthur H., *The clipper ship era.* New York: G. P. Putnam's Sons, 1910.

Cook, James, *The voyage of the Endeavour, 1768–1771,* ed. J. C. Beaglehole. Cambridge, England: Hakluyt Society, 1955.

Dannenfeldt, Karl H., *Leonhard Rauwolf, 16th century physician, botanist and traveller.* Cambridge: Harvard University Press, 1968.

Dodge, Bertha S., *Plants that changed the world.* Boston: Little, Brown, 1959.

———, *Potatoes and people.* Boston: Little, Brown, 1970.

Doughty, Charles H., *Travels in Arabia Deserta* (introduction by T. E. Lawrence). New York: Random House, 1936.

Duran-Reynals, Marie Louise, *The fever bark tree. The pageant of quinine.* New York: Doubleday & Co., 1946.

Erneholm, Ivar, *Cacao production in South America.* Dissertation, Gothenburg 1948, 279p.

Evelyn, John, *The diary of*———, ed. William Bray. London: Walter Dunne, 1901.

Farwell, Byron, *Queen Victoria's little wars.* London: Allen Lane, 1973.

Fletcher, Francis, *The world encompassed by Sir Francis Drake.* London: Nicholas Bourne, 1628. Reissue Bibliotheca Americana, World Publishing Co., Cleveland, Ohio, 1966.

Fuller, John C., *The day of St. Anthony's fire.* New York: Macmillan, 1968.

Gage, Thomas, *Nueva relación que contiene los viajes de Tomás*

Gage en la Nueva España . . . 1625. Biblioteca "Goathemala," Vol. XVIII, 1946.

Gerard, John, *The herball or generall historie of plantes . . . very much enlarged and amended by Thomas Johnson citizen and apothecarye of London.* London: printed by Adam Islip, Joice Norton and Richard Whitakers, 1633. Reissue Dover Publications, 1975.

Gifford, Douglas, and Pauline Hoggarth, *Carnival & cocasleaf: some traditions of the Quechua Alyllu.* Edinburgh: Scottish Academy Press, 1976.

Gill, Richard C., *Curare: misconceptions regarding . . . in Anesthesiology,* 7:14–23, 1946.

————, *White water and black magic.* New York: Henry Holt & Co., 1940.

Griffiths, Percival, *The history of the Indian tea industry.* London: Weidenfeld & Nicholson, 1967.

Hakluyt, Richard, *The principall navigations, voiages and discoveries of the English nation.* London, 1589. Reissue with introduction and index, Cambridge University Press for the Hakluyt Society in 2 vols., 1965.

Historicus (pseudonym), *Cocoa: all about it.* London: Sampson Low, Marston Co., 1896.

Howe, Sonia E., *In quest of spices.* London: Herbert Jenkins Ltd., 1946.

Humboldt, A. von and A. Bonpland, *Voyage aux régions équinoctiales du nouveau continent. . . .* trans. Thomasina Rose. London: George Bell & Sons, 1881–85, 3 vols.

Kreig, Margaret B., *Green medicine: the search for plants that heal.* London: George G. Harrap & Co. Ltd., 1965.

Lewis, Walter H. and Memory P. F. Elain-Lewis, *Medical Botany: Plants affecting man's health.* New York: John Wiley & Sons, 1977.

Ly-Tio-Fane, Madeleine, *The triumph of Jean Nicolas Céré and his Isle Bourbon collaborators (Mauritius and the spice trade).* Paris: Mouton & Cie, 1970.

McIntyre, Archibald Ross, *Curare: its history, nature and clinical use*. Chicago: University of Chicago Press, 1947.

Mangelsdorf, Paul C., *Corn, its origin, evolution and improvement*. Cambridge: Belknap Press, Harvard University, 1974.

Mitchell, Mairin, *Friar Andrés de Urdaneta O.S.A.* London: Macdonald & Evans Ltd., 1964.

Monardes, Nicholas de, *Joyfull newes out of the Newe Founde Worlde, written in Spanish by Nicolas Monardes, physician of Sevilla and Englished by John Frampton, Merchant, Anno 1577.* London: Constable & Co. Ltd. New York: Alfred A. Knopf (reissue), 1925.

Morison, Samuel Eliot, *The maritime history of Massachusetts, 1783–1860.* Boston: Houghton Mifflin Co., 1921.

Motley, John Lothrop, *History of the United Netherlands*. New York: Harper Brothers, 1867, in 4 vols.

Munilla, Fray Martín de La Australia de Espíritu Santo, *Journal of———and other documents relating to the voyage of Pedro Fernández de Quirós to the South Sea (1605–6)* Trans. and ed. Celsus Kelly O.F.M. Cambridge: Hakluyt Society, at the University Press, 1966, in 2 vols.

Parry, John W., *The story of spices*. New York: Chemical Publishing Co., 1953.

Pauli, Simon, *A treatise on tobacco, tea, coffee, and chocolate, 1635.* Trans. Dr. James. London: T. Osborne, 1746.

Petch, Thomas, *The diseases of the tea bush*. London: Macmillan and Co. Ltd., 1923.

Pigafetta, Antonio Francesco et al., *The first voyage around the world*. Trans. from the accounts of Pigafetta and other contemporary writers, with notes and introduction by Lord Stanley of Alderley. London: Hakluyt Society, 1874. Reissue Burt Franklin, New York.

Polo, Marco, *Travels of Marco Polo the Venetian*, with John Masefield's introduction to Marsden-Wright eds. (1818, 1854). New York: E. P. Dutton & Co., 1926.

Raleigh, Walter, *The discoverie of the large, rich and bewtiful empire of Guiana performed in the year 1595*, ed. Robert Schomburgk. London: Hakluyt Society, 1848.

Remesal, Antonio de, *Historia general de las Indias occidentales y particular de la gobernación de Chiapa y Guatemala*, 1619. Reprinted Biblioteca "Goathemala," 2 vols., 1932.

Rock, Joseph F., *The chaulmoogra tree and some related species: a survey conducted in Siam, Burma, Assam, and Bengal*. U.S. Department of Agriculture Bulletin 1057:1–29, 1922.

Rock, Joseph F., *Hunting the chaulmoogra tree. National Geographic, 41:242–276, 1922.*

Schomburgk, Richard, *Botanical reminiscences in British Guiana*. Adelaide, Australia: W. C. Cox, 1876.

———, *On the urari: the deadly arrow poison of the Macusis, an Indian tribe in British Guiana*. Adelaide, Australia, 1879.

Schomburgk, Robert, *On the urari, the arrow poison of the Indians of Guiana. Annals and Magazine of Natural History*, I Ser. 7:407–427, 1841.

Schouten, William Cornelison, *The relation of a wonderful voiage made by William Cornelison Schouten*. London: imprinted by T. O. for Nathaniel Newberry, 1619. Reissued for Bibliotheca Americana by World Publishing Co., Cleveland, Ohio, 1966 (bound with F. Fletcher).

Spruce, Richard, *Notes of a botanist on the Amazon and Andes* . . . London: Macmillan & Co. Ltd., 1908, 2 vols.

Stavorinus, Jan Splinter, *Voyages to the East Indies* . . . Trans. Samuel Hull Wilcocke, London, 1798. Reissue 1969, Dawsons of Pall Mall, 3 vols.

Stephens, Thomas, *The voyage of Father Stephens unto Goa in 1579*, in *Hakluyt's Principall navigations* . . . , pp. 160–162.

Strong, Richard P., *Stitt's diagnosis, prevention and treatment of tropical diseases*. Philadelphia: Blakiston Co., 1944, 7th ed.

Sturtevant, Edward Lewis, *Notes on edible plants*, ed. U. P. Hedrick. Albany, N.Y.: Report New York Agricultural Experiment Station, 1919, II.

Suppan, Leo, *Three centuries of cinchona.* Proc. Celebration 300th anniversary first recognized use of cinchona, 29–138, 1931.

Terry Robert J., *Dr. John Sappington, pioneer in the use of quinine in the Mississippi valley.* Proc. Celebration 300th anniversary first recognized use of cinchona, 165–180, 1931.

Thorne, Robert, Letter to Henry VIII, in *Hakluyt's Principall navigations.*

Thorold, C. A., *Diseases of cocoa.* Oxford: Clarendon Press, 1975.

Thorwald, Jürgen, *Science and secrets of early medicine.* London: Thames & Hudson, 1962.

Ukers, William H., *All about coffee.* The Tea & Coffee Trade Journal Co., New York, 1935 (2nd ed.).

———, *All about tea.* The Tea & Coffee Trade Journal Co., New York, 1935.

Vasco da Gama, *The three voyages of*———, *and his viceroyalty,* from the *Lendas da India* of Gaspar Correa. Trans. and ed. Henry E. J. Stanley, Hakluyt Society, 1869. Reissue Burt Franklin, New York.

Waterton, Charles, *Wanderings in South America.* London: Macmillan and Co., 1879.

Willoughby, Westel W., *Opium as an international problem: the Geneva Conferences.* Baltimore: The Johns Hopkins Press, 1925.

INDEX